I0230361

BHAJANAMRITAM

Devotional Songs of Sri Mata Amritanandamayi

Volume 7

Compiled from Bhajan Supplements
2011 - 2017

Mata Amritanandamayi Center
San Ramon, California, USA

Bhajanamritam Volume 7

Published By:
Mata Amritanandamayi Center
P.O. Box 613, San Ramon, CA 94583-0613
USA
www.amma.org

Copyright© 2017 by Mata Amritanandamayi Center, California, USA
All rights reserved.
No portion of this book, except for brief review, may be reproduced, stored in a retrieval system or transmitted in any form or by any means–electronic, mechanical, photocopying, recording or otherwise–without permission in writing from the publisher.

First printing by MA Center: April 2017

Address in India:
Mata Amritanandamayi Mission Trust
Amritapuri, Kollam Dt.
Kerala 690546, India
www.amritapuri.org
inform@amritapuri.org

Europe: www.amma-europe.org

About Pronunciation

The following key is for the guidance of those who are unfamiliar with the transliteration codes used in this book:

A	-as	a	in America
AI	-as	ai	in aisle
AU	-as	ow	in how
E	-as	e	in they
I	-as	ea	in heat
O	-as	o	in or
U	-as	u	in suit
KH	-as	kh	in Eckhart
G	-as	g	in give
GH	-as	gh	in loghouse
PH	-as	ph	in shepherd
BH	-as	bh	in clubhouse
TH	-as	th	in lighthouse
DH	-as	dh	in redhead
CH	-as	ch-h	in staunch-heart
JH	-as	dge	in hedgehog
Ñ	-as	ny	in canyon
Ś	-as	sh	in shine
Ṣ	-as	c	in efficient
Ṅ	-as	ng	in sing, (nasal sound)
V	-as	v	in valley
ZH	-as	rh	in rhythm
R	-as	r	in ride

Vowels with a line on top are pronounced like the vowels listed above but held twice as long.

The letters with dots under them (ṭ, ṭh, ḍ, ḍh, ṇ) are palatal sounds. They are pronounced with the tip of the tongue against the hard palate.

Abhivandanam (Telugu)

abhivandanam abhivandanam
ādi gaṇapati nīku abhivandanam

Salutations to Ganapati, the primordial One.

jagadamba oṭilōna gārālu kuṭicēṭṭi
bāla gaṇapati nīku abhivandanam
muddu cūpulatōṭa mahēśu nalariñcu
prathama gaṇapati nīku abhivandanam

Salutations to the child Ganapati, who is pampered in the lap of the Mother of the universe. Salutations to Ganapati who makes Lord Shiva happy by His sweet glances.

vātsalya bhāvāna ṣaṇmukhuni tilakiñcu
vighna dēvara nīku abhivandanam
callani cūpulatō lōkāla nēlēṭṭi
vijaya gaṇapati nīku abhivandanam

Salutations to Ganesh, remover of obstacles, who looks at Shanmukha with compassion. Salutations to victorious Ganapati who rules over all the worlds with kindness.

buddhi siddhula gūrcu ā vakratuṇḍunaku
vighnamula parimārcu ā amba sutunaku
siddhidvāramunēlu mūla gaṇapati nīku
bhakti mirage cētu ātmābhivandanam

Salutations to the Lord with a curved trunk, who bestows knowledge and power. Salutations to the son of the Divine Mother who removes obstacles.

Ādidaivamā (Telugu)

ādidaivamā jēṣṭa rājmā
vighnanāśakā śrī vināyakā

tāpatrayam tolagimpa
kadalirā kadalirā kadalirāvayyā

O Ganesha, first among the gods! You are the foremost King of the gods and destroy all impediments. Kindly come and bless me, eliminating the three kinds of sorrows which torment me.

sūrppakarṇṇāya vakratuṇḍāya
prasannavadanāya mahābalāya namaḥ om

You have large ears, and a curved elephant's trunk! Your face is that of an elephant, and Your strength is infinite. We prostrate before You!

āddhyātmika tāpamulu
nā asura pravṛttulu
buddhi balamumiñci vāṭini
jayimpa kadalirāvayyā

'Adhyatmika-tapas' are my demonic tendencies, the troubles that arise within. Kindly come and bless me with the power of intellect and the discrimination to overpower these negativities.

ādi bhautika tāpamulu
nanu cuṭṭina vighnamulu
kārya siddhi iñcci vāṭini
dāṭimpa kadalirāvayyā

'Adi-bhautika-tapas' are the physical hurdles that surround us, caused by the external world. Please come and bless me with victory in all my actions and undertakings to overcome these obstacles.

ādi daivika tāpamulu
prakṛti saṃkṣōbhamulu
daiva kṛpaniñcci mamu
rakṣimpa kadalirāvayyā

'Adi-daivika-tapas' are the natural calamaties that shatter us. With Your divine grace please come and protect us from those evils that are beyond our control.

Adi sṛṣṭi lōpamā (Telugu)

ammā ī māyā sṛṣṭiki mōhitu ḍaitini, ī sṛṣṭini vīḍi nā dṛṣṭi, ninnu cūḍakunnadi ninnu cērakunnadi

O Mother, I have become captivated by Your beautiful, charming and illusory creation. I am unable to brush aside this creation to see You, I am unable to see You.

adi sṛṣṭi lōpamā nā dṛṣṭi lōpamā
telapavamma īśvari bhuvanēśvari

Is this the fault of Your creation? Or a defect in my vision? O Mother of the Universe, please let me know.

tāḍu pāmugā nāku gōcariñcitē
adi tāḍu lōpamā nā dṛṣṭi lōpamā
līlā vinōdini nī triguṇamāyaku nē vasuḍaitē
adi māyā mōsamā nā vāsana dōṣamā
telapavamma īśvari bhuvanēśvari

If a rope appears as a snake to me, is it the fault of the rope or a defect in my vision? O ever playful Mother, if I succumb to Your illusion of the three gunas, is it the fault of Maya (cosmic delusion) or my vasanas (latent mental tendencies)?

kanakam kānaka naganu mechitē
kamsālilōpamā adi erukalōpamā
śilpa saundaryamunu mechi ā śilpini vismariñcitē
adi śilpi dōṣamā nā samskāradōṣamā
telapavamma īśvari bhuvanēśvari

If I am deluded by the beautiful forms of ornaments and do not see the gold behind them, is it the fault of the goldsmith or an error in my judgment? If I become bewitched by the beauty of sculpture and forget the greatness of the sculptor, is it the fault of the sculptor or a deficiency in my character?

antā unnadi nīvē ani telisēdeppuḍu?
ninnē sṛṣṭigā cūsē dṛṣṭi kaligēdeppuḍu?
telapavamma īśvari bhuvanēśvari.

When will I understand that You are the all pervading Mother? When will I be blessed with the vision of creation as Your manifestation? O Mother of the universe, please let me know.

Aintezhuttu (Tamil)

aintezhuttu vittakan anpar manatai āḷbavan
allaltanai tīrttiṭum ayyanviṭai vāganan

Lord of the five syllabled mantra (na-ma-shi-va-ya), ruler of the devotees hearts, You ride the bull and remove all sorrows!

malaiyarasan makaḷtanakku mēnipāti tantavan
maṇṇavarum viṇṇavarum vaṇankum marai poruḷavan

He shared half of His body with Parvati, daughter of the mountain king. He is the essence of the Vedas, and is worshiped by both human and heavenly beings.

ayyamtannai nīkkinam meytanai uṇarttiyē
jñāna oḷi tantiṭum jñāla mūlamānavan

He is the cause of creation; dispelling our doubts and revealing the truth about our nature, He showers the light of wisdom on us.

nañcatanai pōkkiyē nalamanaittum aruḷiṭum
nānilamē pōttri vaṇankum nāyanmārin nāyakan

Removing the poison, He bestows all goodness. He is the Lord of the Nayanmars and is worshiped by the whole world.

nāḷumkōḷum ennaseyyum nāṭa nīlakaṇṭhanai
innalilā irumaiyilā irainilai unarntezhum

What harm can an inauspicious day and an inauspicious planet do to one who seeks refuge in the blue-throated Lord? The divinity in us, devoid of sorrows and duality, will be awakened.

hara hara hara mahādēva, śiva śiva śiva sadāśiva
gangādhara gaurīnātha, mṛtyunjaya sarvēśa

O One of divine effulgence who is eternally auspicious. You sustain the Ganga river, Lord of Gauri, conquerer of death, Lord of everything!

Akamanatin kāriruḷai (Tamil)

akamanatin kāriruḷai
nīkkiṭumun pēraruḷai
nānmaraiyin nar poruḷai
nāṭivantēn nānumammā
pāvaminta ezhaiyammā

Your grace removes the dark clouds within. I have come in search of She who is the essence of the four Vedas

saraṇam saraṇam kāḷiyamma
saranam durgā dēviyamma

I surrender to Mother Kali, I surrender to Durga Devi!

puviyālum punnakaiyarasi
putirniraința bhuvanamitil
aruḷnirai attiruvaṭiyil
manam kuvintiṭa vēṇḍumammā – en
manam kuvintiṭa vēṇḍumammā

You have a captivating smile, and You are the One who rules this universe full of puzzles. Let my mind be fully focused on Your lotus feet that are full of grace.

tuyarkaḷ nirainta vaiyakattil
tumbakkaṭalil mūzhgukirēn
maraikaḷ pottrum nāyakiyē
piḷḷaiyenai kāppāye, piḷḷaiyenai kāppāye

The world is full of sorrow- I am drowning in the sea of sadness. You who have been praised in all the four Vedas- please come and save this child of Yours!

Akatārilennennum (Malayalam)

akatārilennennum aṇayāte nilkkumō
amṛtaprabhādīpamāyi?
akalāyka orunālumivanil ninnambikē
avalambamārammayenyē?
ammē hṛdayēśvarī ammē hṛdayēśvarī

Will You not remain within me as a constant, unwavering light? Please do not separate from me, O Mother. What do I have but Your compassion? Mother, Queen of my heart.

mada matsarāsura samarāgni jvālakaḷ
aṭarāṭiyurayumī mannil
tava sāntvanaśīta madhumāriyillenkil
gatiyentu gatiyentu munnil?
ammē hṛdayēśvarī ammē hṛdayēśvarī

Negative qualities such as pride and jealousy are burning like fire within me. But for Your cooling, sweet words of consolation, what refuge is there for me? Mother, Queen of my heart.

tava tankanūpuradhvani tēṭiyalayunna
tuṇayatta nissāranām ñān
oru mātra nin tūmizhittellil nizhalikkil
atilēre vērentu bhāgyam?
ammē hṛdayēśvarī ammē hṛdayēśvarī

I am all alone and insignificant, in search of the sweet sound of Your golden anklets. If only I could be a shadow in Your sight- what greater fortune could I hope for? Mother, Queen of my heart.

Akatāril oru nēram (Malayalam)

akatāril oru nēram ōrttāl - amma
amṛtūṭṭi arikiliruttum
arikilēkkyoru kātam aṭuttāl - amma
śaravēgam arikil-āyaṇayum
kanivōṭen nerukayil mukarum - amma
kaṭalōḷam karuṇayatēkum

If we remember Mother just once in our hearts, Mother will draw us close to Her, and feed us divine nectar. If we take a step towards Her, She will reach our side within the speed of an arrow. She will kiss our foreheads compassionately, blessing us with an ocean of grace.

viravilāy ā mantramōrttāl - amma
iruḷatu nīkki udikkum
mizhiyiṇa nirayunnatariññāl - amma
amṛtattin niravatu nalkum
kanivōṭe arivatu nalkum - uḷḷil
kārttika dīpam teḷiyum

If we remember the mantra 'Mother' with yearning, She will dispel the darkness and rise within. Seeing the tears brimming in our eyes, She will give us the fullness of immortality. Full of compassion, She will bless us with knowledge, and the Kartika lamp will shine within our hearts.

ulakattil ariyunnoraṛivil - 'amma'
yennuḷḷorarivalle nityam?
anputtoraṛivinde niravām - 'amma'
yennuḷḷa satyamē nityam
trippāda patmaṅgaḷallē
bhavarōga duḥkhattin-abhayam

Of all the knowledge known in the world, is 'Mother' not the only imperishable One? Mother, the fullness of knowledge imbued with love, is the only truth that is eternal. Her divine lotus feet are the only refuge from the disease of transmigratory existence.

Ālā bhāgyāca kṣaṇ (Marathi)

ālā bhāgyāca kṣaṇ ālā
ayī tava svāgatācha kṣaṇ ālā

The auspicious time of our lives has arrived - the moment to welcome You has arrived!

rāngōḷyā rangavū premācyā
patākā lāvū ānandācyā
bhāvbhaktī ne naṭavū jīvan
gharō gharī tujhē guṇ gān

Let us paint the rangoli of love and decorate everything with banners of happiness. Let us live our lives with utmost devotion and sing Your praises in every household!

bhavāni jai jai bhuvaneśvari jai
jagadodhāriṇi jai jai jai

Victory to Bhavani, who rules the world and sustains the universe!

nānā prakār goḍ dhoḍ
kele tujhā naivedyāla
soḍunī rāg lobh cintā
calā calā re ānand lūṭṭā

As a token of our devotion we offer You a variety of sweet dhoda. Casting aside all feelings of greed, anger and anxiety let us come together to celebrate this joyous moment!

Amala bharatam (English)

ABC 1-2-3, ek do teen india
amala bharatam om
amala bharatam, amala bharatam
amala bharatam om

mananthavady, bangaluru, mysore can't you see?
amma has come to you dear friends!
we are her family.
rise up, clean up, and plant some trees!

O hyderabad, pune, mumbai can't you see?
amma has come to you, dear friends!
we are her family.
rise up, clean up, and plant some trees!

O amdavad, jaipur, new delhi, zindabad!
amma has come to you dear friends!
we are her family.
rise up, clean up, and plant some trees!

Ambapaluku (Telugu)

ambapaluku jagadambā paluku
jaganmātā paluku amṛtavāṇi paluku
palukammā paluku nanu karuṇiñci paluku
palukammā paluku kāḷikāmba paluku

Speak, O Mother! Reveal Yourself, Mother of the Universe! Reveal yourself, eternal voice! Mother, reveal Yourself by showering compassion on me! Reveal Yourself, O Mother, reveal Yourself, Mother Kali!

advaitamai paluku nirdvandvamai paluku
antaṭā paluku anniṭā paluku
andarilō paluku andaritō paluku
nā māṭalalō paluku nā cēṣṭalalō paluku
nēnanu ahamunu tumci nīvē paluku paluku

Reveal Yourself to me as the non-dual truth! Reveal Yourself as I transcend duality. Reveal Yourself everywhere and in everything! Reveal Yourself to everyone, reveal Yourself in everyone. Reveal Yourself always in my speech and actions! Crush my ego, the "I," and reveal Yourself.

satyamai paluku priyamai paluku
hitamai paluku amṛtamai paluku
celimigā paluku aṇḍhagā paluku
nā hṛdayamai paluku nā prāṇamai paluku
nēnanu ahamunu tumci nīvē paluku paluku

Reveal Yourself as truth, reveal Yourself as dear to everyone. Reveal Yourself as good advice, reveal Yourself as nectar! Reveal Yourself as friend, reveal Yourself as protector! Reveal Yourself as my heart! Reveal Yourself as my life energy! Crush my ego, the "I," and reveal Yourself in me.

Ambā śāmbhavī (Sanskrit)

ambā śāmbhavī śankarī
mṛtyuṇ-jaya hara priyakarī
sankaṭa hāriṇi śūbhakarī
tribhūvana mōcini sundarī

Mother, benevolent One! You bring peace and are the conqueror of death, O beloved of Shiva! You remove obstacles, bestow auspiciousness and free us from the three worlds, O beautiful One!

jaya śankarī jaya śrīkarī
jaya śūbhakarī jaya sundarī

Victory to the One who brings peace, auspiciousness and goodness! Victory to the beautiful One!

ādi nāda svarūpiṇī
(jaya jaya jaya jaya śāradē)
ādi śakti mahā-rūpiṇī
(jaya jaya jaya jaya kāḷikē)
sanmati dāyini cinmaya rūpiṇi
śaraṇam śaraṇam caraṇayugaḷam ambē.

You are the personification of the primordial sound, victory to Goddess Saraswati! Primordial strength, great embodiment, victory to Goddess Kali! O Bestower of wisdom, who is the embodiment of pure mind, Mother, please give me refuge at Your lotus feet!

tāṇḍava nāṭya manōharī
(jaya jaya jaya jaya bhairavī)
ānanda rāga priyakarī
(jaya jaya jaya jaya bhāratī)
sṛṣṭi sthitilaya kāraṇipūraṇi
śaraṇam śaraṇam caraṇayugaḷam ambē.

You win hearts through Your dance of dissolution and are beyond the fear of death! Blissful One, who holds dear all the notes of music, victory to You, O cherished One! You are creator, sustainer and destroyer. O ancient one, Mother, grant me refuge!

jaya śankarī jaya śrīkarī
jaya śūbhakarī jaya sundarī

Victory to the One who brings peace, auspiciousness and goodness! Victory to the beautiful One!

Ammā ammā enum (Tamil)

ammā ammā enum mandiram – adu
anaivarukkum sondamāna mandiram
summā adai colli colli pārunka
sorggam pōla vāzhvamaiyum kēḷunka

The mantra 'Mother' belongs to one and all. By the mere chanting of this mantra, life becomes a heaven.

aḷḷa aḷḷa kuraiyāda anbu tān
anaittuyirum sondamenum paṇbu tān
kaḷḷamellām pōkkukindhra kanivu tān
kāṇpavarkku makizhvu tarum kaḷippu tān

Her love never decreases. Her nature is to treat all beings as Her own. Her compassion is the destroyer of envy, and Her presence makes everyone joyful.

mella mella nammaiyavaḷ māttruvāḷ
mēnmai tarum pādayinau kāṭṭuvāḷ
solla solla inikkumavaḷ nāmam tān
solli pārttāl nāṭi varum kṣemam tān

Gradually She changes us and shows us the path of upliftment. Repeatedly chanting Her name brings sweetness and prosperity.

āṭuvōm... pāṭuvōm...
āṭi pāṭi anudinam koṇḍāṭuvōm
tudittāṭi pāṭi anudinam koṇḍāṭuvōm

Let's dance and sing, and make every day a celebration! Let's make every day a celebration glorifying Her!

Ammā dēvī (Kannada version)

ammā dēvī tāni-tandānā
dēvī dēvī tandana nīnā

ninna mogada munkarulāṭṭā
miñcu tiruvā mandahāsā
kaṇḍu nānū sotuhōde - kāḷī... dēvī...

tattva śāstra ontu ariye
sādhane sankalpa ariye
ninna mātra bayasi bandē nā - durgē... dēvī...

puṭṭa magu nānammā
keṭṭa ammā nīnallā
taḍa yāke ettikkoḷḷalu - caṇḍī... dēvī...

Ammā dēvi (Tulu version)

ammā dēvi tānitantānā
dēvi dēvi tantana nīnā

irnā mukhada munkuruḷāṭṭā
miñcōntuppuna mandahāsa
irentūdu mātta madēttē - kāḷī... dēvī...

tattvaśāstra enku gottijji
sādhana sankalpa gottijji
iranmātra tūdu batteyān - durgē... dēvi...

iranā bālē yānammā
īratte ēnkḷēgu māttalā
taṭadāne yenan tūvarē - caṇḍī... dēvī...

Ammā hāsattu (Konkani)

ammā hāsattu yō ammā dhāvattu yō
hāsattu yō dhāvattu yō

Mother, please smile. Smile and come, Mother. O Mother, come running to me!

kōṇājhsō ādhār nāgē mākā
tugēlya caraṇāku khētū mākā

I have absolutely no one to depend on. Your lotus feet are my only refuge.

dukhyāca samsārā paṭlō gē mā
raṭatu raṭatu jagtāgē mā
mujha māy mujha māy dhāvatu yō
mujha māy mujha māy hāsattu yō

In this world of sorrow, I am suffering and crying. For my sake, O Mother, come running to me, please come!

māgēlē māgēlē maṇuttāgē mā
māgēlē kōṇājhsā nāgē mā
tujhsā ādhārē āsāgē mā
tyājhsā āṣecīr jagtāgē mā

They say, 'this is mine; that is mine', but in the end, there is nothing I can call mine. I desire only for Your protection, You are my only hope in this world.

Ammā nāpai (Telugu)

ammā nāpai aligindi
jaganmātā nāpai aligindi
nīvainā ceppavayya śivayya
mā manci tanḍrivi nīvayya

The Mother of the Universe is annoyed with me. O my good father Shiva, please tell Mother!

tappēmiṭṭō ceppadu
nātō asalē palukadu
palukamani ceppavayya śivayya
mā manci tanḍrivi nīvayya

She doesn't tell me what my mistake is, She doesn't even speak to me. O my good father Shiva, please tell Mother to talk to me.

nē palikina māṭṭālu vinadu
nāvaipasalē cūḍadu
cūḍamani ceppavayya śivayya
mā manci tanḍrivi nīvayya

She doesn't pay attention to what I have to say. She doesn't even look at me. O my good father Shiva, please tell Mother to look to me.

gaṇēśa kumārulu cālēmō
kānī nākamma lālana kāvāli
lālimpamani ceppavayya śivayya
mā manci tanḍrivi nīvayya

Ganesha and Kumara may be enough for Her. But I also need Mother's comfort. O my good father Shiva, please tell Mother to embrace me lovingly.

nīvu ceppinā vinadēmō
lōkālanēlē mahārāṇi
mazhī vērē gati lēdu nāku
amma mātramē śaraṇu
nākamma mātramē śaraṇu

Being the Empress of all worlds, She may not listen even to You. Who else is there for me to turn to other than Mother? Mother is my refuge, Mother alone is my refuge!

Ammā ninna prēmakāgi (Kannada)

ammā ninna prēmakāgi kāttarisitē
ammā ninna prēmakāgi hāttoredihe
kāttarisi hāttoredu āttūradi nā hāḍitē
ammā. . . ō ammā. . .ammā. . . ō ammā. . .

Mother, I long for Your love. Longing and longing for Your love, here I sing. Mother, Mother, O Mother!

jagada āgūhōgū gaḷali enna mareteyā?
kālacakra sariyitendu enna toredeyā?
āṭṭa pāṭṭa gaḷali nā muḷugi keṭṭe nendu
enna toredu hōgē biṭṭēyā

Busy as You are with the world have You forgotten me? Time has passed, did You leave me behind? Or did You desert me because I indulged in various games?

nanna biṭṭu hōgabēḍa ammā
nanna dūra māḍabēḍa ammā
nanna anāthē yāgisabēḍā
nanna kai biḍabēḍā ammā

Don't leave me, Mother! Don't keep me away. Don't make me an orphan! Don't let go of my hand!

Amma nīvē sākṣi (Telugu)

amma nīvē sākṣi! amma nīvē sākṣi!
nā manassunu pratikṣaṇam vīkṣiṁcu sākṣi
ātmasākṣi karmasākṣi sarvasākṣi
kāmākṣi mīnākṣi nā manaḥsākṣi

Mother, You are the witness! You witness my mind at every moment. You are the witnessing Self, You witness all actions and everything. You have compassionate, eternally open eyes that witness every thought.

sarvvamunnu kāñcesākṣi
sarvatra niṇṭṭina sākṣi
sarvamu tānai vunna sākṣi
sarvakāla mandunna sākṣi

You are the witness who perceives everything and pervades everywhere; You are the witness who has become everything. You are the witness of all times.

annī āṭagā darśiñcu sākṣi
dvandvātītamai vunna sākṣi
buddhini epputu yerugu sākṣi
ahamu māyayani telupu sākṣi

You are the witness, perceiving everything as a play. You are the witness who is beyond duality. You are the witness of the intellect; You are the witness who reveals that the ego is just an illusion.

Ammē enuḷḷu (Malayalam)

ammē enuḷḷu turannu viḷikkumbōḷ
anpōṭe arikil nī ettiṭunnu
māyāmarubhūvil vīṇu piṭaññīṭum
manassil nī maññāyi peytiṭunnu
ammē peytiṭunnu

When we call out 'O Mother' with all our heart, You lovingly come close to us. You manifest as dewdrops in the arid heart of delusion.

ende daivamāṇamma amma tannende amma
ennennum uyirēkum nitya satyamāṇamma

O Mother, You are my God, my very own. O eternal truth, You infuse life into us.

vātsalyamazhayil nanaññu nanaññuḷḷil
ñānenna bhāvam aliññupōke
hṛdayaviśuddhikkāy kēzhunnu makkaḷ
hṛdinilayē mātē kaṇturakkū
ammē kaṇturakkū

My ego has dissolved in the rain of Your compassion. O Mother, we, Your children, pray for the purification of our hearts. O Mother, who dwells in our hearts, please open Your eyes. O Mother, open Your eyes!

nin kṛpa prāṇanāyi nirayunna tanuvitil
ninniccha vazhipōl naṭanniṭaṭṭe
nin kazhal pulkiya pūjāmalarivaḷ
nityavum vāṭāte kākkukammē
ammē kākkukammē

May everything unfold as You wish through this body, which is infused with the vital force of Your grace. I am a flower that has been offered as worship and which is hugging Your feet. O Mother, protect me that I may never wither. O Mother, protect me!

Amṛtalayam ānandalayam (Malayalam)

amṛtalayam ānandalayam
en ātmāvu śruticērum madhuralayam
pūvum prakṛtiyum pōle
ponnalakaḷum kaṭalum pōle
śruti cērumī laya bhangiyil
śruti cērumī laya bhangiyil

My soul is content and immersed in bliss - like a flower within nature, like waves within the ocean. I am immersed in sweet song.

pramada mānasavaniyil viriyum saugandhikaṅgaḷil
nī viral toṭumbōḷ praṇavamantra
dhvanikaḷuṇarum oru tamburuvāy mārum
praṇava tamburuvāy mārum
divya tamburuvāy mārum

At the touch of Your fingers, the flowers growing in the garden of my mind transform into a tambura playing the Omkara.

ātma harṣam tuḷumbi nilkkum
indīvaradaḷa śobha pōlum
nin nayanaṅgaḷil manassinde cippiyil
muttukaḷ tīrkkum oru māya mantramuṇḍō?
divya māya mantramuṇḍō?
dēvī māya mantramuṇḍō?

When the glance from Your lotus eyes shining with bliss falls upon me does it not have the power to create a pearl within the shell of my heart?

Ānandamē ānandam (Tamil)

ānandamē ānandam ennē enadu ānandam
anubhavamē anubhavam bhakti tanda anubhavam

O bliss, bliss! Intense is my bliss! O experience, experience! The experience that devotion gives me!

kaṇkaḷ raṇḍum kaṇṇanadu divyarūpam kāṇudē
kādiraṇḍum kāṇṇanadu venkuzhalil mayankudē
kaigaḷ raṇḍum kaṇṇankku veṇṇeyinai ūṭṭudē
kāliraṇḍum kaṇṇanoḍu āṭi āṭi kaḷikkudē

I behold Krishna's form with my two eyes. I become intoxicated hearing Krishna's flute with my two ears. I feed butter to Krishna with my two hands. I dance with Krishna with my two feet!

nāvumavan mīdivaitta avalin suvaiyai rusikkudē
nāsiyavan vanamālai narumaṇattai rasikkudē
vāyumavan līlaigaḷai pāṭippāṭi magizhudē
mēniyavan tīṇḍalilē mellatannai izhakkudē

The taste of the puffed rice He has eaten is on my tongue. I inhale the sweet fragrance of His garland of wild flowers. With my lips, I blissfully sing about his lilas. My body slowly merges into His form.

nirmalamām idayamavan kōyilāga ānadē
nittiyamum isaimalarāl pūjaitanai ceyyudē
arivumavan gītaiyenum amudattinai parugudē
āṇavamum avanaṭiyil sevaganāy paṇiyudē

My heart is becoming pure; now it is His temple! In my daily worship of Him, songs are the flowers I offer at His feet. My mind drinks the nectar of the Gita, and my ego falls at His feet. I am His servant.

Annaiyē unnaiyē (Tamil)

annaiyē unnaiyē eṇṇiye vāzhntiḍum
ariyāta makkaḷ emaiye
ponnaiyē maṇṇaiyē peṇṇaiyē eṇṇāta
peruvāzhvu vāzha vaippāy

O Mother, bless us—Your ignorant children who think only of You—so that we may lead exalted lives, without desiring wealth or sensual pleasure.

mōhamum bhōgavum rōgamum emmaye
suṭṭri cuzhaṭṭrukiratē
yōgamum tyāgamum yāgamum sādhanaiyum
emma nī seyyavaippāy

I have become ensnared by delusion, material pleasure and disease. O Mother, please lead me to the path of yoga, renunciation, self-sacrifice and spiritual practices.

sarkkarai pākenḍrum vellattin pākenḍrum
eṇṇi ēmārukinḍrēn
tunba narakattil vīzhāmal nārāyaṇī
kaṭṭi emai kāpāṭṭruvāy

Imagining we can find sweetness and bliss, we fall headlong into trouble. O Narayani, please ensure that I don't fall into the hell of suffering, and thus save me.

āpattu āpattu devī nī kāpāṭṭru
nānum katarukinḍrēn
tāmatam inḍri nī tāriṇī vantiḍu
tāymayē kāpāṭṭriḍu

"Save me from danger!" Thus I cry out to You. O Bhavatarini, embodiment of motherhood, please come soon and save us.

Antardarśanattinuḷḷa (Malayalam)

antardarśanattinuḷḷa cintayum prayatnavum
varttamāna hṛttilum pravṛddhamānamākki nī
antarangatantriyil prapañcasāramantramāy
sañcaricciṭunnu nī svatantrabhāvadhārayāy

Even in current times, You inspire people to strive for self-realization. You are the Omkara mantra in the soul of every man. As said by the scriptures, You are the absolute.

āgamiccezhiccuninnulaññazhiññupōvatin
āgamōktiyōrkkilō nidānabinduvāṇu nī
āgamam vidhiccatokke ācariccupōkilum
ākulaṁ śamikkuvān bhavāni, nin kṛpāśrayaṁ

Only if self-effort is blessed by the grace of the Guru will we attain realization. In the heart blossoming with innocent love, You are the essence of poetry

bhaktiyāluṇarnnularnna niṣkkaḷanka cētasil
śuddhabhāvavaikharī nisargakāvyadhāra nī
maṇṇilēkkurannolicca veṇṇilāvupōle yenn-
-uḷḷil nin madhusmitābha sāndrasaukumāryamāy

When the mind is moving, You act as the force of creation. In a still mind, You shine as the power of God.

cittatārcalikkavē kriyātmakatvaśaktī nī
niścalam vasikkavē śivatvamennariññiṭām
śaktiyum śivatvavum parasparānupūrakam
buddhiyekkaviñña, vēda tattvasāramē, tozhām

Creativity and stillness are mutually complementary. I bow down before You, who are above the intellect and embody the essence of the Vedas.

Anudinamum (Tamil)

anudinamum unai ninaindu urugudamma neñjam - adu
arukil nindru ezhil mukhattai kaṇḍu rasikka keñjum
tiruvaruḷai tēḍivandun tiruvaḍiyil tañjam - guru
vaḍivām tāy umayē unai aravaṇaittu koñjum

Thinking of You daily, my heart melts. I yearn to move close to You and enjoy Your beautiful face. Seeking divine grace, I reached and took refuge at Your feet. O Goddess Uma, who are of the form of the Guru and Mother, we take comfort in Your embrace.

piñju manam unnaruḷāl parugum anbu vellam
neñjuruki unnizhalil nilai marandu tuḷḷum
añjukindra tīvinaikaḷ allal yāvum akalum - anku
pañjupōla manamiḷaki paramānandam koḷḷum

By Your grace, the waters of love have softened my mind and melted my heart, making me jump joyfully in abandon. All the fears and miseries that affected me have disappeared. My tender heart has attained supreme bliss.

aruḷamudē! ānandamē!
anbin vaḍivē! aḍaikkalam nīyē!

O Mother of grace! O blissful One, embodiment of love! You are my refuge!

māyaiyadin piḍiyinilē matiyizhandu uzhalum
makkaḷ manam amaidipera nin kazhalinai nizhalum
sēykaḷ nilai uyara un tiruvizhi malarndaruḷum - anbu
tāyundan sannidhikku taraṇi ellām tiraḷum

Those ensnared by Maya (cosmic delusion) act without discernment. To find peace of mind, they seek solace at Your feet. Your divine gaze uplifts souls. Hence, millions flock to Your divine presence, O loving Mother.

unadu padam dinamum manam paṇindiḍa manankanivāy
ninadaruḷāl paramapada nilai aḍaindiḍa aruḷvāy
guruvaḍivē tiruvaruḷē parivuḍan emai kāppāy - nān
maraimuḍiyinil maruvum nindan padamalaraḍi sērppāy

O Mother, bless us so that we may worship Your feet daily. By Your grace, may we reach the abode of the Supreme. O Divinity in the form of the Guru, protect us with love and affection. Help us attain Your feet, which hides the precious gems of the four Vedas.

Aparādham-endētu (Malayalam)

aparādhamendētu mātram – nītanna
tanuyōjya jīvita pātram
daivīka sthānattahantaye vāzhiccor-

aparādhamendētu mātram
anyayajanam dōṣam-āriyāteyācari-
ccaparādham-endētu mātram, nītanna-
tanuyōjya jīvita pātram

The fault is mine alone. You are the life that shines within the body, which is losing its luster, and that is entirely my fault. You are the life that shines within the body. The fault of letting the ego rule in place of the divine is mine also. The unknowingly committed fault of being needy of others is also mine.

azhivallahantaykkoratirillateppozhum
nizhalennapōleṅgum-anugamikkum
cerumaṇtariyilum tāzheyāṇennu ñān
karutumbozhum tāne ahamezhikkum

The ego grows without any boundaries. The ego follows like a shadow. But when I consider myself to be smaller than a grain of sand, the ego falls away.

arppaṇam ceytāl-aham tezhikkum, svayam
arppitamāyāl-aham dahikkum
arppitamākunna śunya hṛttil svayam
nirbharamakunnu daivīkata

When I surrender, the ego dissolves. When my surrender is accepted, the ego is burnt. The heart, emptied by surrender, becomes filled, overflowing with divinity.

aparādhamellām kṣamikkū
aparādhamellām porukkū
aparādhamellām kṣamikkū
aparādhamellām porukkū

Forgive all my faults, please pardon all my faults!

Āreyāṇāreyaṇiṣṭam (Malayalam)

āreyāṇāreyaṇiṣṭam
uṇṇiykkālila kṛṣṇaneyāṇō?
uṇṇiykkālila kṛṣṇanettanne
iṣṭam ālila kṛṣṇanettanne

Whom do you love the most? Whom do you love the most, little One? Do you love Krishna on the banyan leaf? It is Krishna on the banyan leaf that unni loves!

veṇṇayum pālum kavarum kaḷḷa
kaṇṇanāmuṇṇiyeyāṇō?
kōlakkuzhalu viḷikkum bāla
gōpālakṛṣṇaneyāṇō?
gōkkaḷe mēyccu naṭakkum hari
gōvinda kṛṣṇaneyāṇō?

Do you love child Krishna, the thief who steals milk and butter? Do you love Gopala Krishna who plays the bamboo flute? Or the cowherd Krishna who roams with his cows in the meadow?

gōvarddhanam uyarttīṭān vanna
gōpakumāraneyāṇō
vṛndāvanattilalayum cāru
nandakiśōraneyāṇō
rādhāhṛdayam kavarnna
muraḷīdhara kṛṣṇaneyāṇō?

The youthful Krishna who came to lift the Govardhana Mountain? Or the bewitching Nandakishora of Vrindavan? Or is it Krishna the flute player, who stole the heart of Radha?

śrīvatsa kaustubham cārttum sākṣāl
śrīkṛṣṇanettanneyāṇō?

dēvaki dēvitan puṇyam pūtta
śrīvāsudēvaneyāṇō ?
nāradarennum vāzhttum śrīman
nārāyaṇamūrttiyeyāṇō ?

Is it Krishna who wears the Srivatsa kausthubham (jewel of Vishnu) that You love? Or Krishna who was born as a result of Devaki's merits? Or Krishna in the form of Narayana, forever praised by Narada?

Aridu aridu (Tamil)

aridu aridu māniṭarāy pirappadu aridu
adanin aridu muktiyilē nāṭṭamum aridu
mikavum aridu guruvin vaṭivil daivattin uravu – inda
mūnḍrum peṭṭrum vīṇaṭittāl kūriruḷ iravu

To be born as a human being is very rare. It is rarer still to have an interest in liberation. And extremely rare to have a relationship with God in the form of a guru. If we waste our life even after gaining these three, it is like a pitch dark night.

ulakapporuḷil inbam tēṭi alaindavar – yārum
nirai manadil amaidiyōṭu vāzhndadum illai
ānmanāṭṭam koṇḍu sukhattai turandavar yārum
vīṇarāgapaśiyil vāṭi irandadum illai

Those who search for pleasure in worldly objects never experience the peace of contentment. Those who renounce worldly pleasures to follow spiritual pursuits never die from hunger.

sondabandham vēṇḍi vāzhndadu ettanai kālam?
sottu sukham tēṭi alaindattenai kālam?
pirandu vanda nōkkamtanai ninaippadekkālam?
piravippiṇi tīrkkum aruḷaipperuvatekkālam?

How long have we lived for our families? How long have we wandered in search of wealth and pleasure? When will we realize the purpose of our birth? When will we receive the grace that will remove the affliction of the cycle of birth and death?

indanāḷaippōla nallanāḷum vērillai
indanēram pōla nalla nēram vērillai
guruvin vākkai kēṭṭu manatil cindippadālē
uṇmaiyinai uṇarvvadu pōl tavamum vērillai

There is no day better than today. There is no time better than now. There is no austerity equal to listening and contemplating the Guru's words, and thus realizing the eternal truth.

Arikiluṇḍenkilum (Tamil version)

arugilirundum arindiṭa iyalāmal
alaigintrēn ammā
kaṇgaḷirundum kāṇaviyalāmal
tēṭugintrēn ammā... unnai
tēṭugintrēn ammā

mārgazhi iravil nīlavānil pūtta
veṇmadi nītānō...
vānattai sēra muṭiyāmal karaiyil
talaimōdum alaiyāga nān – ammā
talaimōdum alaiyāga nān

ulagattin sukhamellām nilaikkādentruḷḷa
uṇmaiyai uṇarndadinālē...
iravum pagalum kaṇṇīr perugi
ariyattuṭittēn ammā – unnai
ariyattuṭittēn ammā

tuyarattin sumaiyāl tuvaṇḍiṭum enniṭam
ārudal aḷittiṭa vārāy
varuvāy enḍruḷḷa āsaiyuṭan nān
nittamum kāttirukkinḍrēn - ammā
nittamum kāttirukkinḍrēn

Arivenum akakkaṇ (Tamil)

arivenum akakkaṇ tiranditumō - endan
iruḷenum maṭamai akandriṭumō
aruvamāy anaittilum viḷankiṭum annaiyin
anumati atarkkāy kiṭaittiṭumō

Will my inner eye of wisdom ever open? Will the darkness of my ignorance ever be dispelled? Will I gain the blessings of the divine Mother, who abides in all as the formless Self?

arivāy ātavan aruḷ purindiṭinum
māyaiyām mēgham maraikkiratē
manatinil avaḷuru oḷiyena viḷankiṭa
taṭaikaḷum māyamāy maraindiṭumē

Even as rays pour from the sun of wisdom, the dark clouds of delusion eclipse divine grace. But when the splendor of the divine Mother manifests in my heart, all impediments vanish instantly.

pēruṇarvenappaṭum perumpātaiyilē
pētaiyām nānum naṭandiṭavē
bētamaiyillā tāyāmavaḷum
kaippiṭittennai naṭattiṭuvāḷ

An ignoramus am I, attempting to walk the path of inner awakening. The divine Mother, unconditional in Her love for all, will surely hold my hand and guide me to the goal.

Ariyāte ceytoraparādham (Malayalam)

ariyāte ceytoraparādham-ākilum
anivāryamō śikṣa kaṇṇā
āśikṣa satyattil-itrayum dussahamāvēṇam-
ennuṇḍō kaṇṇā?
ārūṇd-enikk-ende kaṇṇā?

O Krishna, is it really necessary to punish mistakes made unknowingly? Kanna, does that punishment have to be so painful? Who is there for me, Krishna?

pala-pala-tettukāl kuttaṅgaḷ ñān
ninnōṭu paraññu
pala nāḷum ninmunnil kaṇṇīrozhukki ñān
nilaviḷikkārille kaṇṇā?
nī sāntvanam coriyāruṇḍallo?

I used to tell You many of my mistakes and problems. Many days I would cry aloud before You, tears streaming. You are the one who showers compassion, aren't You?

niravadhi aparādham ceytālum munpokke
nī porukkārille kaṇṇā?
svaramezhum pāṭe pizhaccālum nī mugddha
svaramākkiṭarille kaṇṇā?
nī sāramillennu paraññu

Even when I commit many mistakes, don't You forgive me, Krishna? When my voice loses it's timber, don't You make it sound sweet, Kanna? You told me it was ok.

orunōkku kaṇān koticcum kitaccum
ā tirunaṭayil ñān ōṭivannāl
paribhavam tōnnēṇḍa- yenn-ōrttu
yāt-onnum parayāte ninmunnil ninnāl

vāripuṇarān nī arike varille?

If I come running with the urge to catch a glimpse of You, will You approach me? If I stand before You without saying anything, hoping You won't get upset, will You come to hug me?

Aśrutīrtthattāl (Malayalam)

aśrutīrtthattāl nin tṛkkazhal tazhukām ñān
arppita-hṛdayattil avatarikkū
centāraṭiyūnni, cintāmalaril nī
mandānilan pōle avatarikkū
dēvī dēvī dēvī dēvī
mandasmitānvitam avatarikkū

With tears, I will caress Your lotus feet. Please awaken in my heart, that is surrendered to You. Awaken with a smile, O Devi!

manassinde ēkānta nikuñjattil tapassinde
kanalūtiyūti ñān kāttirippū
ariya-jñānattinde aruḷābhayāluḷḷam
abhiṣiktamākki nī anugrahikkū
dēvī dēvī dēvī dēvī
amṛtākṣaraṅgaḷāl anugrahikkū

In the lonely cave of my heart I am awaiting You, in deep austerities. Please bless me with eternal knowledge. O Devi, please bless with me with immortal bliss.

kadanaṅgaḷ kaṭalōḷam karinīla nirabhēdam
karadūramini-yetra kātam
karaḷile kaṇṇīrum kadanavum cālicha
kavitayāl kazhaltāru tazhukām
dēvī dēvī dēvī dēvī
kanivōlum mizhiyālonnuzhiyū

The sorrows are infinite, the flowers are colorless, how much suffering must I endure? I will caress Your feet with my tears and sorrows. O Devi, will You caress me with Your compassionate glance?

Āṭalarasē (Tamil)

āṭalarasē āṭalarasē
āṭumivarai pārumarasē
tattuvankaḷ kēṭṭarintār
tannil atanai uṇarvatenṭrō?

O Lord of Dance! Look at these people dancing in illusion. They have listened to many philosophical treatises, but when will they realize them within themselves?

vīzhntuviṭum uṭalitanai
enatu enṭrē ivarninaippār
kozhuntuviṭum tīyatuvō
tanatu enṭrē tān ninaikkum

People think that the body which falls off in course of time is their own; but the blazing fire which consumes the body at the end will think 'this is mine'.

pirakkayilē ivar azhuvār
irakkayilē pirar azhuvār
pirappumillā irappumillā
tannaiyarintāl evar azhuvār

People cry when they are born, others cry when they die, but who will cry when they know their own Self?

jñāniyinai yārumpukazhvār
jñāniyāka yārmuyalvār?
jñālamkātta nīlakaṇṭhā
jñānam aruḷ naman talaivā

All glorify the enlightened person, but who strives to become one? Bestow real knowledge on us, O Lord of Death!

āṭiyapādā aruṇaiyin īsā
pārvatinēsā paramēsā
tēṭiyatiruvē pāṭiyaporuḷē
nāṭiya aruḷē naṭarājā

O One with dancing feet, Lord of Arunachala, beloved of Parvati, supreme One, Nataraja! You are the wealth sought by all, the essence of all hymns, the ultimate grace that everyone seeks.

Āṭi bā ō ranga (Kannada)

āṭi bā ō ranga angāla toḷedēnu
gandha sugandha candā

O Ranga, come back after play.

gandha sugandha candanadinda
cinnada pāda toḷedēnu

With fragrant ingredients, I shall wash Your golden feet.

gopike sakhiyaru gopa bālakaru
kaṇṇāmuchālē āṭi
kaṇṇāmuchālē āṭi nin ondige
daṇidu malagavarilli

The gopis and gopas, having played hide and seek with You, are now tired and resting here.

rādheya jotegūdi rāsalīleya āṭi
rājīva nētra nī bāro
rājīva nētra bārayya mane kaṭege
rātri gāḍa vāguva munna

O Lotus-eyed One, after having played rasa lila with Radha, come home before it is too late in the night.

mussanje musukide godhūḷi eddide
sandhyā lakṣmi minugavaḷe
sandhyā lakṣmi nakṣatra minugi
ninagāgi dārī beḷagavaḷe

It is twilight. The dust of dusk is rising, the evening star is shining. That evening star is showing You the path.

gogaḷu kādive hālanūṭalu bāla
amma yaśode kādavaḷe
amma yaśodeya ede tumbi bandide
hālanūṭuvaḷu bābārā

The cows are waiting to feed You their milk. Mother Yashoda is waiting. Her heart is overflowing, wanting to feed You milk.

Āvo mā ammā (Gujarati)

āvo mā ammā, hṛdayamā mārā banīne gīt koyī
tārī stuti karū, tārī bhakti karū
tārā bhajanmā rācū ammā
tārā bhajanmā rācū

Mother, come to my heart in the form of a song. I'll sing Your glories. I'll worship You with devotion. Singing Your praises, I'll lose myself.

āvo mā ammā hṛdayamā mārā
banīne mūrat kōyī
tāro abhiṣek karū, tāro alankār karū
tārī āratīmā rācū ammā
tārī āratīmā rācū

Mother, come to my heart in the form of my deity. I'll do abhishekam to You, I'll adorn You. Performing arati to You, I'll forget myself.

āvo mā ammā hṛdayamā mārā
banīne joḍ mārī
tārī sāthe rās ramu
sāthe tārī nṛtya karū
tujhmā hu samāvū ammā
tujhmā hu samāvū

Mother, come to my heart as my soul-mate. I'll dance with You Mother, with You I'll play the rasa dance. I'll merge in You.

tu mārī ambā tu bahucarā māḍī
tu mārī santoṣī ambikā
jai jai ho mā tārī jai jai maiyyā tārī

You are my Mother, Mother Bahuchara, Santoshi, my Mother Ambika. Victory to Mother!

Āyā he sārā (Hindi)

āyā he sārā jahā yahā
milke ye sārā jahā yahā
ek mantr bole ek svar me bole
jag me ho śānti samādhān
om lokāḥ samastāḥ sukhino bhavantu

The whole world has come. All of us are here together. Let us chant this mantra in chorus, 'let there be peace and harmony in the world.' May all the beings in all the worlds be happy!

ham sabhe īśvar kī santān
ye duniyā ke khelse anjān
rāh dikhānā prabhu sāth hame le ke caltu
mānava dharma sikhānā
om lokāḥ samastāḥ sukhino bhavantu

We are children of God. We are ignorant of this play. Show

us the way, O Lord. Take us along with You and teach us what man's dharma is. May all the beings in all the worlds be happy!

ham sāre mil jul ke rahe
sab kā dard apnā samjhe
nā koyī dukhse roye sab cainki nīnd soye
prabhu dedo aisā vardān
om lokāḥ samastāḥ sukhino bhavantu

Let us live together happily. Let us feel others' pain as our own. Let no one cry in sorrow, let everyone sleep peacefully. O Lord, grant us such a boon.

niṣkām sevā ham kare
karm yog ke pathpe cale
cāhe ham sabkā bhalā jiye to aisā yahāṁ
dharttiko svarg banāde
om lokāḥ samastāḥ sukhino bhavantu

Tread the path of selfless service and karma yoga. Desire everyone's well-being. Live in such a way that this earth becomes a heaven. May all the beings in all the worlds be happy!

Āye hān tvadde (Punjabi)

āye hān tvadde darbār vich sāre, śera valiye
dukhān nu pul kke, sukhān de kinare

We have all come into Mother's arms, forgetting all sorrows at the banks of happiness.

ditta hai janam ikk navān jo sānu, jota valiye
pyar te karuna di pāśa vi sikhade – o ma

Giving us this new birth, teach us the language of love and compassion.

mata rani di (jai)

śeravali di (jai)
jotavali di (jai)
latavali di (jai)
pahadavali di (jai)
meharavali di (jai) bolo sāche darbār di (jai)ki
galat ki tīk na patā hai sānu, lātā valiye
har kadam te cirāg jyot jalade – jalade ma

We don't know what is right or wrong, so illumine our path for every step we take.

Āyī bhavāni tū (Marathi)

āyī bhavāni tū āmuci mātā
kuṭhe śodhū tulā āmhi sāṅg ātā

O Mother Bhavani, You are our Mother. Tell us, where should we search for You?

jai jai āyī bhavāni jai jai
jai jai āyī śivāni jai jai

Victory to Mother! Victory to Bhavani and Shivani!

jaḷī sthaḷī nabhī an pāṣāṇi
tuc naṭali ga vividha rūpāni
pari kase śodhū māuli
mayecyā āvaraṇi āyī tū lapali

You are hiding in the universe disguised as water, air, sky, and mountains. You are residing in these various forms. How do I search for You, hidden as You are under the cover of maya?

māyāvi sansāri āmhās bhulavi
jāḷe nijamāyece ase ṭākuni
sukhalipt jhāli ga naśvara kāyā
durlabh naratanu cālali vāyā

You have engrossed us in this illusive world by putting a net of delusion over us. Our mortal body is attached to seeking pleasures and this rare chance of a human birth is getting wasted.

viṣaya vihacha nivaruni kata
davī amha navadha bhakticya vata
carni visava deī ga satvar
par kar majha ha bhavasagar

Removing the poisonous throne of sensual pleasures, show us the way of nine-fold devotion. Please give me rest as soon as possible at Your feet. Take me across the ocean of samsara!

Azhagukku azhagu (Tamil)

azhagukku azhagu etuvō?
atu kaṇṇanin karuniramē
azhagukku azhagu etuvō?
atu kaṇṇanin kuzhikannamē
inimaikku inimai etuvō?
atu kaṇṇanin salankai-oliyē
inimaikku inimai etuvō?
atu kaṇṇanin kuzhalisaiyē
iḷamaikku iḷamai etuvō?
atu kaṇṇanin pun-sirippē
iḷamaikku iḷamai etuvō?
atu kaṇṇanin tirumukhamē
kṛṣṇā madhusūdanā gōvindā nārāyaṇā

Among all that is beautiful, which is most beautiful? It is Krishna's dusky hue. Among all that is beautiful, which is most beautiful? It's His dimples. Among all that is charming, which is most charming? It's the tinkle of Krishna's anklets. Among all that is charming, which is most charming? It's the melody of His flute. Among all that is youthful, which is most youthful? It's Krishna's smile. Among all that is youthful, which is most youthful? It's His sacred face. O Krishna, slayer of Madhu! O Lord of Speech, supreme Lord.

putumaikku putumai etuvō?
atu kaṇṇanin kaṇṇoḷiyē
putumaikku putumai etuvō?
atu kaṇṇanin kurumbutānē
perumaikku perumai etuvō?
atu kaṇṇanin rāsalīlayē
perumaikku peruma ietuvō?
atu kaṇṇan kāḷiya naṭanamaṇdrō
kṛṣṇā madhusūdanā gōvindā nārāyaṇā

Among all that is new, which is newest? It's the luster of Krishna's eyes. Among all that is new, which is newest? It's His mischief. Among all that is exalted, which is most exalted? It's Krishna's rasa-lila (mystic) dance. Among all that is exalted, which is most exalted? It's the dance He enacted on Kaliya's head. O Krishna, slayer of Madhu! O Lord of Speech, O Supreme Lord.

Azhaku azhaku (Tamil)

ammā un paṭaippellām orānanda naṭanam
aṇumutal kāṇpatellām unnōṭu pāṭukiratu
tāḷamiṭṭu āṭukiratu unnai
ānandattōṭu vazh-ipaṭukiratu
azhum kural kēṭṭu jñāna pālūṭṭiya tāyē
ānandattil-āzhttiṭa bhuvanattil
naṭanamāṭi vantarūḷvāy

O Mother, Your creation is a blissful dance. From the atoms to all that is seen, everything is singing with You. Dancing with rhythmic steps, all worship You blissfully. Hearing the cries of a child, You fed the milk of wisdom. Please come dancing to the world to immerse us in that bliss!

azhaku azhaku azhaku azhaku
ammā untan naṭanamazhaku
azhaku azhaku azhaku azhaku
dēviyāṭum bhuvanamazhaku

Your dance is beautiful, and the world You dance in is also beautiful.

naṭanamāṭum naṭanamāṭum
kaṇkaḷ mūṭi naṭanamāṭum
ennammā enkaḷ ponnammā
pāṭal pāṭi por kaimaṇiyāl tāḷamiṭṭu
paravasamāy parantāṭum
paṭṭāmpūccipōl ennammā
dēviyavaḷ nāmam solla
dēva dundubhikaḷ muzhanka

O Mother who is dancing with closed eyes, You are our dear Mother. Mother, You are dancing like a butterfly in an elated state, singing with golden cymbals in rhythmic beat. Chanting Devi's name, the gods are playing divine instruments.

mātārāṇī ku - jai
mahārāṇī ku - jai
mahādēvī ku - jai
mahālakṣmī ku - jai

Hail to the Mother Empress! Hail to the Queen Empress! Hail to Mahadevi! Hail to Mahalakshmi!

āyiram nāmam koṇḍu pūmāri tūviṭuvōm
kōlāṭṭam karakāṭṭam kōṭi makkaḷ āṭiṭuvōm

āyiram kaṇṇuṭayavalē ankāḷa māriyamma
ammā mahāmāyiyavaḷ anpumazhai pezhintiṭuvāḷ

We worship You, chanting Your one thousand names and showering flower petals. Millions of people are dancing the folk dances Kollattam and Karagattam in worship of You. O Mariyamma, You have a thousand eyes. Shower the rain of love, O Mahamayi!

jīvanellām śivanilaṭanka śivakāmi nī āṭumāṭṭam
anpu koṇḍu azhaittiṭṭāy anaivaraiyum un āṭalukkuḷ
kalipuruṣan āṭṭattai kāḷi nī oṭukkiṭamma
kallyāṇa guṇankalē nī kallyāṇī vaḷarttiṭamma

Shiva's dear One, You are dancing, merging all souls into Shiva. You are attracting everyone lovingly through Your dance. O Kali, please stop the dance of the dark-age. O Kalyani, please nurture good and auspicious qualities.

Azhalingu puzhayāy (Malayalam)

azhalingu puzhayāy mizhinīru mazhayāy
aliyāttatentē ghanaśyāma mānasam
irulērumī rāvil-oru nāḷa-manayāte nī -
yaṇayunnatum kāttu-kāttirikkunnu kaṇṇa

Why does my dark-clouded mind not melt and flow as a river of grief, a downpour of tears? In this dark morning, I keep a flame ablaze and wait for You to come, O Krishna.

karinīla vipinattil ēkānta-yāmattil
kuyilēttu pāṭunnu nin gānam-ippōl
ariyāte nī vannu pōyitō kaṇṇā
ninavārnnu mātrayō nilayattorōrmmayō

In this dark blue sky, at this solitary hour, the cuckoo echoes Your song. Did You come and leave without my knowledge? Was it just my imagination? Or was it a memory?

virayārnnu pozhiyunnoril-apōlayen manam
nilayatta-tozhukunnithalayāzhi tēṭi
alayārkkum ā nīlavarṇṇamen kaṇṇā
ārālumariyāte nīyēkiyallayō

My mind trembles like a leaf. It flows blindly searching for the ocean to which You have secretly given Your blue hue.

tirumāril vanamāla aṇiyikkumōrmmayil
malarcūṭi nilkunnu vāsanta śākhikaḷ
ārōrumariyāte malar cūṭuvānen kaṇṇā
nīyalōla vāyū pōlaṇayunnatillayō

These trees bear their blossoms in the memory of adorning Your divine chest with the Vanamala garland. Did You secretly pass by as the gentle breeze to accept their garland, O Krishna?

Azhutāl unnaiperalāmē (Tamil)

azhutāl unnaiperalāmē
ammā aruḷai peralāmē
tozhutāl unnai peralāmē
tutittē anpai peralāmē

We get Mother's grace and blessings when we cry for Her. We receive Her love if we worship Her.

unakkō āyiram tirunāmam
uḷḷam tannil orunāmam
enakkō ammā nīyē gati
enrum nīyēyen śaraṇāgati

Though You have a thousand names, I have only one name in my mind. You are the only refuge for me, I am forever surrendered to You.

śorpadam kaṭanta paramjyōti
sōrnta manattil uyirjyōti
porppadam paṇintāl nī varuvāy
bhuviyil vaḷattai nidam taruvāy

The supreme Self cannot be described in words. The individual soul is just behind the weary mind. If we surrender, You will come. Please give prosperity to this Mother Earth!

anpai pozhiyum mazhaiyānāy
amṛtānanda vaṭivānāy
unnai paṇiyum makkaḷukku
uyarvai koṭukkum iraiyānāy

You shower the rain of eternal love. You are in the form of blissful nectar. You are God to those who surrender to You. You are the God who is uplifts us.

Bā bhṛngavē bā (Kannada)

bā bhṛngavē bā
mana bhṛngavē bā
ammana karēyitu kēḷisadē?
ētakē aḷutiruvē?

Come, O Honey-bee of the mind! Don't you hear Mother calling? Why are you crying?

hoḷeva dhavaḷa hṛdaya kamala
miḍididē prēma taranga
madhuva saviye savidu kuṇiye
makāra moḷaguta bā

The resplendent, white lotus of the heart throbs with vibrations of love. Come, chanting the divine syllable, 'Ma', so that you may taste the nectar and rejoice!

bēganē bantu madhuva uṇḍu
mēlakēruva bā
allidē ānanda allidē āmōda
amṛtapāna allidē bā

Come soon to drink the nectar, and then let us ascend. Come! There is real bliss, there is real joy. There is the real drink of immortality.

hē manabhṛnga! hē manabhṛnga!
hē manabhṛnga! hē manabhṛnga!

O Honey-bee of the mind!

Balē ambikē (Tulu)

balē ambikē jñāna dēviye
balē ambikē appē lakṣmiyē
dēvī balē balē appē pārvati
jayatu ambikē jayatu tāyē
jayatu jayatu jayatu jayatu jaganmayi

Come, Mother, Godess of wisdom. Come, Mother Lakshmi! Come, O Mother Parvati. Glory to You, Mother of the World!

balē ambikē jagakku boḷpādu
balē ambikē manakku boḷpādu
ētu vismayō īrēna mahimē
irana prēma jyōtiyē bālugu boḷpu

Come, Mother, and light up the world. Come, Mother, and light up the mind. Your greatness is such a wonder! The light of Your love is the light of our life.

balē ambikē korlē santōṣā
balē ambikē korlē sāntvana
balē appē tojālē daivī śaktinu
appē prēmōḍē ī jōklēnu kāpūlē

Come, Mother, and give us happiness. Come, Mother, and grant us consolation! Come and reveal Your divine power. O Mother, protect these children with Your love!

jayatu jayatu jayatu jayatu jaganmayi

Glory to You, Mother of the World!

Bandaḷō bandāḷō (Kannada)

bandaḷō bandāḷō amma
bandaḷō bandāḷō
bandaḷō bandāḷō hṛdayēśvarī
kāruṇyarūpadī bandāḷō

Here comes Mother, Goddess of my heart, in the form of compassion!

paṭṭusīre dharisi bandāḷō
honnageya bīrutali
kaiyeraḍu bīsutali
ōṭi banni makkaḷe yentu karedāḷō
kāruṇyarūpadi bandālō

Decked in golden silk, beaming with golden smiles, swinging both of Her hands, calling "Come running, O children!" She comes in the form of compassion.

ellarannu tabbikkoḷḷalu
tabbikkoṇḍu muttanīḍalu
ellarannu anugrahisalu
anugrahisi varanīḍalu bandāḷō
kāruṇyarūpadī bandāḷō

She comes to embrace every one of us, to kiss every one of us, to bless us all and grant us our wishes. She comes in the form of compassion.

kaṣṭakaḷa pariharisalu
nijānanda tōrisalu
ajñānikaḷāda namannu
ānandadi muḷugisalu bandāḷō
kāruṇyarūpadī bandāḷō

She comes to solve our problems and to show us real bliss. She comes to drown us, ignorant ones, in bliss. The Mother in the form of compassion is coming!

Bandaḷō bandāḷō (Gujarati version)

āvi amba āvi amba
āvi amba āvi amba
āvi amba āvi ḥṛdayeśvari
kārunyarupini padhāri

lāl cundaddi odhine āvi
mand muskān karti
hāth banne pasāri kaheti
doddi āvo ballako badha
padhāri kārunyarupini padhāri

sahune haiye lagāvavā
haiyye lagāvi cumbana devā
ballakone āshish deva
āshish āpi var deva
padhāri kārunyarupini padhāri

kaṣta badhā dur karavā
nijānanda varsāvavā
agnāni aevā āpanane

ānandamā magna karvā
padhāri kārunyarupini padhāri

Bandhamu nīttō (Telugu)

bandhamu nīttō ērppaṭanī - bhava
bandhamu lēvō viṭipōnnī
spandana edallō mōdalavanī
sāndrappuṭṭalalā muñcēttanī

Let my bond be with You and let my bondage drop away. Let the quest for God begin in my heart and let me be submerged in its waves.

dentamunīkkayyī parugiṭanī
sarvamunīvani sthirapaṭanī
cīkaṭi tṛṭṭīlō cittavanī
cittappa vṛttalu layamavanī

Let my heart and mind run after You. Let it be established that You are everything. Let darkness take flight in a fraction of a second. Let my desires cease to exist.

satyappu kāntulu aguppaṭanī
nityānandamu nilappaṭanī
ammala gannā ammava nī
biṭaggā nī oṭi cērcamanī

Let the beams of truth appear. Let eternal bliss be established. Mother of mothers, take me in Your lap as Your child.

ammā jagadambā nannu kāvaga rāvammā
ammā jagadambā nā śaraṇamē nīvammā

Mother, Mother of the Universe, come and protect me! Mother, Mother of the Universe, You are my sole refuge.

Bandu biḍabāradē (Kannada)

bandu biḍabāradē bāgilanu tērēdu ni
hṛdaya bāgilanu tērēdu ni
ariyalārenu nānu bāgilanu tērēyalu
hṛdaya bāgilanu tērēyalu

Why don't You come, and open the door Yourself, the door of the heart? I don't know how to open the door of my heart.

mareyutihēnu nāni manada māyeyalī ninna
endendu mareyada hāge
bandu ni nelesabāradē

Caught in the maya of the mind, I forget You. Why don't You come and settle in my heart so that I may never, ever forget You?

ammā ammā endu kareyutiruvēnu ninna
kāyutiruvēnu tāyē ninna baruvikege nānu

I call out to You, O Mother, I am waiting for You to come.

Bārayya śiva (Kannada)

bārayya śivā bārayya śivā bārayya śivanē
nōḍuvē ninna manadaṇiye bārayya śivanē

Please come, my dear Lord Shiva. Let me behold You to my heart's content.

kailāsadi vāsipane umākāntanē
rudrākṣiya dharisihanē nīlakaṇṭhanē
bhaktarige oliyuva paramēśvaranē
nōḍuvē ninna manadaṇiye bārayya śivanē

Consort of Uma, You reside in Kailash. O blue-throated One, You wear the rudrākṣa bead. O supreme Lord, You readily offer boons to devotees. Let me behold You to my heart's content.

ruṇḍamāla dharisihane rudrēśvaranē
gangēyannu hottiruva śaśiśēkharanē
bhaktarige oliyuva paramēśvaranē
nōḍuvē ninna manadaṇiye bārayya śivanē

O fearsome One, You are adorned with a garland of skulls. Your wear the crescent moon on Your head, from which flows the cascading Ganga River. O supreme Lord, You readily offer boons to devotees. Let me behold You to my heart's content.

triśūlava hiḍidiha trilōkanāthanē
śmaśānadi vāsipanē bhūtanāthanē
bhaktarigē oliyuva paramēśvaranē
nōḍuvē ninna manadaṇiye bārayya śivanē

Lord of the three worlds, You wield the trident. O Lord of ghouls, You dwell in charnel grounds. Supreme Lord, You readily offer boons to devotees. Let me behold You to my heart's content.

śaśidhara śikhinētrā purahara girivāsā
trinayana suranāthā jaya! hara! jitakāmā

Victory to Shiva, whose head is adorned with a crescent moon, who has the eye of fire, who destroyed the demon known as Pura, who dwells in the mountain, who is three-eyed, who is Lord of the gods, and who has conquered desire.

Barutihaḷu (Kannada)

barutihaḷu barutihaḷu tāyē kāḷī
viśva jananī tāyē viśva mātē

Mother Kali is approaching! She is the Mother of the universe.

puṭṭa hejjeyaniṭṭu paṭṭu sīreyanuṭṭu
barutihaḷu barutihaḷu tāyē kāḷī
kembu kunkuma biṭṭu cinna dōḍyāna toṭṭu
barutihaḷu barutihaḷu tāyē kāḷī

Mother Kali is approaching with dainty steps and wearing a silk sari. She is approaching with a saffron mark on Her forehead, wearing a golden girdle.

ruṇḍa māleya dharasi caṇḍamuṇḍa samharisi
barutihaḷu barutihaḷu tāyē kāḷī
jagavanne manemāḍi manavanne guḍimāḍi
barutihaḷu barutihaḷu tāyē kāḷī

Mother Kali is approaching, wearing a garland of skulls, having annihilated demons Chanda and Munda. She is approaching, having made the whole universe Her abode and the mind Her shrine.

Beḷḷi beṭṭadoḍeya (Kannada)

beḷḷi beṭṭadoḍeya śivanu
kubēranā geḷeyanivanu
himavantana aḷiyanivanu
bhaktajanara hṛdayanivanu

O Shiva, Lord of the silver snowy mountains, friend of Kubera, son-in-law of the king of the Himalayas, heart of the devotees.

om namah śivāya om namah śivāya
om namah śivāya om namah śivāya

Salutations to Lord Shiva!

sutagaṇapati skanda sahita
nandīśvara gaṇa sēvita
bhuvanakkella oḍeyanīta
maruḷanante tōruvāta

Accompanied by Your sons Ganapati and Skanda, served by Nandishwara and other ganas, the Lord of the worlds pretends to be ordinary.

bhaktarā jīvanivanu

śaraṇajanara prāṇanivanu
yōgijanara dhyēyanivanu
prēmavāgi baruvanivanu

He is the soul of devotees, the very life of saints, the goal of spiritual seekers. He comes as love.

yatiyu mēṇ brahmacāri
sādhu matte samsāri
pārvati pati jagadādhāri
carācarātma vihārī

Sage and celibate, saint and family man, Parvati's husband, rescuer of the world, Self of all living and non-living beings.

Beyond the most beautiful words

beyond the most beautiful words in the world
above the most glorious hymns ever heard
too wonderful to be expressed with fine art,
is our devi dayambike, queen of my heart

a writer whose mind is as clear as the heavens
can easily find the right words for a scene
words that will fail time and again,
to tell of the wonder I feel
when her silence and peace is revealed

a painter beholds endless colors in a rainbow,
and easily finds the right yellow for the sun
paintings will fail time and again
to convey the beauty I see
in her face that is formless and free

a singer who holds all the knowledge of the ragas
can easily choose the right one for the dawn
melodies fail time and again
to reach the most beautiful key
one she holds for a door within me

Bhaktigē sōpāna (Kannada)

bhaktigē sōpāna harināmavu
nija muktigē sādhana harināmavu
ānanda koḍuvanta śubhanāmavu

The name of Hari is a stepping-stone to devotion. It is a spiritual practice that leads to eternal liberation. The auspicious name bestows bliss.

nintalle endare ānandavu - hari
nintalle endare kaivalyavu
ānanda koḍuvanta śubhanāmavu

Chanting the name of Hari while standing gives bliss and liberation. The auspicious name bestows bliss.

kuntalle endare santōṣavu - hari
kuntalle endare akṣayavu
ānanda koḍuvanta śubhanāmavu

Chanting the name of Hari while sitting gives happiness and abundance. The auspicious name bestows bliss.

hariyanu bhajisalu anavaratavu
śāśvata sukhavu khaṇḍitavu
ānanda koḍuvanta śubhanāmavu

Chanting the name of Hari incessantly guarantees eternal happiness. The auspicious name bestows bliss.

hari hari hari hari gōvindā

jaya hari jaya hari nārāyaṇā
hari nārāyaṇā gōvindā
jaya nārāyaṇā gōvindā

Victory to Hari, Govinda, the protector of cows, and Narayana, the all-pervading One.

Bhuvanasundarī (Tamil)

bhuvanasundarī śankaran tuṇaivi
ṣaṇmukhan vaṇankiṭum umayē – ammayē
ṣaṇmukhan vaṇankiṭum umayē
sahaja samādhi nilayē

O Uma You are the beauty of the universe. You are the consort of Lord Shankara. You are worshipped by Lord Shanmukha, Your son. You are ever dwelling in a state of supreme bliss.

tāmarai kaṇkaḷ amaiti tarum – atu
karuṇaiyinālē nīr tatumbum
mānuṭa janmattin poruḷ vizhantāl nī
bōdhippatellām atil teḷiyum

Your lotus like eyes bestow peace of mind. They are filled with crystalline tears because of Your exceeding compassion. If one desires to understand the meaning of human life, all that You teach will be shining in Your eyes.

malayinai kuṭaintu vīṭamaippāḷ – anku
katavinai tirantu varavērpāḷ
tāyavaḷ namakkena kāttiruppāḷ – nam
varukaiyinālē akam kuḷirvāḷ

You abide in mountain caves, and keep the doors open so as to receive everyone. O Mother, You await our arrival at the door. You will feel exhilarated upon seeing us arrive.

kēśavan sōdarī gajamukhan ammai nī āpadbāndhavi
anātharakṣaki bhārggavi saundari ambikai īśvari
mugguṇa māyai nīkkiṭum tāy nī tavattiru tēnmozhi
muttamizh kalaiyē sattāna poruḷē ānanda bhairavi
ammē ānanda bhairavi

You are the sister of Keshava and Mother of Gajamukha. You are the protector at all times, the savior of the destitute! You are the Mother that destroys the illusion of the three gunas. You are the exponent of the three arts, and the power behind everything. O Mother, You are the Goddess of bliss!

Birhā ki in (Hindi)

birhā ki in havāvom me
terā khoyā lāl pukāre
ungili thāmlecal ab janani
jag kī bāzī me ham hāre

In this atmosphere heavy with the feeling of separation, Your long-lost child is calling You. O Mother! Now at least please hold my hand and lead me, as I feel completely defeated in this game of 'world!'

mā kā ācal thām liyā hai
riśte nātom ko ṭukrāyā
saccā ēk sahārā pākar
jag mithyā hai samajh me āyā
- samajh me āyā

Now that I am holding on to my Mother's saree, I have done away with all worldly relations. Only upon finding a true support have I come to know the hollowness of this world!

pichle karm māne jalāye
ab duṣkarm na hone pāye

sevā bhakti prem kā var le
jīvan apnā dhanya banāye
- dhanya banāye

Mother has burnt away all my earlier karma. Now let me be cautious not to create more bad karma. Let us all seek the blessings of service, devotion and love, thus making our lives blessed forever!

durge durgatihāriṇi mātā
sāsom kā har tār pukāre
ghar vāpas ab lecal janani
terā khoyā lāl pukāre
- lāl pukāre

O Mother Durga, You eliminate misery and pain. My each and every breath calls out to You aloud: 'It is enough now! Mother, Please take me back home! Your long-lost child is crying out to You!'

Callaga cūḍu (Telugu)

callaga cūḍu nī pillalamu
nīvu tappa dikkevaru māku
cintalu tīrci centaku cērcu
cittamulo nī cintane nimpu

Protect us. We are Your children. We have no other refuge than You. Allay our anxieties and draw us close to You. Fill our mind with remembrances of You.

nī dayalēka dorakadu mārgam
nī dīvena tō kalugunu mōkṣam

Without Your compassion, we cannot find the path to spiritual liberation. Without Your blessings, we will not attain liberation.

nī caraṇamulē śaraṇamu māku
nī sannidhiyē pennidhi māku

Your feet are our sole refuge. Your presence is our wealth.

devi bhavānī sakalavēdarūpiṇī
devi śivānī dēvalōkapālinī

O Goddess Bhavani, embodiment of all the Vedas. O Goddess Shivani, Protector of the world of Gods.

Candracūḍa (Telugu)

candracūḍa pādamulaku praṇāmam
śrīśailavāsunaku praṇāmam
hara praṇāmam praṇāmam
śrīnīlakaṇṭhunaku pranāmam

Salutations at the feet of Shiva, the One who wears the moon on His head. Salutations to the One who resides in Srisailam. Salutations to Hara. Salutations to He who has a blue throat!

veṇṭi koṇḍalalō ānanda-nṛtyamāḍu
naṭarāja pādamulaku praṇāmam
rāmuni hṛdayamulō nityanivāsi
rāmēśvara pādamulaku praṇāmam – ā
bhakta-jana-sulabhunaku praṇāmam

Salutations at the feet of Nataraja who dances with ecstasy. Salutations to One who resides in the heart of Rama eternally. Salutations to the One who is easily attainable by devotees.

hara praṇāmam praṇāmam praṇāmam
praṇava-svarūpunaku praṇāmam

Salutations to Hara, salutations to the embodiment of Om!

sarvāntar-ātmunaku kaivalya-dhāmunaku
ādyanta-rahitunaku praṇāmam
praḷayānta-kālamulō bhīkara-tāṇḍavamāḍu
kālarudra-pādamulaku praṇāmam – ā
ādipraṇava-rūpunaku praṇāmam

Salutations to the One who resides in everyone, to the One whose abode is liberation. Salutations to the One who is without beginning and end. Salutations at the feet of the One who dances fiercely during dissolution, salutations to the primordial One.

Cēnmilē (Hindi)

cēnmilē ārām milē
śānti ōr viśrām milē
vō hē mā kigōd vimal
jahā bhaktōn kō prēm milē

Our sweet Mother's lap is so soft. Her devotees find quietude, peace, and unconditional love there.

snigdhasnēh apār mile
karuṇā aparampārmilē
vō hē mā kā hṛdayakamal
jahā hari ōmkār milē

Our sweet Mother's heart is like a lotus flower where Her devotees experience divine union and limitless compassion. In Her heart Lord Hari resides and the divine sound Om resounds.

duḥkh dard santāp miṭē
ādhivyādhi abhiśāp miṭē
vō hē mā kā hṛdaycaman
jahām kānṭō kā uttāp miṭē

Our sweet Mother's heart is like a beautiful garden. Her presence removes curses, pain and suffering. In Her lap, grief-stricken hearts find inner peace.

lōbh mōh sē trāṇ milē
kāmkrōdh kō virām milē
vō hē mā kā hṛdaygagan
jahā gangā kī dhār milē

In our divine Mother's heart flows the holy river Ganga. In Her lap devotees find freedom from greed and material attachments. Mother's presence purifies the hearts of Her darling children by bringing an end to lust and anger.

Cinna cinna kaṇṇā (Tamil)

cinna cinna kaṇṇā sinkārakaṇṇā
cintaiyil kalandiṭum kārmēghavarṇṇā
cinnañciru itazhināle anpumozhi pēsavā
sīraṭṭi pāraṭṭi pālūṭṭi tālāṭṭa ōḍi vā kaṇṇā

O little Kanna (Krishna), beautiful Kaṇṇā, Your dark-hued form merges into the mind. Utter a few loving words with those tender lips! Come running, O Kaṇṇā, so that we may cuddle and praise You, give You some milk, and sing You a lullaby.

yaśōdayin karampiḍittu taḷirnaḍai naḍantāy
yārumariyā līlaiseydu makkaḷai kāttāy
yātumariyā siruppiḷḷayāy viḷaiyāḍināi
yādavā mādhavā māyavā kṛṣṇā
yādavā mādhavā māyavā manamōhana kṛṣṇā

You toddled, holding Yashoda's hand. Engaging in divine play without anyone's knowledge, You saved the people. You frolic like an innocent, little child. O Yadava, Madhava, who wields the power of illusion, You captivate the mind!

tunpam tarum asurarai māyaiyāl māittāy
kurumpāle gōpiyarai anpuḍan īrttāy
enna nī seydālum unnōḍu kōpamillaiyē
ennavā mannavā cinnavā kṛṣṇā
ennavā mannavā cinnavā śrī bālakṛṣṇā

With Your power of illusion, You destroyed the evil demons. And with Your loving mischief, You captivated the milkmaids' hearts. No matter what You do, we can never get angry with You, O Lord, little One, child Krishna!

piñjukālāl nañjutarum kāḷiyanai azhittāy
añjaneñcil tañjamtandu ānandam aḷittāy
inampuriyā makizhvaḷitta uravāṭināy
anpane naṇpane āyanē kṛṣṇā
anpane naṇpane āyanē gōvindakṛṣṇā

With those tender feet, You stamped out the ego of the poisonous Kaliya snake. You bestow bliss that removes fear from the heart and that grants refuge. You forge a bond that confers indescribable bliss, O Companion, Friend, cowherd Krishna!

Cuṭṭri cuṭṭri (Tamil)

cuṭṭri cuṭṭri varukirēnē teriyalayō
unnai cuttrum inda bālakanai ariyalayō
pattri undan kāl piṭittēn pārkkalayō
unne pattrum endan mēl unakku parivillayō

Mother, don't You know that Your child is going round and round You? Have You not seen me holding Your feet? Don't You have compassion towards this child who is surrendered to Your feet?

ēnki ēnki azhukirēnē teriyalayō en
ekkamadai nīkkiṭavum manamillayō
tūnkāmal tavikkirēnē puriyalayō
tūnkudal pōl naṭikkirāyē kanivillayō

Don't You know that I'm longing and crying for You? Do You not intend to remove my suffering? Don't You understand that I am suffering, unable to sleep? You are pretending to sleep. Won't You have compassion towards me?

pārkka eṇṇi tuṭikkirēnē pārkkalayō
pārkka maṭṭum undanukku manamillayō
vākkadanāl azhaikkirēnē kēṭkkalayō en mēl
vātsalya mazhai pozhiya manamillayō

Do You not see me longing to see You? You have time to see everything else. Do You not have the mind to see me? Don't You hear me calling out to You? Do you not want to shower Your motherly love upon me?

valaiyil vīzhā mīnuṇḍu vaiyagattil
vāñcayilā tāyumuṇḍō sēyiṭattil
imaikākkā nilaiyuṇḍu kaṇṇiṭattil bhakti
valayil varā daivamuṇḍō ivvulakil

In the world, fish are caught in nets. Is there any mother who is not caught in the net of their child's affection? It may come to be that the eyelid fails to protect the eye - but will any god be able to escape from the net of devotion?

ennammā cellammā ennai kaṇ pārammā
kaṇṇammā ponnammā kaṇṇin kaṇ nīyammā

My Mother, dear Mother, please glance at me. Darling Mother, You are the eye of the eye.

Ḍam ḍam ḍum ḍum ḍamarū bōle

(Gujarati)

ḍam ḍam ḍum ḍum ḍamarū bōle
har har har har mahādevā
śiv śiv śiv śiv śivagaṇa bōle
namaḥ śivāya ōm namaḥ śivāya

The damaru is chanting 'har har har har mahadeva'- in response the Shiva Ganas are chanting 'namah shivaya om namah shivaya'

nīla nīla ākāś bōle
har har har har mahādevā
garjjanā kartā mēgh bōle
namaḥ śivāya ōm namaḥ śivāya

The blue sky chants 'har har har har mahadeva'. In response, the blue clouds roar 'namah shivaya om namah shivaya'.

sāgar nadī sarītā bōle
har har har har mahādevā
ghāṭ ghāṭ ne kinārā bōle
namaḥ śivāya ōm namaḥ śivāya

The oceans, the rivers and streams chant 'har har har har mahadeva,' and all the coasts and banks chant 'namah shivaya om namah shivaya' in response.

dhartti van parvat bōle
har har har har mahādevā
vṛkṣa latā ne śikharo bōle
namaḥ śivāya ōm namaḥ śivāya

The earth, the forests and the mountains chant 'har har har har mahadeva'. The trees, the creepers and the mountain tops chant 'namah shivaya om namah shivaya' in response.

ḍāḷ ḍāḷ par pankhī bōle
har har har har mahādevā
nṛttya karantā mōr bōle
namaḥ śivāya ōm namaḥ śivāya

The birds on every branch chant 'har har har har mahadeva'. In response, the peacocks dance, chanting 'namah shivaya om'.

vāṇi vidyā vādya bōle
har har har har mahādevā
sūr sangīt ne sār bōle
namaḥ śivāya ōm namaḥ śivāya

Speech, knowledge and musical instruments chant 'har har har har mahadeva'. All of music, every tune, and every essence chants 'namah shivaya om namah shivaya' in response.

sādhu sant bairāgi bōle
har har har har mahādevā
tum ham sab milkar bōle
namaḥ śivāya ōm namaḥ śivāya

The sages, the saints and the renunciates chant 'har har har har mahadeva'. Let us all chant 'namah shivaya om namah shivaya' in response!

Dānavāntakā rāmā (Kannada)

dānavāntakā rāmā
dāśarathē raghu rāmā
dīna dayaḷō rāmā
dhīra vīra śrī rāmā

O Rama, destroyer of demons, son of Daśaratha, and scion of the Raghu dynasty, You are compassionate to the fallen. You are wise and valorous.

rāmā jaya jaya rāmā
rāmā jānaki rāmā
rāmā paṭṭābhi rāmā
rāmā kōdaṇḍa rāmā

Victory to Rama, consort of Janaki! You hold arrows, and are heir to the throne.

prēmabhakti tā rāmā
prārabdhava kaḷe rāmā
pavana suta priyanē rāmā
parama pāvanā rāmā

O Rama, give me love and devotion, and remove my karmic burden. Beloved of Hanuman, You are of utmost purity.

vairāgya taḷeso rāmā
viśva caitanya rāmā
vārija nayanā rāmā
vāmadēva sakha rāmā

O Rama, who is the divine consciousness of the universe, give me dispassion. O lotus-eyed One, You are Lord Shiva's friend.

niṣkāmi māḍo rāmā
nisvārthi māḍo rāmā
nirupama guṇanē rāmā
nityānandane rāmā

O Rama, grant me freedom from desires and selflessness. O Lord of incomparable virtues, You are ever blissful.

Dayānidhiyē (Kannada)

dayānidhiyē kṛpāsāgaranē
pāṇḍuranga viṭṭhala jai pāṇḍuranga

O treasure of compassion, Ocean of divine grace! Victory to Pāṇḍuranga and Viṭṭhala !

bālyadalli mugdhate tāruṇyadi kāmāsaktatē
vṛddhāpyati rōga rujinatē matte sāvige siddhatē
intu vyarthadi jīvipa ī narajanmakēnīḍu ninna
nāmasmaraṇē anavaratā acyutanē
viṭṭhala viṭṭhala jai jai viṭṭhala viṭṭhala

Innocence in childhood, attachment to sensual pleasures in youth, illness in old age, and then preparation for death–if we live thus, life will be in vain. O Achyuta, bless me that I may always chant and remember Your name. Victory to Viṭṭhala!

mangana ī enna manasu yocisutā halavu holasu
ninna mareyutā yēnē kārya māḍalēnu sogasu
ēkāgratē mūḍhisi dṛḍha bhakti irisu
prēma viśvāsa nīḍi namma munde naḍēsu

The mind, restless like the monkey, dwells on impure matters and thus forgets Your name. What then is the point of doing selfless service? Bestow on me concentration, firm devotion, love and faith, and thus show me the right path.

janma saphala jnāna nīḍi muktipathada dāri tōri
nirantara ninna bhajipa mati nīḍu mādhavanē
sajjana sangavanittu nisvārtha sēvē gaiva
samājakē sārthaka rīti pālisenna bandhuvē

To make my life blessed, please bestow wisdom on me and show me the path to liberation. O Madhava, bless me that I shall always sing Your praises. By associating with the holy and engaging in selfless service, may my life become beneficial to the world.

Dayatoru hē kāḷikē (Kannada)

dayatoru hē kāḷikē karuṇāmayī kāḷikē
anugrahakkāgi nā kādiruvē
kṛpākaṭākṣa mātravē rakṣē

Be merciful, O compassionate Kalike! I am waiting for Your grace. Your merciful sidelong glance is my only protection.

centāvarē hū mogadavaḷē
pādadaḍi śiva malagiruva
nī ruṇḍamāleyā dharisiruvē
vyōmakēśī nī mukaṇṇiyē
dayatōru hē kāḷikē, karuṇāmayī kāḷikē

You have a beautiful red lotus-like face, and Shiva lies at Your feet as absolute pure consciousness in its inert form. You are the manifested energy of potential creative power. You wear a garland of skulls and have the sky as Your hair, and You have three eyes.

kōpāgniyanu badigirisi
kāppāḍu ninna makkaḷanu
ā rudhira nālage oḷaseḷedū
mandahāsa mātra bīrutta bā
dayatōru hē kāḷikē, karuṇāmayī kāḷikē

Set aside Your fearful wrath - protect us, Your children! Pull in Your fierce tongue. Come showering only Your sweet smile on us!

Dayayālē urukoṇḍu (Tamil)

dayayālē urukoṇḍu
tān tōtri tāyē
ātmāvin aṭayāḷam nī
jīvarāsikaḷ yāvum
paṇiyum karupporuḷ
pārāṭṭa vākkētammā

O Mother, by mere will driven by compassion, You ever materialize Yourself in human form. You are the icon of the all-pervasive Atman. O Mother! You are the essence of the Self to whom all beings bow down in reverence. It is ineffable to praise Your greatness.

nī eṇṇi tān pinnē
tān eṇṇum jīvan
tirumūlakāraṇiyē
maraipporuḷē yugayugam
avatāram seytāy
viḷaiyāṭal arputamē

O Mother, source of everything! Each thought originates in You before coming to the jiva's mind (living being). You are the subtle supreme aspect (of the entire creation). You incarnate Yourself in all ages. Your divine play is really amazing!

ariyātu pōnālum
prapañcattil yārum
tānāga tuṇai seyyum nī
atarkāka aruḷayē
uruvāka ēnti
bhuvanattai idamākkum nī

Even though the entire universe fails to know You, You voluntarily extend Your help to living beings. Taking a body that is none other than grace itself, You support them, soothing and consoling one and all.

Dēvādidēvā (Telugu)

dēvādidēvā ō mahādēvā
nīvē śaraṇayyā darijērcavayyā

O Lord of lords, O great Lord, we take refuge in You, take us to the goal.

jangamadēvarā janimṛtināśakā
mangaḷadāyakā amangaḷahārakā
kāḷahastīśvarā kalimalanāśakā
nīvē śaraṇayyā darijērcavayyā

O Lord of the ascetics with matted hair and ash-marks over their bodies, destroyer of birth and death, giver of auspiciousness and destroyer of inauspiciousness! Lord of Kalahasti, destroyer of evils of Kali Yuga we take refuge in You, take us to the goal!

rakṣimpavayyā darijērcavayyā nīvē śaraṇayyā

Protect us, take us to the goal, we take refuge in You.

bhūtagaṇanāthuḍā śavabhūmivāsuḍā
praṇavākāruḍā nīpraḷayakāruḍā
śrīśailavāsuḍā bhramarāmbanāthuḍā
nīvē śaraṇayyā darijērcavayyā

O Lord of ghouls (Shiva's companions), dweller of the cremation grounds, the form of the primordial sound, Om, the cause of dissolution. Lord of Srisaila, Lord of Goddess Bhramarambha, we take refuge in You, take us to the goal.

duḥkhamayasāgaram dāṭimpavayyā
nī nāmamepuḍu pāḍedamayyā
ōm namaḥ śivāya śiva ōm namaḥ śivāya

Take us across this ocean of misery, we sing Your name always, prostrations to Lord Shiva!

Dēvi dayākari (Kannada)

dēvi dayākari tāyē
paripālaki pūraṇi mātē
tūṣṭiyu nīnē puṣṭiyu nīnē
annapūrṇēśvari tāyē

Compassionate Mother Goddess, protecting and fulfilling mother! You are nourishing, You are nurturing! O Mother Goddess, Annapurneswari.

jalanidhi battide bhavāgni suṭutide
bēgeyā tāḷevu tāyē
hasiranu uḷisu usiranu uḷisu
karuṇeya tanbanu nīṭe

Underground water sources have dried up, and the fire of worldliness is blazing. We cannot bear this heat, O Mother! Save the greenery, protect the air and breath. Give us Your compassionate, cooling relief!

anāvṛṣṭi undeṭe ativṛṣṭi bēreṭe
ellellu hāhākārā
āśraya nīṭe sāntvana nīṭe
bāramma bēgane tāyē

Heavy rains here, drought elsewhere, everywhere is in panic! Give us support, please give us comfort. Come quickly Mother!

durāse biṭiri atyāse tyajisi
prakṛtige vandisi makkaḷe
prēmati porēvaḷu prakṛtiyu nammanu
prakṛtiye pratyakṣa daiva

Give up greed and excessive desire. Children, show reverence to nature. Nature protects us with love. Nature is verily God's form revealed.

Devī mahādevī (Hindi)

devī mahādevī
kāḷī mahākāḷi

O Devi, supreme Goddess, O Kali, great Kali.

śyāme nāthe māye
vānī gaurī lakṣmī
bāle līle durge
śaktī devī kāḷī

O dark-hued One, Empress, great Illusion, Goddess of speech, auspicious One, Goddess of true wealth, youthful One, playful Mother, Mother Durga, supreme energy, Mother Kali.

vedye vidye hṛdye
dhanye ramye punye
satye śantye vandye
saumye rudre bhadre

You are the embodiment of the Vedas and supreme knowledge, blessed One, beautiful One, You are merit itself. Supreme truth, peaceful One, You are worshipped by all. You are gentle as well as fierce, O excellent One!

devī tu mahākāli sāvale rang vāli tu sab kī mā
pyārī mayyā tu māyā mē chip khelne vālī mōhinī
śāradā kamalālayā durgā pārvatī sab tuhī he
tere dās brahmā-hari-śiv dev dānav sāre jīv

O Devi, Great Kali with a dark-complexion, You are the Mother of all. Darling Mother, You are the enchantress, hiding behind the veil of maya and playing with us. Goddesses Durga, Parvati, and Saraswati seated in the lotus - they are all You. You are served by Brahma, Vishnu, Shiva, all the host of gods and all living beings.

mayyā tu līlāmayī sārā viśv terī līlā jananī
tū sarvaloka rānī carācar tere me janm lete
tū pālan poṣan kartī duniyā kā nāś bhī tūhī kartī
kāl bhī terā svarūp sabhī-me-tū bastī he mātārānī

O Mother, You are the Creator of all these lilas - indeed, this entire universe is Your play. O Queen of all the worlds, everything takes birth in You. You nourish the world, and are also the cause of its destruction. Time itself is also nothing but Your form. You reside in all, O Queen Mother.

Devī triloki (Hindi)

devī triloki men vyāp rahī tū
khel anokhā rūp anek
tū dhar mohan rūp sabhī par
barsātī hai kṛpā aur neh

Devi You are present in the three worlds. All these different forms are Your strange play. Assuming an attractive form, You shower Your blessings and love on everyone.

devī pyārī jananī main
terā śaraṇārtthī - mujhe
denā tū sahārā
sab pīḍā har lenā

O dear eternal Mother Devi, I have taken refuge at Your feet. Please give me Your support and remove all my sorrows.

vaiṣṇavī devī ghaṭ ghaṭ vāsī
kānti bharī hai sūrat terī
ye duniyā hai tujhse hī rośan
ghaṭ-ghaṭ main tum jyoti jagānā

Vaishnavi Devi, You are present in every form. Your face is always full of beauty and brightness. This world is illuminated by You. Please illumine all the forms with Your light from within also.

tū santoṣī kṣīr bhavānī
vindhyānivāsini śailanandini
tū kharvāhini śītalā dēvi
tan man śītal karnī jananī

O Santoshi, Mother of contentment, Bhavani, You dwell in the Vindhya Mountains and rejoice on the peaks. O Mother Seetala Devi, You cool down the body and mind of the afflicted.

jal thal agan samīr kāriṇī
gagan sarīkhī sirmal rūpiṇī
nirakh mane tū niraj locanī
nit nav mangal modavarṣiṇi

You are the cause of water, earth, fire, and space. Your form is soft and vast like the sky. O Mother with eyes bright like the sun, You shower the bliss of eternal happiness.

ma jai jai ma ma jai jai ma

Victory to the divine Mother!

Dil me terī (Hindi)

dil me terī ās hai
darśan kī pyās hai
taras rahā hai yē man
āj bhakto ke sang khel holī kā rang
sārī duniyā ko apne hi rang me rangālo mā
jagadiśvari! prema ke rang me rali

There is only one desire in my heart: to attain Your darshan. Please play holi with Your devotees and color the entire world with Your divine colors. O Goddess of the world, who revels in the colors of love!

meri sun le araj banke mamtā baras
tere dāman me mujhko samāle
sāre jagse judā dekhū tujh me khudā
pyār bhakton kā tujhko bulāye

Please listen to my prayer and shower Your compassion on me. Keep me tied to the end of Your sari, close to You. I see the world as different and see God in You. The love of the devotees is calling You.

ye jīvan ḍagar hai muśkil magar
tere hātho ne hamko sambhāle
cāhe tujhse dulār āye bande hazār
tere āhaṭ ke vyākul hai sāre

This path of life is extremely difficult, but your hands are here to protect me. There are thousands of people who crave to be dear to You. Everyone is just eager to hear Your voice.

Durge durgati (Hindi)

durge durgati harane dinodharane
devi dayāmayi jananī
lalite līlā lole māte
manme basnevālī

O Goddess Durga, remover of misfortune, uplifter of the down-trodden, Devi! Compassionate Mother, Goddess Lalita who revels in divine play! O Mother who resides in the mind!

bhuvan racānevālī sāre
bhuvan me rahnevālī
duḥkh daridra miṭānevālī
dīna janāvani jananī

O Creatrix of the world, You permeate the entire Universe! You are the Mother who alleviates sorrow, eradicates poverty and cares for the downtrodden.

śakti traya mūrte bhakta priya citte
tū he varalakṣmi nit terī jai gāve ham
terī duniyā me tūhī he sab me basī

You are the embodiment of shakti, the consciousness worshipped by the devotees. You are Lakshmi who bestows boons. We will always sing Your glories- You alone exist within Your whole creation!

jai mā... jai jai mā... jai mā... mā... jai jai mā

Victory to the divine Mother!

satyavrata vandye mukti prada haste
kīje karuṇā tū vinatīye sunle mayyā
mere dil me tū āve he devī mayyā

O Mother, You are worshipped by the sage Satyavrata, and You grant liberation, please be compassionate! Hear this prayer and come into my heart, O divine Mother!

sāre jag ko tū var dettī mā
sohe tavamūrttī hṛdayo me sab ke sadā
nāce sab me tū śubhjyoti jagajāye mā

May Your divine form reside always in the hearts of all! You dance in all of creation. O Mother, may divine light dawn within!

Ēkantatayuṭe āzham (Malayalam)

ēkantatayuṭe āzham tōrum
vēdana ninnu miṭippū
nīla kaṭalinuḷḷil tēṅgum
pōya yugaṅgaḷ pōle, pōya yugaṅgaḷ pōle

Pain is pulsating in the depths of loneliness, like bygone ages, like bygone ages moaning in the depths of the blue ocean.

vannīṭaṇam hṛttil vanniṭaṇammē
ammē ammē atmarūpiṇi

Come to my heart Mother, please come, Mother, my Mother who is none other than my own Self!

ēkāntatayuṭe gaganapathattil
tārakaḷ ninnu tuṭippū
nī pāṭumbōḷ kūṭe mūḷum
māmaka hṛdayam pōle, māmaka hṛdayam pōle

In the loneliness of the paths of the sky, stars keep pulsating, like my heart, like my heart that hums along with You as You sing!

ēkāntatayuṭe pātayilellām
ninde mukham kāṇunnu
ārō kaṇṇukaḷ tēki nanakkum
pūjā puṣpam pōle, pūjā puṣpam pōle

In all the pathways of loneliness, I see Your face, like a flower nurtured by someone's tears, like a flower for worship.

Ēlappulayēlō (Malayalam)

ēlappulayēlō ēlappulayēlō
ēlappulayēlō ēlappulayēlō
kalluṇḍē mulḷuṇḍē karimalayēṛi varunnuṇḍē
kāṭallē mēṭallē kālitu tellumariññillē

We didn't feel any pain in our legs while climbing up the mountain forest full of stones and thorns!

pon mala mēṭu kaṭannu patineṭṭu paṭi kaṭannu
ayyappa svāmiye kāṇān kāttin kāṛ ēraṇa pōle

When coming to see Lord Ayyappan, we cross the holy mountain and climb the eighteen steps- we feel like a cloud in the wind!

uḷḷāle onnāke ottu śaraṇam viḷichāṭṭē
kayyāle meyyāle ellām marannu viḷichāṭṭē

Let us all chant 'Ayyappa sharanam' with complete devotion! Let us chant 'Ayappa sharanam', forgetting our mind and body!

pēṭṭayil cuvaṭu vechu tāḷattil meyyuzhiññē
āṛkkaṇa āṛppu kaṇḍā āzhittira ēraṇa pōle

Seeing the devotees dancing to the rhythm in 'petta', one is reminded of waves rising in the ocean.

kai tozhutu munnil ninnāl antimegha cintu pōle
ney viḷakkin nērariññāl neñcilennum dīpa śōbha

Standing with devotion in front of the Lord feels like a cloud in the evening sky. Arati lamps fill my heart with divine light.

uḷḷariññu kaṇṇaṭachāl svāmi pādamuḷḷuṇarum
uḷḷunontu nām viḷichāl ayyanuḷḷilōṭiyettum

Standing with my eyes closed, I can see the Lord's holy feet in my heart. If You call the Lord with devotion, he will certainly come.

kāladōṣa kanmaṣangaḷ nīkki-yennum kāttiṭunnē
pambāvāsā ninde nāmam pārinennum puṇyapūram

O Lord, please remove all my obstacles and protect me all the time. Lord of Pamba River, Your name is a blessing for the world!

Ēlō ēlō (Malayalam)

ēlō ēlō ēlēlō ēlō ēlēlō ēlēlō
ēlō ēlō ēlēlō ēlō ēlēlō ēlēlō
ādiyum antavum ētumezhāttoru
ādi parāpara gaṇapatiyē
nādam gītam rāgarasāmṛtam
gānam aruḷuka ivanini nī

You are beyond beginning and end, You are the highest of the high, O Ganapati! Please bestow on me the nectar of music.

buddhiyum śaktiyum ottizha cērnnoru
śakti ivanini nīyaruḷū
śankara nandana akṣara hṛdayā
jnānamēkuka ivanini nī

Please bless me with the combination of intellect and power, O son of Shiva, immortal heart!

vāraṇa vadanā vārija nayanā
nīyē varaṇam tuṇayatināy
kadanam kadaḷikkulayāyaṭiyan
vayppūyiviṭe aṭimalaril

O One with the elephant face and lotus eyes, please come, You are my only refuge. I take refuge at Your feet. Please remove my sorrows!

avilum malarum śarkkarayum itu
vaypū hṛdayam nākkilayāy
manassō uṭayum kēramatallē
nilpū munnil guṇanidhiyē

We offer You parched rice and jaggery with all our heart. You have all the auspicious qualities!

śankaranumayum arumukhanum nin
tiruvuṭalanpilaṇaykkunnē
dēvanmārum munijanavum nin
tiruvuṭaluḷḷilaṇaykkun nē

Lord Shiva and Parvati embrace You with affection. The gods and the sages reside in Your Self.

Enakkuḷḷē nīyum (Tamil)

enakkuḷḷē nīyum unakkuḷḷē nānum
irukkinṭra pōdu īṭar enbatētu
kaṇakkillai ammā piṇakkillai ammā
kanivilum kanivē nī kāṇbadu niraivē

O Mother, when You are in me, and I in You, how can there be sorrow? Mother, Your love is limitless, and You are free of enmity, for You behold fullness everywhere, O most merciful One.

kaṇmūṭi unnai kāṇbadu dhyānam
kaṇtirandetilum kānbaduvum dhyānam
annilaiyil dhyānam seydiṭa munaindēn
ammā unaittānē anaittilum ninaindēn

Visualizing You with eyes closed is meditation. So, too, is seeing You everywhere with open eyes. As I strove to meditate in that state, I beheld only You everywhere.

kaipiṭitittu ennai kāl naṭatti senṭrāy
kāl naṭandu vandēn kaiyaṇaittukkoṇḍāy
un aruḷāltān nān unniṭattil vandēn
enseyalāl ēdum āvatinkuṇḍō

Holding my hands, You led me every step of the way. When I

stumbled, You caught hold of me. I came to You by Your grace alone. Can my mere effort achieve anything?

Enkirundu vandōm (Tamil)

enkirundu vandōm
edai koṇḍu vandōm
ematenḍru kūriṭavē
edai izhandu ninḍrōm

Where did we come from? What did we bring? What have we lost that we can say belonged to us?

edanai iccittōm
epporuḷil pattru vaittōm
pārtannil kaṭṭuṇḍē
paritavittu nirkkinṭrōm

What did we desire? What did we have attachment towards? Bound by the objects of the world, we are suffering.

kayirinai pāmbenṭrōm
kāṭci tanil añcukinṭrōm
maṇ peṇ pon enṭru
matimayanki vāzhukinṭrōm

We mistook the rope for a snake and became afraid of its appearance. We are fascinated by wealth and physical pleasure.

pirantiṭavittiṭṭōm
irappinilē sikkuṇṭōm
mummalamum nīkkiṭuvōm
muktiyinai aṭaintiṭuvōm

We sow the seed for birth, we are tied to the fear of death. Let us remove the ego, the sense of doership and illusion, and thus attain liberation.

Engum annaiyun (Tamil)

engum annaiyun vaṭivām
edilum annaiyun vaṭivām
ponkum kaṭalilum pudunilavadilum
pozhundiṭum un ezhil amudām...

Mother, Your form pervades everywhere. Your form pervades everything. The rising ocean and moon light shower Your nectarean beauty.

makkaḷin manam tanil oḷirvāy – nī
makizhvuṭan vāzhndiṭa aruḷvāy
kāttrāy mazhaiyāy kanalāy nilamāy
vānamumāy nī tikazhvāy

You shine in the hearts of Your children and bless them with a happy life. You manifest as breeze, rain, fire, earth and sky.

pārpukazh annai pādam tudittē
pāriṭamellām pāṭiṭuvōmē

Let us sing everywhere the glory of Your lotus feet!

En mannassiloru maunam (Tamil)

en manadil oru maunaṁ
maṇivaṇṇan varādadin maunaṁ
kaṇṇane kāṇādurugi urugiyen
kaṇgaḷil kaṇṇīr perugum

ānirai mēyttu varādadō – kaṇṇan
āzhtuyil nīnki ezhādadō
kārmukil vaṇṇanai kāṇattuṭikkumen
vāṭiya kōlam marandadō

pālveṇṇayum kiṭaikkādadō – piñcu
pādaṁ iṭari vizhundadō

nin malaraṭigaḷil tēn nukara
bhaktavaṇḍukaḷ mūṭi maraittadō

ēn vara tāmadaṁ innuṁ - kaṇṇan
ennai marandiruppānō
kaṇṇā varuganī kārmukilvaṇṇā - en
kaṇṇīr vizhigaḷin munnē

Ennadu yāvudammā (Kannada)

ennadu yāvudammā - tāyē
anyaradyāvudammā?
ellā saubhāgyavu ninadāgiralāgi -
ennadu yāvudammā tāyē?

What is mine, O my Mother? What is others'? When all good fortune is Yours alone, what can be mine, O Mother?

aihika sukhabhōga bēḍuve nādare
aitindriyavū ninninda vimukha
aihika sukhabhōga iruvalli nī nilla
endu nā aritu ēnanu bēḍali ?

If I ask for worldly pleasures, all five senses will turn away from You. Where there is only worldly pleasure, You are not there. Realizing this, what shall I beg of You?

ommana bēḍuve ondē mana bēḍuve
ondare kṣaṇavū agaladiru
ondē manadali ninnanu dhyānisi
ondāgi hōguve ninnalli jagadamba

I beg for one-pointedness of mind. Do not leave me even for a second. Let me meditate upon You with one-pointed concentration, mother. Let me become one with You, O Mother of the world!

Ennai nān maranda (Tamil)

ennai nān maranda vēḷai
unnaiyē ninaikka vēṇḍum
unnai nān maranda pōdum
ennil nī irukka vēṇḍum

When I forget myself, I should be thinking of You. Even if I forget You, You should remain with me.

kaṇṇil nī maṇiyumāvāy
karuttinil oḷiyumāvāy
uṇṇum poruḷ nīyumāvāy
ulakattin tāyumāvāy
enkenku senḍrālum en vizhi kāṇbadu
ammānin ponrūpamē

You are the pupil of my eye. You are the light of my thoughts. You are my nourishment, You are the Mother of the universe. O Mother, wherever I cast my eyes I see Your effulgent form

tāyāvāy makaḷumāvāy
tānkiṭum tōzhiyāvāy
anbirkku viḷakkamāvāy
ammā nī anaittumāvāy
enkenku senḍrālum en vizhi kāṇbadu
ammānin ponrūpamē

You are Mother, daughter and supportive friend, O embodiment of love, You are everything. O Mother, wherever I cast my eyes I see Your effulgent form.

Ennō ennō (Telugu)

sarva-svarūpē sarvēśē
sarva-śakti samanvitē

bhayēbhyastrāhi nō dēvi
durgē dēvi namōstutē

You exist in all forms. You possess all powers. O Devi, please protect us from all fears. Salutations to You, Goddess Durga!

ennō ennō ennō rūpālu
upādulanni nīvēle nīvēle

How many myriad forms there are! You are verily all of them.

ennō dehālani meghālu - avi
kadile cidākāśam nīvēle
ennō bhāva-tarangālu - avi
pongē mano kaḍali nīvēle
ammā nīvēle antā nīvēle

How many bodies move like clouds in the sky of consciousness! How many emotional vibrations rise like waves in the ocean of the mind! O Mother, You are that! That You are!

ennō jīvita-dṛśyālu - avi
kanabaḍe darpaṇam nīvēle
visvamantā unnadi nīvēle
nīvu nīvēle nēnikā lēdūle
ammā nīvēle anta nīvēle

How many scenes of life are reflected in the mirror that You are! You pervade the entire universe. I, too, am You; and therefore, 'I' do not exist. O Mother, You are that! That You are!

ammā nīvēle antā nīvēle
ambā nīvēle jagadambā nīvēle
ammā nīvēle antā nīvēle
ambā nīvēle jagadambā nīvēle

O Mother, You are that. That You are. O Mother of the Universe, You are everything.

En piravi muṭindiṭumō (Tamil)

en piravi muṭindiṭumō ammā - unai ariyāmal
en jīvan pirindiṭumō - un anbai parugāmal
gangaiyin karaiyinilē dāhattil tavippaduvō
karppaka nizhalinilē śōkattil tuṭippaduvō

O Mother, will my life end without my knowing You? Will my soul depart without my drinking the nectar of Your love? Is it right for me to feel the pangs of thirst while sitting on the banks of the Ganges? Is it right to grieve while sitting in the shade of the kalpaka (wish-fulfilling) tree?

poyyuruvai meyyuruvāy ittanai nāḷ eṇṇi vandēn
meyyuravāy nī vandum mēnmayinai nānariyēn
unniraṇḍu tāḷkaḷaiyē tañcamena koḷkkinṭrēn
enniraṇḍu kaipiṭittu un vazhiyil naṭattiṭammā
un vazhiyil naṭattiṭammā

All this time, I mistook false relationships for true ones. Though You came, the only true kin, I failed to understand Your glory. I took refuge at Your feet. O Mother, please take my hands in Yours so that I may walk in Your path.

nāṭkaḷum ōṭiṭudē āṇḍukaḷum maraindiṭudē
nānirukkum nilaiyeṇṇi nāḍiyellām taḷarndiṭutē
ettanai pirappeṭuttu iḷaittappin unai kaṇḍēn
ippirappum tappiviṭṭāl eppirappil śaraṇaṭaivēn
eppirappil śaraṇaṭaivēn

Days and years are passing. Thinking of my state, my body and mind are becoming fatigued. I have met You after many a tiresome birth. If this lifetime, too, is wasted, when will I ever take refuge with You? I must do it now.

Etayō tēṭi (Tamil)

etayō tēṭi alaintu inṭru unai tēṭukirēn
kaṇmaṇiyē karuṇaimazhayē iruppiṭam tanai sol

All these years, I ran after worthless things. Today I look for the one who is full of compassion- please tell me where You live.

maunattil lakṣam pāṭhankaḷ tantāy
purintatellām appōt
sūzhnilai vantāl ellām marantēn
iggati toṭarntāl narggatiyuṇḍō ?

Through silence, You teach me millions of lessons, and I understand it all quite clearly, but when new situations arise, I forget it all. Is it possible for me to progress with such a mind?

pāpangaḷ janmangaḷāyi sumantēn
inṭr tān bhāram enṭruṇarntēn
dēhattil sañcarittiṭumbōtē
bhārattai irakkiṭa mārggam kāṭṭu

For all of my previous births, I have been carrying a load of sins; only today did I realize that they are nothing but burdens. Show me the way to unburden myself of this weight while in this present body.

Ettanai vēdanai (Tamil)

ettanai vēdanai unakku nān tantālum
ittanai karuṇayō unakku enmēl
vaḷayā neñcattil ahankāram sumantēn
kaṇḍu en ammakku vēdanayō – vēdanayō

Though I caused You great pain, You have so much compassion for me. In my brittle heart, I only held on to my ego. When You observed this, I caused You great pain.

iṭayūru kaṇḍu varunneccarittu
tirukkaikaḷ iruka kōrttennai piṭittu
kāttiṭum sumayai muzhuvatum ēttru
enakkāka tāy paṭum pāṭṭai kaṇḍēn

Cautioning me about the obstacles, You held me tightly in Your divine arms. I saw how much You suffered by accepting the total responsibility of protecting me.

uyarvāna cintai paṇikintra guṇamum
taṇintiṭum idayam teḷivāna pārvai
nōkkam mārātu ūkkankaḷ tantu
enakkāka tāy paṭum pāṭṭai kaṇḍēn

I see how much You strive to nurture noble thoughts in me such as having humility, a compassionate heart, and clear vision, without deviation, for my journey towards goal.

Gajānanā he gajānanā (Tamil)

gajānanā he gajānanā
gajānanā he gajavadanā

O Gajanana, elephant-faced Lord!

vezha mukhattu vināyakanē
viḷanku sindūra vināyakanē
aindu karankaḷ uṭayavanē
ankuśa pāśam koṇḍavanē

O elephant-faced Lord, destroyer of our miseries! You wear kumkum, have five arms and bear the goad and the noose.

aimpula vēṭkai aṭakkiṭuvāy
añcēl eṇṭrē kāttiṭuvāy
allalakaḷ nīkki aruḷ taruvāy
anbāl emmai āṇṭiṭuvāy

You keep our five senses in control. You show the mudra of fearlessness. You remove our worries and rule over us lovingly.

Gaṇanāthā he gaṇanāthā (Tamil)

gaṇanāthā he gaṇanāthā
gaurīnandana gaṇanāthā
gaṇanāthā he gaṇanāthā
gaurīnandana gaṇanāthā

O Ganesh, Lord of the Ganas, son of Parvati!

gaṇanāthā ena azhaittiṭuvōm
kāriyankaḷ tamai tuvankiṭuvōm
kālaṭiyil talai vaittiṭuvōm
kavalaikaḷ yāvum venṭriṭuvōm

Let us pray to Ganesh, the remover of all obstacles, before we begin our activities. Let us surrender to His lotus feet and thus overcome all our difficulties.

ōmkāram un vaṭivamanṭrō
ulakamellām atil aṭankumanṭrō
āṇavam tannai akattriṭuvāy
ānma oḷiyinai tandiṭuvāy

You are the embodiment of the sacred syllable Om, wherein the whole world is contained. O Lord, please remove our egos, thereby making us Self-realised.

Gaṇaṅgaḷin nāthā (Tamil)

gaṇaṅgaḷin nāthā kaitozhutōm
kavalaikaḷ tīrkka kaitozhutōm
guṇaṅgaḷin adhīpā kaitozhutōm
kuṭṭrankaḷ poruttiṭa kaitozhutōm

O Lord of divine beings, we worship You! We worship you, seeking an end to our worries. O Lord of all good things, we worship You! We worship You that You may forgive our bad actions!

seyalkaḷai toṭankiṭa unai paṇivōm
jayankaḷai aruḷi kurai kaḷaivāy
uyyum vazhi tannai emakkuṇartta
uvapputaṇ unnai kaitozhutōm

We surrender to You that You may give us strength to act. Grant us success in all that we do and correct our mistakes. Show us the correct path! We worship you with great sincerity.

kavalaikaḷ ellām tīrttiṭuvāy
kaṭum pakai tannai azhittiṭuvāy
abalaikaḷ enkaḷai kāttiṭave
anbarin tuṇaivā vandiṭuvāy

Remove all our worries, destroy the hatred that arises in our minds. O Savior of good people, please come and protect helpless ones like us!

ādimudalvanai ānaimukhattanai
aindkarattanai vaṇankiṭuvōm
vēdamudalvanai jñānakozhundinai
iruvinai nīnkiṭa vaṇankiṭuvōm – nām

You are the first leader, elephant-faced One. You have five arms, and are the first knower of the Vedas. Quintessence of all Knowledge! We worship You, that You may remove our bad karmas!

Gaṇapati guṇanidhi (Hindi)

gaṇapati guṇanidhi tērē
guṇgāyak ham pyārē
sab vidhi tū rakhvārē
har lē duḥkh hamārē

O Lord Ganapati, You are the protector of Your devotees. We sing Your glories; please remove our sorrows.

gaṇapati karuṇā karnā tū
guṇanidhi sab var dētā tū
gajamukh mangaḷ bharnā tū
gaṇanāyak bhay harnā tū

O Lord Ganapati, treasure-house of compassion, O Lord who bestows boons, fill our lives with auspiciousness and remove our fears.

bahuvidha kaṣṭ mē paḍkē
din banē ham rōkē
ab tū rakṣak bankē
ājā gajmukh dōḍ kē

We are in deep sorrows; we are helpless. O Lord Ganapati, we are crying. Please come running and free us from the burden of sorrows.

sundar kajñara vadanā
jana par karuṇā karnā
muda mangal sab bharanā
tū karuṇā kā jharanā

O Lord, You speak beautifully and are the river of compassion. Grace us Your compassion and bring prosperity to our lives.

girijā nandan var dē
pada vandana ham kartē
tērā yaś jō gate
unke bandhan miṭ tē

O Lord Ganapati, son of Goddess Parvati, we worship Your lotus feet. We sing Your glories: please bless us that we may be freed from the bondage of worldly attachments.

Gōkula bālā gōvindā (Malayalam)

gōkula bālā gōvindā
gōkula pālā gōvindā
gōpakumāra gōvindā
gōvindā hari gōvindā

O boy of Gōkul (cowherd clan), Protector of cows and the cowherd clan, cowherd boy, O Vishnu!

vārmuṭiyil cārttiyatārī
varṇṇappīli mayilppīli
vākaccārttinu vannavarō
vṛndāvanattile gōpikaḷō

Who adorned Your beautiful locks with the colorful, peacock feather? Was it those who came for the morning worship or the milkmaids of Vṛndāvan?

pūntānam nalkiyatallē
ponnuṇṇikkīvanamāla
mēlppattūr nalkiyatallē
muktakamāla maṇimāla

Wasn't it Puntanam who offered You, O darling Kṛṣṇa, the garland of wild flowers? Wasn't it Melppattur who offered You a poem of free verse?

tirumadhuram nēdikkām
tuḷasippūkkaḷ cūṭikkām
tarumō tarumō kārvarṇṇā
tāmarakkaiyyile tūveṇṇa

We shall offer You sweet pudding and tulasi (basil) flowers. O dark-hued One, won't You offer us some of the butter from Your lovely hands?

Gopiyara usirē (Kannada)

gopiyara usirē kṛṣṇa gōpālakṛṣṇa
govarddhanadhara kṛṣṇa gītānāyaka kṛṣṇa

The very life breath of the gopis, O Krishna, Gopala Krishna. The One who lifted the Govardhana Mountain, Lord of the Gita...

yaśoda nandana kṛṣṇa yadukulatilakane kṛṣṇa
yamunā taṭadī kṛṣṇa rāsavihāri kṛṣṇa

Son of Yashoda, King of the Yadukulas, the One at the banks of the Yamuna. The One who revels in the Rasa (the divine dance).

kṛṣṇā harē kṛṣṇā kṛṣṇā giridhara kṛṣṇā

O Krishna, O Hari...

sarōjanētrane kṛṣṇa ninnaya samayār kṛṣṇa
varṇisalasadaḷa kṛṣṇa guṇasāgaranē kṛṣṇa

Lotus-eyed Krishna, who can be equated with You? Krishna is beyond description, Krishna is the Ocean of divine qualities.

kṛpārdra hṛdayane kṛṣṇa karuṇārasanē kṛṣṇa
dāsara prāṇanē kṛṣṇa dāsara dāsanē kṛṣṇa

Your heart is soaked in grace, You are compassion personified. You are the soul of Your servants, and You are also the servant of Your servants.

Gōpiyarkaḷ (Tamil)

gōpiyarkaḷ ellōrum gōpālan tanakkenṭrē
kōṇḍāṭi avan mukhattai pārttirundanar
āyarpāḍi māyavanum āmām nān unakkenṭrē
anaivarukkum adaikkūri pūttirundanan

Imagining Gopala to be theirs alone, the gopis gazed at him in celebration. With a mischievous smile, the rogue of Gokula reassured each one of them that he belonged to her alone.

pankiṭṭāl kuraivatillai pazhiyiṭṭāl veruppatillai
kumbiṭṭāl maruppatillai kūppiṭṭāl viṭuvatillai
vambiṭṭāl vazhiyumillai vazhakkiṭṭāl kiṭaippatillai
nambiviṭa kēṭumillai avanaruḷa taṭaiyumillai

His love does not diminish when shared. He does not hate when blamed, and has no objection to being worshipped. He forsakes none who calls, and can never be annoyed. He is not attained by argument. Faith in Him removes difficulties. His grace flows without any hindrance.

paśiyenbatavan ēkkam pālamudam avan ninaivu
kasiyā manamenum kallinuḷḷum īram vaittān
attanaiyum turanduviṭṭāl anaittum nam sondamenṭrān
aṭiyeṭuttu vaittuviṭṭāl avan namadu bandamenṭrān

Intense longing for him is hunger, thoughts of Him are nectar. He has filled even the hardest of hearts with the waters of tender love. He declares that one gains everything by total renunciation. He says that if we take even one step towards Him, He becomes our very own.

Gōpiyarkaḷ uḷḷankaḷai (Tamil)

gōpiyarkaḷ uḷḷankaḷai koḷḷai koṇḍavā
gōkulattil ōṭiyāṭi gōkkaḷ mēykkavā
gōvindā gōpālā gōkulēśvarā
kōṭiyinbam tandiṭuvāy kōdai nāyakā

O Thief who captivated the hearts of the gopis (milkmaids)! O Krishna who frolicked in Gokula as the cows grazed! Hey Govinda, Gopala, Lord of Gokula! Shower eternal bliss on us!

āṭippāṭi kaḷittiṭavē nīyum vārāyō
āyarppāṭi āṇḍavanē ānandakkaṇṇā

uttamanē pittanānēn un ninaivālē
uṇṇavillai urankavillai un pirivālē

Denizen of Gokula, blissful Krishna, come to dance and play with us. Supreme One, we have become crazed by thoughts of You. In our separation from You, we have forgotten food and sleep.

edarkku inda poykkōpam enkaḷin nāthā
ēn inda pārāmukham vēnkaṭanāthā
azhaippadanai nīyum inṭru kēṭakka kūṭādō
anbil tōynda idayam tanai ērkkakūṭādō

O Krishna, why do You pretend to be angry with us? Why are You ignoring us, O Venkateswara? Won't You hear our calls? Won't You accept our hearts, steeped in love for You?

nin nāmam ennāḷum enkaḷin vēdam
nin ninaivē ennāḷum enkaḷin dhyānam
nīyinṭri vāṭiṭutē enkaḷin uḷḷam
nittiyanai vandiṭuvāy nirmmalakaṇṇā

O Krishna, Your name is scripture to us. Thoughts of You are our meditation. Without You our hearts are pining. Eternal and pure One, O Krishna, come running to us!

Gopiyarkoñcum (Tamil)

gopiyarkoñcum rādhaiyin kaṇṇā
mālē maṇivaṇṇā
kuvalayam keñcum kuzhalisai kaṇṇā
malarmakaḷ mannā maṇivaṇṇā

O Krishna, darling of the gopis, beloved of Radha, emerald-hued One. Lord of Lakshmi, the whole world yearns to hear the mesmerizing music of Your flute.

kaṇṇanai kaṇkaḷ kāṇavum vēṇḍum
kaṇamum imaiyā kaṇkaḷē vēṇḍum

Bless me so that my eyes never blink and are thus able to see You always.

ennatān seyvēn edai nān taruvēn
enadenbadēdu unadu tān ellām
ennaiyē tandēn unai nān koṇḍēn
ennilē uraiyum unai nān kaṇḍēn

What can I do for You? What can I give to You? What is mine anyway? Everything is Yours. So, I offered myself to You. You gave Yourself to me. I then beheld You within me.

vānamun siramē vaiyamun aṭiyē
kānamun ezhilē kaṭalun niramē
ennilum nīyē edilum nīyē
uḷḷad yāvum nīyē nīyē

The sky is Your head, and the earth Your feet. Nature is Your beauty, and the ocean, Your hue. You reside in me and in everything else. All that exists is nothing but You alone.

gōkulakṛṣṇā gōvindakṛṣṇā
gōpālakṛṣṇā rādhēśyām
sanmayakṛṣṇā cinmayakṛṣṇā
ānandakṛṣṇā rādhēśyām

Krishna of Gokul, cowherd Krishna, protector of cows, beloved of Radha. You are existence, knowledge and bliss!

Hanumat bal do (Hindi)

hanumat bal do bhagvān
amar vīr hanumān

gun sāgar pehcān terā
param śiṣya kā sthān

O Lord Hanuman, give us strength! Immortal, valorous Hanuman, You are known as the ocean of virtues and the foremost amongst disciples.

bhagvān, balvān, hanumān, terā gun gān

Lord Hanuman, mighty One, we sing your glories!

siyāvar rāmacandra kī jai!
pavan sut hanumān kī jai!
bolo bajrang balī kī jai!
bolo mahā dhīr vīr kī jai!

Victory to Lord Rama, consort of Goddess Sita and son of the Wind-God! Victory to the One who is as powerful as thunder, as fast as lightning and foremost amongst the valorous!

rām rām jo gāve tere
man ko vo bhāve
aisā var vo pāve
śraddhā amṛt pāve

You are pleased by those who sing the divine name of Lord Rama. You bestow upon them the boon of awareness and the nectar of immortality.

atulit bal kā dhām
kiñcit nahi abhimān
kar ye śakti pradān
dhṛḍh bhakti kā dān

Abode of unparalleled power who has not even the least of pride! Bless us with strength and grant us unflinching devotion!

Harē śankha cakra dhāri (Kannada)

harē śankha cakra dhāri
harē dēva kṛṣṇa

O Hari, bearing conch and disc, O Lord Krishna!

biḷigiri ranga kṛṣṇa
uṭupiya svāmi kṛṣṇa
guruvāyūra kṛṣṇa
nanna ninna celva kṛṣṇa

O Krishna in Biligiri as Ranga, the Lord in Udupi, Krishna of Guruvayur- he is the same Krishna dear to me and to you..

kṛṣṇa kṛṣṇa gopi kṛṣṇa
kṛṣṇa kṛṣṇa gopala kṛṣṇa

Krishna! O Gopikrishna, Gopalakrishna!

mīrābāyi bhajipa kṛṣṇa
rādhā dēvi smaripa kṛṣṇa
ānḍāḷu sēvipa kṛṣṇa
ninna nanna canda kṛṣṇa

O Krishna, praised by Mirabai, and remembered by Radhadevi! O Krishna, served by Andalu- He is the same Krishna, dear to you and to me.

kanakana natha kṛṣṇa
sūradāsa kanḍa kṛṣṇa
narasi mehta nāpta kṛṣṇa
nammellara amṛta kṛṣṇa

O Krishna, worshipped by Kanakadas! O Krishna, seen by Surdas, the blind devotee! O Krishna, dear to Narsi! He is the same immortal Krishna dear to all of us.

namellara amṛta kṛṣṇa
snighdhāpānga lōla kṛṣṇā

mandasmita vadana kṛṣṇa
citta cōra īśvara kṛṣṇa

Immortal Krishna, dear to all of us, looks at us with love. Krishna has a smiling face, he is the Lord that steals our hearts.

Harē tū hamārē (Hindi)

harē tū hamārē
hṛdaya kō curākē
virah kī agan mē
hame kyō jalātā

O Lord Hari, You have stolen our hearts. Why do You burn us in the fire of separation?

hare kṛṣṇa śaurē
vibhō viśvamūrttē
mukundā murārē
yaśōdā kē pyārē

O Lord Krishna, Lord of the universe, destroyer of the demon Mura, You are the darling son of Yashoda.

kabhī bānsurī mē
madhura tān chēṭakē
lubhātā tū hamkō
dars tō na dētā

You enchant us by playing sweet music on Your divine flute, but You never show us Your divine form.

niṭhūr hōkē dilsē
madhur muskurātā
nacātā hē apanē
īśārē par sabkō

You have become so uncaring, and yet You smile at us and make us dance at Your command.

nichāvar hē mādhav
pagōm par ham cākar
hamē tū na chōḍnā
abhī āke milnā

O Madhava, this servant of Yours is an offering at Your lotus feet. Please do not leave us, come and grant us the vision of Your divine form.

Harim śyāmavarṇam (Sanskrit)

harim śyāmavarṇam vidhum vārijākṣam
mudā cārurūpam sadāmālyagātram
priyam lokapālam atīndram mukundam
vasum vaiṣṇavam viṣṇumādyam namāmi

I salute Vishnu the primordial One, treasure of the Vaishnavas. O Hari of dark complexion, You please all and You have lotus eyes. You are ever cheerful, Your form is beautiful, always adorned with garlands. Dear One, protector of the world, You are unfathomable to the sense organs. O Mukunda!

kare pāñcajanyam tanau pītavastram
mahāviśvarūpam mahāviṣṇudevam
trayīpālanātham bhuvam pālayantam
vasum vaiṣṇavam viṣṇumādyam namāmi

I salute Vishnu the primordial One, treasure of the Vaishnavas, who has the Panchajanya conch in His hand and wears a yellow garment. Your form is that of Vishwarupa, you are the great Lord Mahavishnu, protector of the three Vedas and protector of the Earth.

gale puṣpahāram sadā dhārayantam
caturbāhurūpam hṛṣīkeśadevam
samudre vasantam murārim mahendram
vasum vaiṣṇavam viṣṇumādyam namāmi

I salute Vishnu the primordial One, treasure of the Vaishnavas, who always wears a garland of flowers on His neck. You have four arms and are Lord of the sense organs. You dwell in the milky ocean, and you are enemy to the demon Mura, O great Lord!

anante śayānam jagadrakṣakam tam
gadāśamkhacakram ca padmam dharantam
sadānāradādiprapūjyam harīndram
vasum vaiṣṇavam viṣṇumādyam namāmi

I salute Vishnu the primordial One, treasure of the Vaishnavas, who reclines on the serpent Ananta. You are protector of the universe, bearing the mace, discus & lotus. You are always worshipped by Narada and others. You are the best among devas!

jagadpālakam tam ramākāntadevam
gurum śrīpatim divyavaikuṇṭhanātham
daśākāradevam trilokādipālam
vasum vaiṣṇavam viṣṇumādyam namāmi

I salute Vishnu the primordial One, treasure of the Vaishnavas, who is the maintainer of the worlds and the Lord of Lakshmi! You are the Guru, the consort of Shree, and You dwell in Vaikuntha; You took ten forms, and You are the protector of the three worlds.

Harsut akhila (Hindi)

harsut akhila amangala har
mud mangala dātā
hāthī mukh hasmukh sundar
candra mukuṭ vālā

O Lord Ganesh, Son of Shiva, You eliminate all inauspiciousness in the world and bestow auspiciousness. O Elephant-faced One, You have a beautiful smile and bear the crescent moon on Your crown!

āgē baḍhe pagpag par bole vignarāj kī jai
pāve vidyā vijay viśvame lāve śānti gaṇeś

Moving ahead, chant at every step: "Victory to the Lord who removes obstacles! May we achieve success in our quest for knowledge!". Lord Ganesh brings peace to the world.

jai ekadant kī jai
jai vakratūṇḍ kī jai
jai vighnarāj kī jai
jai divyarūp kī jai

You have a single tusk and a big belly, victory to You! You are the destroyer of obstacles and have a divine form, victory to You!

tume vandan śankar nandan sundar dantikāy vande

We sing Your praises, son of Lord Shiva. We bow before the One with the beautiful tusk!

kalmaṣ bhañjan kari vadana
karma bandha hārī
dhavala kalebar dharma niketan
bhīma deh bhārī śrī gaṇeśa varadānī

You eliminate impurities. You are the Elephant-faced One who removes the bondage of karma. Your complexion is white, Your body is mighty, and You are the Embodiment of Righteousness. O Lord Ganesh! You are the Bestower of Boons.

vighna nivārak śvetāmbaradhar
tū antaryāmī
bhagat janāvan gaṇapati śivsut
ho prasann svāmī śrī gaṇeśa varadānī

You eliminate all obstacles and are dressed in white. You are the indweller and the protector of devotees. O Lord of the Ganas, Son of Shiva, may You be pleased!

Hē mañjunāthā (Konkani)

hē mañjunāthā karttā praṇām
kailāsavāsa karttā praṇām

O Lord of the snowy mountains (Lord Shiva), I bow down to You. O One who resides on Mount Kailash, I bow down to You!

vyāgrāmbara tū dhāraṇ kōrnu
sarppā bharaṇāna śōbhita jhāvnō
vṛśabhāva vāhanāri savāri evnu
jaṭājūṭadhara yōre dhāvun

Covered with a tiger skin, adorned with a serpent, riding on the sacred bull, please come soon and elate the world!

hē mañjunāthā kailāsavāsa
hē mañjunāthā kailāsavāsa

O Lord of the snowy mountains, residing on Mount Kailash!

paśupati tū paramadayāḷu
kaśśi sāgūre manāntle taḷamaḷ
karttā smaraṇa sarvākāḷu
dākkāyi karuṇa kōrṇuka vēḷu

Lord of animals, You are the kindest. How do I express my desperation to You? I remember You all the time. What is keeping You for so long?

himaparvatā vairi ityatu baslā
bhagutāle bhagutiku parvatu kirlā
manamandirāntu baisūn paḷe
daruśana mātrāna dhanyatī dhōḷe

He resides on the peak of the Himalayas- those mountains have turned due to the sheer devotion of this devotee. Look into the temple of your soul, and your eyes are sanctified by the very sight of the Lord.

jaya jaya śambho he mañjunāthā
hē mañjunāthā kailāsavāsa

Victory to You, O Lord Manjunatha!

He śrīnivāsa (Kannada)

he śrīnivāsa he ṛṣikēśa
karuṇadi pālisō hē pāṇḍuranga
bhavasāgaradi bendu bendu nondenayya
tande bandu salahayya śrī mukunda

O Srinivasa, O Rishikesa (names of Vishnu), please take care of us with compassion, O Panduranga. I've been in pain, burning in the ocean of transmigration. Please come and console me, O Sri Mukunda!

kāmakāñcanagaḷige mōhitanāgi nā
ninnanu stutisadē matihinanāde
janmada lakṣyava tiḷiyade vyartthavāgi
pāramārtthava toredu ninnane marete

I have been disillusioned by desire and greed. I was foolish for not remembering You. Not knowing the goal of this life, I wasted it. I forgot You and lost sight of the ultimate goal

hē śrīnivāsa hē ṛṣikēśa hē padmanābha hē pāṇḍuranga

O Srinivasa, O Rishikesa, O Padmanabha, O Panduranga!

mōhada baleyalli siluki oddāḍide
dāriya kāṇade baḷalide toḷalide
nijavanu aritu śaraṇu bandihenīga
tvaritadi kāyō hē pāṇḍuranga

I lost my way getting caught in the net of desires. I lost sight of my path and suffered for it. Now I understand the truth and I have come in surrender to You. Please come and save me right away!

viṭhala pāṇḍuranga viṭhala pāṇduranga

O Vithala, Panduranga! (names of Lord Vishnu)

Holi hai āyī (Hindi)

ye hai vraj ke holī holī holī
kāhā kī anokhī holī holī
āvo sab mil kānhā sang
khele ye holi nirāli

This is the festival Holi of Vraj, this is the unique Holi of Krishna. Let us all come together and play this exceptional Holi with Krishna!

holi hai āyī rangīlī
nikli kānhā kī ṭoli
rādhā sang vraj khele āj
fāgun kī ye holī
holī... holī... holī... holī... hoy... hoy... hoy...

Colourful Holi has come, Krishna's troupe has come out! Radha and the whole of Vraj are playing today - the festival Holi in the month of Phagun.

yahān vahān gopiyān dauḍe
āpas me rang vo fenke
hāthon me lekhe pichkārī
rang chiṭke giridhāri
holī... holī... holī... holī... hoy... hoy... hoy...

Gopis ran here and there, throwing colours at each other. With piston in hand, Lord Giridhari sprayed colours.

rang me ḍubāye kānhā
jo bhī āye vahān
khele aisa madhur holī
vraj vāsī hogaye rangīle

holī... holī... holī... holī... hoy... hoy... hoy...

Krishna drenched everyone present in colour. They played such a sweet Holi that all the inhabitants of Vraj became colourful!

kānhā kyā rang jamāye
vraj me khuśiyā chāyī
ānand se nāc uṭhe dekh ke
prabhu kī mastī bharī holī
holī... holī... holī... holī... hoy... hoy... hoy...

Krishna made a colourful impact, the whole of Vraj rejoiced. All came to see the Lord's prank-filled Holi.

jaya rādhe rādhe rādhe rādhe śyām rādhe
govinda gopāla hari kṛṣṇa murāre

Victory to Radha and Shyam!

Hṛdoye ācho mā tumi (Bengali)

hṛdoye ācho mā tumi
tobu pāina tomāre
ekī khelā tomār
kemone bujhibo, tumi nā bojhāle

Though You reside in my heart, I don't feel Your presence. How am I to understand Your game if You don't explain it to me?

kakhono dāo je dhorā
kakhono adhorā lūkāo chokote kotha?
keno je tumi omon karo mā?
a kemon dhārā tārā, a kemon dhārā?

Sometimes You are within reach and sometimes You hide, going out of bounds. What is this way of Yours, Mother Tara (Kali)?

tārā tārā tāro tāro tāro mā

O Tara, please rescue me!

snehamoyi tumi karuṇāmoyi
tobe keno chalonā, niṭhūr chalonāmoyi?
śudhu tomār mojā ār amar ṣājā?
a kemon khela tārā, a kemon khela?

You are full of love and compassion. Then why this cruel deception? You have all the fun and I get only punishment? What kind of game is this, Tara?

ār keno karo chalonā?
tomār chele āmi ṣeṭā bhūlonā
tomāy āmi kobhu chāḍbonā
jatokhon nā tumi debe dhorā

Why do You fool me? Don't forget, after all I am Your son. I'll not stop pursuing You until You come to me.

Illāmai enbatilum (Tamil)

illāmai enbatilum uḷḷāḷ avaḷ
illāmai āgavē illātavaḷ
kallātavan anbōṭaizhaittālavaḷ
nillātu parivōṭu selvāḷ avaḷ

She exists even in nothingness. So there is no nothingness for Her. Even if an unrefined person calls out to Her, She will run to help without delaying even one second.

pollātavan pōttra mayankātavaḷ
nallōruṭan avanai iṇaikkindravaḷ
ariyāmai rōgattin marundānavaḷ
piravāmaikkuriya vazhi tānānavaḷ

She will not fall prey to the flattery of a wicked man. She will instead connect him to the supreme soul in order to elevate him. She is the medicine for the disease of ignorance. She Herself becomes the sole way to escape the cycle of birth and death.

arugāmayāl neñcil pularvāḷ avaḷ
tīmai viḷai seyalinai porukkātavaḷ
tuvaṇḍu viṭum aṭiyārin balamānavaḷ
akhaṇḍajapam seyvittu kanivāḷavaḷ

By Her nearness, She will manifest herself in our hearts. She will not put up with any ill-wished actions. She is the source of support for the devotees who lose hope in their pursuits. She rejoices by inducing them to chant incessantly and bestows grace upon them.

varaṇḍuviṭṭa idayattil nīrānavaḷ
aruḷamudam tiraṇḍuvarum kāṭṭāravaḷ
marayōtum periyōr mun nirppāḷavaḷ
kurai kūruvōreyum sahippāḷavaḷ
sirai iruntu viṭuvikka varuvāḷavaḷ
ammā endrāl kural taruvāḷ avaḷ

She becomes water for those hearts in dryness. She is an abundantly flowing thunderous river of nectar. She will give heed to those souls who sing the hymns of the Vedas. She is absolutely unaffected by any criticism against Her. She will release one from the jail of material bondage. She will respond to the sincere calls of Her devotees.

Indu nammamma (Kannada)

indu nammamma na mūrige bandaḷu
harṣada varṣava karedihaḷu

Today my Mother has come to our town. She has brought down a rain of joy.

makkaḷa kāṇalu tavakisī nannamma
bēgane lōkava suttāṭi bandaḷu
hōdalli bantalli muddina maḷegaredu
duḥkhavu mithyavu entutā nuṭivaḷu

My Mother, eager to meet her children, travels all over the world at good speed. Wherever she goes she showers love and kisses, and tells us that sorrow is unreal.

kaicācci baḷigenna seḷedukoṇḍihaḷu
maṭilalī malagisī maidaṭa vidaḷu
muddū maguvē bhayapaṭadirentu
tabbimuddāṭī prasāda koṭṭaḷu

She stretched out her hand and pulled me to Her. She put me in Her lap and patted my back. She told me, darling child, don't be afraid. She hugged me, kissed me and gave me prasad

ībhavasāgara dāṭisu tāyē
dīnaḷa īmore kēḷamma tāye
mōhakke bedaruve kapaṭakke hedaruve
dāriya kāṇadē dikkeṭṭu aledihe

O Mother, help me cross this ocean of worldliness. O Mother, please listen to this helpless one. I fear attachment and I fear deceit. I have lost my way and am wandering aimlessly.

mithyava nīgū satyava tōrū
kattale nīgū beḷakannu tōru
mṛtyuva nīgū amṛtatva nīḍū
lōkakke śānti nīḍu – tāyē
samastake sukhava nīḍu tāyē

Lead us from untruth to truth; From darkness to light; From death to immortality. May all beings in all the worlds be happy.

Iniyoru janmam (Kannada version)

innondu janma nīḍadiru kṛṣṇa
madamōha rāṭige dūḍadiru
nīḍidare nina dāsānudāsiya
janmava enage karuṇisayyā

nina nāma manadali sthiravāgali kṛṣṇa
nina pādapatmā sadā beḷagali
sakalava ninna pratibheyāgi kanḍu
samaniladali mana sadā nillali
kṛṣṇa karuṇānidhē
karajōḍisi kaimugive

avaniyilupakāra pradavāgali janma
avināśa sukhadāna ennindāgali
adakāgi janma nīḍuve yādare
agaṇita narajanma enage nīḍu

Inkē irukkum (Tamil)

inkē irukkum unnaikkāṇā alaikirārē śankarā
enkēcenṭru etanai kāṇpār yārarivār śankarā
ankē inkē alaintu ōṭi taḷarumvarai śankarā
śankēseviṭan kātilpōla muzhankiṭumē śankarā

O Shankara (Lord Shiva), You are right here but people are wandering to see You elsewhere. Where will they go and what will they see? No one knows. People wander here and there till they get exhausted, like a conch sounding before deaf ears.

āśaiyatan āttralālē tavaruseyvār śankarā
arivin āttral kūṭumbōtu uṇarntiṭuvār śankarā

uṇarntavarō varuntumbōtu tiruntiṭuvār śankarā
tiruntiyavar unataruḷāl uyarntiṭuvār śankarā

O Shankara, people make mistakes because of the power of their desires. They realize this when their knowledge increases. They change themselves when self-realized people repent their mistakes. Changed people will reach a high status by Your grace.

tannil unnai kaṇḍukoḷḷa tavariyavar śankarā
mattravarai tāzhntavarāy kaṇḍiṭuvār śankarā
tannil unnai kaṇḍukoṇḍa uttamarō śankarā
enkum etilum unnaikkaṇḍu vaṇankiṭuvār śankarā

O Shankara, those who don't find You in themselves will see others as inferior. Great are those who find You within- they worship You in each and every thing.

śankarā śiva śankarā śiva satguru nāthanē śankarā
śankarā śiva śankarā tiru kailāsa nāthanē śankarā

O Shankara, absolute One, Self-realized Master, Lord of Mount Kailash.

Īrattē tūpanāru (Tulu)

īrattē tūpanāru ammā īrattē kāpunāru
sakala jīva rāśiga ādhārō īrē
nambuduḷḷe ammā īrēnu pādonē
śuddha bhakti kōrdu kāpulēmma dēvi

O Mother, aren't You the one who protects and looks after me? You are the sole support of all beings. Goddess, You are my sole refuge. Bestow on me pure devotion and save me.

dinja duṇḍu uḍuluḍu duhkha duritōlu
enka enna panpi malla svārtthōlu
parōpakāra malpare manasa kōrpadu
kanalē namana badukugu śānti saukhyonu

Owing to selfish and egoistic thoughts, my heart has become filled with sorrow and strife. Give me a mind that yearns to help others. Thus, fill my life with peace and well-being.

janmōlētu yānu nashta malte ammā
īrēna pāda smaraṇē malpande
sampattu sambandhō dālu kēnujamma dēvi
nijala kanala smaraṇē kōrdu kāpulēmma dēvi

I have wasted many lives because I neither remembered You constantly nor surrendered at Your feet. I do not desire wealth or good relationships. Bless me that I may remember You while awake and when dreaming, and in this way redeem me!

Iyarkaiyammā (Tamil)

iyarkaiyammā iyarkaiyammā
enkaḷiṭam irakkam koḷvāy
uyirkaḷellām vāṭudammā un kōpam taṇindiṭuvāy
erimalaiyāy kodikkinṭrāy veḷḷamāga azhikkinṭrāy
puyalāga aṭikkinṭrāy bhūkambamāy veṭikkinṭrāy

O Mother Nature, please have mercy on us. The earthly creatures are suffering. O Mother, may Your rage be appeased. Volcanoes are exploding, floods are swelling, cyclones are raging, and earthquakes are striking.

eṭuppadpōl koṭuppadu tān ivvulakin niyatiyanṭrō
eṭuttukkoṇṭē irunduviṭṭōm koṭuppadarkku marandviṭṭōm
unnarumai marandviṭṭu tannalamāy irundatināl
unporumai maraindviṭa maṇṇulakam tavikkudammā

Although it is nature's law that one should give as much as one takes, we have forgotten Your sublime ways, and have been taking without giving. Seeing this, You have lost Your patience, making us tremble in fear.

pālūṭṭi aṇaittavaḷē kainīṭṭi aṭippaduvō
sōrūṭṭi vaḷarttavaḷē tīmūṭṭi erippaduvō
uḷḷattil valiyirundāl unniṭattil uraittiṭuvōm
unnālē valiyenṭrāl yāriṭattil muraiyiṭuvōm

Will a mother who has breastfed her baby punish the child? Will a mother who has nourished her child prepare the funeral pyre for her child? When difficulties arise, we take refuge in You. But if You punish us, where else can we find refuge?

un sēvai seydiṭuvōm unaivaṇanki vāzhndiṭuvōm
munnōrkaḷ sonnavazhi ennāḷum naṭandiṭuvōm
tattaḷikkum kuzhandaikaḷai dayaikoṇḍu kāttiṭammā
tavarizhaikkum makkaḷuṇḍu dayayillā tāyumuṇḍō

We will adore and save You. Henceforth, we will follow the wisdom of our ancestors. Save Your children who are in the throes of suffering! There may be children who err. But can there be a mother without compassion?

jagajananī kaitozhutōm jaganmātē kāttiṭammā

Mother of the world, our prostrations to You! Mother of all, protect us!

Jagajjananī (Marathi)

jagajjananī ambā bhavānī ālō mī darśnālā
vāṭ pāhū kitī ambā darśan dē tū malā

O universal Mother, we have come for Your darshan. We have been waiting for You since so many days. O Bhavani, please give us Your darshan.

andhārātun rastā chuklā jhālō bējār
ṭēch lāglī tarīhī nāhi sōḍū nirdhār
pāy śīṇlē cāl cālunī ālō tujhiyā dāri
vyākuḷ jhālā jīv ambā kṛpā karī majhvarī

I had lost my path in darkness. Even though there are difficulties, I am not shattered by them. My feet are becoming feeble. Still, I have come to see Mother. My heart is in pain. Please shower Your blessings.

phulē bhaktīchi nirmaḷ arpaṇ tujhiyā charṇī
jyōt ḍōḷyānchī ambābāī ōvāḷū āratī
besūr mājhī vāṇī tarī gāvūn tujhīch gāṇī
ambē bhavānī mahān mahimā pāvan kar tū malā

I have pure love for You. I am offering that love as flowers at Your feet. I offer arati to You with the lamps of my eyes. Though I don't know to sing, I still sing Your glories. O Mother, I heard of Your greatness. Please shower Your blessings!

Jai jai rāma (Kannada)

jai jai rāma sannuta nāma
jānaki jīvana vandanam
kuśalavatāta kuśalapradāta
daśaratha putrasu vandanam

Victory to Rama of praiseworthy name, the very life of Janaki. Prostrations to the father of Kusha and Lava, the son of Dasharatha, the one who makes action skillful.

raghupati rāghava rāja rām
patita pāvana sīta rām

Hail King Rama, Lord of the Raghu dynasty, who uplifts the downtrodden, and who is Sita's consort!

lōka bhayankara rākṣasa mardana
lōka śubhākara vandanam
karuna samudra suranara vandita
carana sarōjake vandanam

Salutations to Rama, the demon slayer feared by the world, and who lends auspiciousness to the world. Prostrations at the lotus feet of Rama, who is an ocean of compassion and whom the celestials and humans worship.

ayōdhyavāsi ahalyōdhāraka
vānara sēvita vandanam
mangalānga hē ananga pālaka
tunga vikrama vandanam

Salutations to Rama, citizen of Ayodhya, who liberated Ahalya, and whom the vanaras (monkeys) serve. Prostrations to the auspicious-limbed Rama, who protects the God of love and is of immense valor.

raghupati rāghava rāja rām
patita pāvana sīta rām
jai jai rām sīta rām
jai jai rām sīta rām

Hail king Rama, Lord of the Raghu dynasty, who uplifts the downtrodden, and who is Sita's consort! Victory to Lord Rama and Goddess Sita!

Jamuna kināre (Hindi)

jamuna kināre muraḷi bajāne
madhuban me nit rās racāne
gopī ghar navanīt curāne
giri kānan me dhenu carāne

To play the flute on the banks of the Yamuna river, to blissfully dance in the gardens, to steal butter from the house of the gopis, to feed the cattle on his mountain...

navghan nīla kaḷebar āyā
vṛndāvan kā pyārā

kṛṣṇa kṛṣṇa kṛṣṇa kṛṣṇa kṛṣṇa
kṛṣṇa kṛṣṇa kṛṣṇa kṛṣṇa kṛṣṇa

...the dear One of Vrindavan with a dark blue complexion has come! O Krishna.

āyā sāvrā, pyārā sāvrā
ayā pās bajāyā bāsuri

Playing the flute, the dear dark One has come close to us.

māyā me nij rūp chipāke
nitnit navnav līlā karne
mere dilme jyoti jagāne
gokul me to śor macāne

Concealing His true form behind the veil of illusion, performing new lilas again and again. to awaken the light in my heart, and create a commotion in Gokul.

madhurhasī se sabko lubhāne
muh me sārā viśv dikhāne
braj jan manme madhubarsāne
govardhan giri karme lene

To endear everyone with His sweet smile, and show the entire cosmos in His mouth. Showering bliss in the minds of the people of Vraj, lifting the mountain with His hand.

Janmāntarapathikan (Malayalam)

janmāntarapathikan ñān tēṭiṭum
ambikē nin caraṇam
janma marīcikayām kanavakalān
nin kṛpa tān śaraṇam

I'm a pilgrim travelling through many a birth in search of You. Your flowing grace is my sole refuge, please make this mirage of births dissolve.

sankaṭamōcinī nin kaṭamizhitan
amṛtoḷi puraḷānāy
ulkkaṭa mōhamatonnuṇḍennil
uḷkkaṭalāyennum

O Mother, remover of all sorrows, within me lies an ocean of hope. The hope of being engulfed at least for once by the splendor of Your glance.

ennile ñānākē ninnilaliññiṭaṇē
en matiteḷiyān anpoḷi paṭarān
amma kaniññiṭaṇē - ennum
amma kaniññiṭaṇē

Let the 'I' in me become merged completely with Your Self. Be kind, and make my mind so pure that the light of Your love will shine through.

nīrava niśatan vīthiyilalayum
oru virahārtta vilāpam
priya jana caraṇadhvanitēṭīṭum
vijana vimūka vihāram

I am just a smothered cry that roams the streets of silent nights. An empty home - listening out to hear the familiar steps of someone dear.

viṇtala śobhini nī
mṛṇmaya bhājika ñān
nin mṛduhāsa nilā mazha pozhiyān
amma kaniññiṭaṇē - ennum
amma kaniññiṭaṇē

You shine so bright in the night so high. Me, down here - mere earthenware. Shower Your grace and fill me with the cool beams of Your gentle smile.

Japo re (Hindi)

japo re japo re japo re japo
rām kā nām japo
subah ke vakt japo
aur har śyām japo

Chant, chant, chant the name of Ram! Chant it in the day and chant it in the night!

rām nām japune se
hote hai kaṣṭ dūr sabhī
rām nām japune se dil
ko mile surūr sabhī
rām jī kā nām japo
subah aur śyām japo

Chanting Ram's names expels sorrow, chanting his name gives peace of mind. Chant his name day and night!

rām nām aisā he jiskī
na koyi kīmat hai
rām nām esā hai jo
khud hī ek dolat hai
rām jī kā nām japo
subah aur śyām japo

Ram's name is such that it cannot be equaled in value, His name is itself the biggest wealth. Chant His name day and night!

rām kā nām japo
rām rām rām rām rām kā nām japo

Chant Ram's name!

Jaya jaya hō! (Telugu)

jaya jaya hō! śrī mātā!

sṛṣṭi-sthiti-laya-kāriṇi jōta!

Hail, hail, O divine Mother! Salutations to the creator, maintainer and destroyer of the universe, hail!

nī sankalpamē praṇava nādamai
sṛṣṭiki ūpiri ūdinadā!
pracānda tējamē bhānukōtiyai
rōdasi kāntula merasinadā!

Your resolve resonates as the sound 'aum', creating the universe. Your astounding brightness radiates more brilliantly than millions of suns illuminating the cosmos. Hail!

apāra prēmayē amṛta dhārayai
pālapuntalalō ponginadā!
mūrtībhavincina mātṛ prēmayē
avanī mātaga velasinadā!

Your unlimited divine love, transformed as nectar, overflows throughout the Milky Way. Mother Earth is an embodiment of Your motherly love. Hail!

avyāja karuṇē ambu rāśiyai
kṛpā sindhuvula ninpinadā!
caitanya dīptiyē pavana vīcikai
prāṇikōti prabhavincinadā!

Your unconditional kindness is like a huge ocean of grace. The brilliance of Your cosmic consciousness has become the wind, giving birth to billions of beings. Hail!

kanureppa pāṭuna kālayavanika!
śṛuti laya vinyāsa viśva vēdika!
ānanda tāndava ṇṛtya kēḷika!
andapinda brahmānda prahēḷika!

The wink of Your eye becomes the curtain of time. The Universe, vibrating with divine musical harmony and cosmic rhythm, forms a dais upon which Your eternal dance of bliss is the sacred play. Your maya creates the mirthful magic of the magnificent Universe with all its splendid beings. Hail!

Jaya jaya rāma jānaki rāma (Kannada)

jaya jaya rāma jānaki rāma
mēghaśyāma raghukula sōma

Hail to You O Rama, dark as clouds, moon of the Raghu clan.

āgali ennaya hṛdaya rāma
nitya ninnaya prēma dhāma
dēha vīṇeya mīṭalu rāma
mūḍali sumadhura tārakanāma

May my heart become Your abode of love for ever. When the veena of my being is played, may Your saving name be the only sound emerging from it!

rāma ennalu gadgata svaravu
hṛdayadi bhaktiya bhāvada honalu
nayanadi prēmada mēghada maḷeyu
bārade ā dina karuṇārāma

O Rama, my throat chokes when I utter Your name. A torrent of devotional fervour shall spring forth from my heart, and rains from clouds of love will pour from my eyes- will a day such as this not come, O compassionate Rama?

janamana rañjaka jagadabhirāma
janimṛti nāśaka jayajaya rāma
bhaktajana prāṇadhana rājārāma
ānandarūpanē ātmārāma

You are the Lord who keeps all the beings in the world happy. O Rama hail to You, destroyer of birth and death! You are the most precious treasure of the devotees. O Rama who reposes in the supreme, You are the embodiment of bliss.

Jaya māt bhavāni (Sanskrit)

bhaktim dadātu me premam dadātu me
viśvāsam dadtvā mama rakṣām karotu jagadambā

Please give me devotion, please give me love, O Mother of the universe, protect me by bestowing faith.

jaya māt bhavāni namāmi śive
śivaśankari śāmbhavi pāhi rame
praṇamāmi śubhankari śrī laḷite
jaya he asurāri mahēśa priye

Victory to Mother Bhavani, I bow down to the auspicious one. Protect me Mother, Shankari, consort of Shiva. I bow down to Sri Lalita who bestows auspiciousness. Victory to the divine One who is averse to negativity

amṛteśvari śrīkari pālayamām
śaraṇāgata pālaya śrī amṛte

O eternal Goddess who bestows prosperity, please protect me. Divine and immortal One, please protect us who have taken refuge in You!

jaya he tripureśi maheśi ume
varadātri nirantari muktiprade
manamohini kṣīrapayodhi sute
amṛteśvari śrīkari pālayamām

Bestower of boons, eternal one who grants liberation. I bow down to the One who captivates the mind and has manifested from the milky ocean.

bhuvaneśi kṛpākari haimavati
paśupāśavimocini mantramayi
bhavasāgaratāriṇi śrī janani
amṛteśvari śrīkari pālayamām

O Parvati! Goddess of the universe, compassionate one who releases from worldly bondages. You are the form of the mantra. O divine Mother, You take us across the ocean of transmigration.

hṛdayeśvari bhairavi bhāvaghane
śivaśakti svarūpiṇi prāṇadhane
sachidānandarūpiṇi bhaktipriye
amṛteśvari śrīkari pālayamām

O Bhairavi, Goddess of my heart, You are adept in divine manifestation. You are of the form of Shiva and Shakti, and the wealth of life-force. Your form is existence, knowledge and bliss, and You are fond of devotion.

Jhala jhalavena (Tamil)

anbu vaṭivānavaḷ annaiyavaḷ varukirāḷ
akilattil vizhākkōlam annai makkaḷin porkkālam
amudamazhayāy avaniyil ānandamē pozhiya
ādiśakti bhuvanattil bavani varukirāḷ

That embodiment of love, the divine Mother, is coming! It is a universal festival, the golden age for the children of the divine Mother. The Goddess of supreme power is coming, leading a procession to shower the nectar of bliss over the entire universe.

jhala jhalavena salankai kulunka
kalakalavena sirittukkoṇḍu
palapalapala līlai purintu bavani varukirāḷ
amma bavani varukirāḷ

Mother is leading the procession, anklets jingling. She is laughing, and performing many, many lilas!

om śakti parāśakti om śakti mahāśakti
akilattai aravaṇaittiṭa bavani varukirāḷ

ammā bavani varukirāḷ

The essence of Om, the ultimate power of the universe, is coming in a procession to embrace the world!

kāḷī mahākāḷī dēvī parāśaktī

Divine Mother Kali, supreme power of the universe!

arttamillā vārttaikaḷai arttamuḷḷatākkivaittu
arttamillā siruvāzhvil anpatanai tantarūḷi
arttamuṭanē vāzhavaippāḷ anbunāyakī
akilalōka rakṣakiye jagadīśvarī

Filling empty words with significance, blessing our short, aimless lives with love, the Goddess of love, protector of all the worlds, the Queen of the universe, will make our lives meaningful.

dēhamēgam sūzhntālum ātmasūrya oḷivīśum
ēkaśakti katiravanām parāśaktiyē
katiravanai tilakamākki tarittukkoṇḍavaḷē
kātaṇiyai veṇṇilāvāy māttri vaittavaḷē

Although we are surrounded by the dark clouds of body-consciousness, You come as the sun that showers us with the rays of consciousness. O Mother! You wore the sun as the tilakam mark on Your forehead and made Your earrings shine like the moon.

manamenum pū malarkiratu tēnenum bakti niraikiratu
manakōvilil niraintiṭa dēvī varukirāḷ
kaliyukattin iruḷ maraya aruḷ vēṇḍumē
kalidōṣam nīkka jñāna mazhai vēṇḍumē

The flower of the mind opens, and is filled with the honey of devotion. Devi is coming to reside in the temple of the mind. We need Her grace to remove the darkness of the Kali Yuga. We need the divine shower of self knowledge to remove the evils of Kali Yuga.

Jñānakkaṭaltannai (Tamil)

jñānakkaṭaltannai mīn aḷakkalāmā
aḷakkintra potu sirikkintrāy tāyē
mīn sintum kaṇṇīrkkaṭal sērumō
sirumīnin kaṇṇīrkku vazhi sollumō?

Can an ignorant fish measure the depth of the ocean of knowledge? If it tries at all, O Devi, You laugh at its attempts. Will the tears of this fish reach the ocean? Will Devi, knowledge personified, offer a solution?

unnai tēṭi aṭaya uḷ nōkkumbōtu
alaimōtum eṇṇankaḷ taṭam māttrakkūṭum
īrkkintra śaktivaṭivāna ammā
varavēṇḍum varavēṇḍum nizhalāka dēvī

As I wander in search of You, unwanted thoughts may come and distract me, pulling me in another direction. O She who attracts the masses! Come and stay with me like a protective shadow.

uyirōṭu uyirāka kalantiruppāyē
kaikūppi siram tāzhtta kaṇ pārppāyē
sodanaikaḷ tantu āzham pārkkintrāy
padam pārttu nal bhakti nalkukintrāy

When I bow in reverence, remaining as one with the Soul, You glance at me with love and compassion. To check the intensity of my search, You test me in different ways, and then grant me pure bhakti.

Kab āye gā (Hindi)

kab āye gā vō din prabhujī
chabi tērī dēkh pāvū me
param prēm kē gangā jal me
har pal nahāvūm me

O Lord, when will that day come when I will see Your image? When I will bathe every moment in the holy Ganges water of eternal love?

tērē vacanō kō suntē prabhujī
bhāv vibhōr hō jāvūn me
man mandir kē vṛndāvan me
divya rās racāvūn me

O Lord, when will I be overcome with love while listening to Your words? When will I perform the diving dance in the Vrindavan of my mind?

ahankār kī ghōr pakad se
mukt hō jāvūn mē
tērē hāthō me basūm prabhujī
tērī bānsuri ban jāvūm me

When will I be free from the strong hold of the ego? It will come to be when, in Your hands, I become Your flute.

prēm kā ras pān karke
prēm hī ban jāvūn me
sāgar me jese saritā mile
tujh me ghulmil jāvūn me

Drinking the nectar of love, when will I become love itself? When will I become one with You, as the river merges into the ocean?

Kadiranu enagende (Kannada)

kadiranu enagende udisidarēnu
tingaḷanu enagāgi beḷagidarēnu
ninna kṛpā kiraṇa enna hṛdayava
hūvāgi araḷisadiralu ammā

So what if the sun rises for my sake? So what if the moon shines for my sake? What is the use unless the ray of Your grace makes my heart blossom into a flower?

jīvana nadiguṇṭu aṭe taṭe anēka
viparītanēka viparyāsanēka
suḷiyali silukadantiralu nā ammā
vilavilā horaḷāḍutiruve ammā

The river of life has many obstacles, many contradictions, many paradoxes. I am struggling, turning around and around, to avoid getting caught in the whirlpool.

śaraṇu bandavagē nī karuṇe tōrammā
pāpa maguvendu ennatta nōṭamma
hūvāgi aralaḷi hṛdayavu indē
minugali kṛpā kiraṇa ammā

Mother, please be compassionate towards those who have come seeking refuge! Please glance at me, in my pitiful state. Please make my heart blossom like a flower, and shine Your grace on me.

Kalamurali (Tamil version)

kuzhalisaiyāl emai mayakkum mukundā
nīyāṭum arankāgaṭṭuṁ en manaṁ

pulavar punaindadu puṣpavimānaṁ
en uḷḷamē undan ratnavimānaṁ
īṭiṇaiyillā ezhilmigu vaiyam
nī naṭaṁ puriyum nāṭṭiya mēṭai

oru piṭi avalāl peruṁ pēraḷittāy
oru sir ilaiyai amudena koṇḍāy
tuyaraṁ migundu kaṇṇīr sindum
draupadikaḷ – tuyar nīkki aruḷvāy

eḷiyavarkkeṇtrum naṇbanaṇṭrō nī
eḷiya kuzhalilum pozhivāy amudai

mayirpīli aṇiyum yadukula bālā
līlai seydālum yōgiyanṭrō nī

Kāḷī kāḷī kāḷī (Gujarati)

kāḷī kāḷī kāḷī tane śāne kahe mā
tārā jevū sundar nathī koyī ā jagmā
kāḷī mā o kāḷī mā

O Kali, why do they call You 'the dark One,' when there is no one as beautiful as You in the whole world? O Kali Ma.

ami bhari tāri draṣṭi
karuṇābharyā tārā nayn
tujhthī chūpū nathī
kayī ā jagmā

Your eyes are full of divine nectar and compassion. Nothing remains hidden from Your eyes.

kāḷī kāḷī mārī kāḷī
vālī kāḷī pyārī kāḷī kāḷī mā o kāḷī mā

My Kali, my dear Kali, my darling Kali Ma.

tū mārī vālī kāḷī
tū mārī bhoḷī kāḷī
bhoḷī chattā śāṇī kāḷī
tārā jevū nathī koyī

You are my dear Kali. Kali, You are so innocent, but no one is as smart as You in the whole world.

tū kāḷī mahākāḷī
darśan de de mātārānī
dauḍī dauḍī āv kāḷī
tane pokārū laḷi laḷi

You are Maha Kali! Give me Your darshan, O Queen Mother. Come running Kali, I am calling out to You!

rūmjhum rūmjhum āv kāḷī
rās ramvā āv kāḷī
jay jay kāḷī mahākāḷī
kāḷī kāḷī jay ho kāḷī

Come, Kali, with Your anklets jingling. Come Kali to dance with us. Victory to You Kali!

Kāḷi māteyē (Kannada)

kāḷi māteyē kāruṇya kīrtiyē
vāñchita phala dāteyē amṛtānanda mūrtiyē

O Mother Kali, You are renowned for Your compassion. Bestower of desires, You are of the form of immortality.

ninna makkaḷu nāvu namma irisu satya mārgadi
kaṣṭaveṣṭe barali koḍu śakti śānti nemmadi
svārtha biḍisi tyāga beḷesi naḍēsu namma avirata
kāma-krōdha mōha-lōbha mada-matsara kaḍiyuta

We are Your children. Please keep us on the true path. Let there be any amount of difficulties in our lives. Please give us strength and peace. Please remove selfishness and may the attitude of sacrifice grow in us. Keep us on this path incessantly. Please remove lust, anger, delusion, greed, pride and envy.

kāli mā jai jai kāli mā
kāli mā jai jai durge mā

Victory to Mother Kali. Victory to Mother Durga.

janani ninna bēḍutihevu bhaktiyinda bhajipevu
irisu namma mukti-pathadi eḍebiḍadē satatavu
māyayinda dūramāḍu svārthavillade duḍivevu

sulabhamukti mārga tōru dēvi ninna stutipevu

O Mother, with devotional hymns, we beg You to always keep us on the path of salvation. Please keep delusion away from us, and we will strive selflessly. Kindly show the easy path to liberation while we sing Your glories.

Kallum avanē (Tamil)

kallum avanē kaṭavuḷum avanē
ellām śivamayamē
ellām śivanē ellām śivanē
ellām śivamayamē

Everything is Shiva. He is the stone idol. He is also God, everything is Shiva.

sattenum sollum śivamayamē
cittenum sollum śivamayamē
akattinil ānanda naṭanam puriyum
anbin vaṭivum śivamayamē

The word existence is Shiva. The word consciousness is also Shiva. The One who dances the ecstatic dance inside of us is Shiva in the form of love.

tiruccittrambalam, tiruccittrambalam
tiruccittrambalam, tiruccittrambalam

Shiva resides in Tirucitrambalam (a famous Shiva temple in Tamil Nadu)

dēvarkaḷ palarāy irundiṭinum
pēraruḷ enbatu śivamayamē
uruvangaḷ palavāy irundiṭinum – atil
aruvamāy iruppatum śivamayamē

Even though the gods are many, true grace is Shiva. In all these forms, the formless One is Shiva.

śivanena vaṇankiṭa śivanāvān
hariyena vaṇankiṭa hariyāvān
kumaranām guhanē endriṭinum
kumbiṭum poruḷāy avanāvān

One who worships Shiva becomes Shiva. One who worships Vishnu becomes Vishnu. Even if it is Lord Muruga, his son, Shiva is the ultimate truth.

eppeyar yār yār kūppiḍinum
appeyarālavan vandiṭuvān
epporuḷai nām vaṇankiṭinum
apporuḷāy avan tōndriṭuvān

Whatever name one worships, Shiva will come in that form. Whatever truth one worships, Shiva will come in that truth.

śivāya namaḥ om śivāya namaḥ om
śivāya namaḥ om namaḥ śivāya

I prostrate to Lord Shiva..

Kanasu maṇigaḷa (Kannada)

kanasu maṇigaḷa māle māḍide
ninna muddu koraḷige
bēga bandu svīkarisu
bayake īḍērisu

I have made a garland from the beads of my dreams to adorn Your lovely neck. Come accept it quickly and satisfy this yearning.

hṛdaya mandira oppa māḍide
pīṭhavidō kādide
ōṭi bandu alamkarisu
bayake īḍērisu

The temple of my heart is open and a seat awaits You. Come running and grace it with Your presence. Satisfy my yearning.

attu kareva kaṇṇugaḷige
ninna darśana nīḍu
baḷige bandu eduru nintu
bayake īḍērisu

To these crying eyes please give Your darshan, come and stand by me. Satisfy this yearning.

duḥkha buguḍa mṛtyu rōga
bhavada bhaya nivārisu
prēma dinda baḷasi nanna
ninnalondu māḍiko

Please quell my fears of this world, the sorrows, the fear of death. Make me one with You. Satisfy this yearning.

Kaṇḍariyātana (Tamil)

kaṇḍariyātana kaṇḍēn śivanē
kaṇkaḷ panittana nandriyil aranē
kaṇḍēn ārivin kaṇṇāl śivanē
kāṇacheytatu mukkaṇ āranē

I saw truth with the eye of wisdom. It was You, with Your third eye of wisdom, who enabled me to see it.

aranum ariyum vērendrirundēn
aruvē uruvil iraṇḍena kaṇḍēn
bhaktiyum jñānamum pakay endrirundēn
muktiyai īndra tāy tandaiyum kaṇḍēn

I thought that Shiva and Vishnu were different. Now I realize that the formless appears in these two forms. I imagined that devotion and knowledge were mutually contradictory. Now I see they are mother and father of spiritual liberation.

enkō kayilaiyil nī endrirundēn
inke ennūḷḷēyum irukka kaṇḍēn
ālayachilayē nī endrirundēn
anbē śivamāka irukka kaṇḍēn

I thought Your abode was Kailash. I now see that You also dwell in my heart. I thought You were confined to the temple idol. Now I realize that Your essence is true love.

hara hara hara śankarā śiva śiva śiva śankarā
śankarā śiva śankarā śankarā abhayankarā

Hail to Lord Shiva! Victory to Shankara! Glory the one who protects!

Kandarppakōṭi sundarā (Telugu)

kandarppakōṭi sundarā
mandaragiri śūradharā
vanamāli nagadharā
jagadīśvarā bhavabhayahara kēśavā

God who is infinitely beautiful and extremely capable, who lifted Mandhara mountain, who wears the garland of wild flowers around His neck. Lord of the world, who removes the fear of the world.

kēśavā jay mādhavā gōpikā
vallabhā madhusūdanā muraharā

Glory to Madhava, beloved of the gopis, the one who killed the demon Mura.

kamalākṣa laṣmīpati
vāsudēva nārāyaṇa
śrīdharā bhudharā
puruṣōttamā karuṇākarā kēśvā

Lotus-eyed One, consort of Goddess Lakshmi. Son of Vasudeva, Lord of the world. You support Lakshmi and You support the Earth. You are the best among men, O compassionate Keshava!

nanduni varasuta
sumanōhara suguṇākarā
dvārakā purapālakā
puruṣōttamā karuṇākarā kēśavā

Blessed child of Nanda, beautiful One, embodiment of all good qualities, ruler of Dwaraka. You are the best among men, O compassionate Keshava!

bhadrārchita śrīcaraṇā
śaraṇamu sarvēśvarā
śamkhacakra maṇidharā
puruṣōttamā karuṇākarā kēśvā

O Lord of all, I surrender to Your auspicious feet that bestow protection for those who worship them. You wear the jewel, conch, and disc. You are the best among men, O compassionate Keshava!

Kaṇṇan kaḷḷa kaṇṇan (Tamil)

yaśodayin cinna kaṇṇan
gōpiyarin cella kaṇṇan
bṛndāvanattin cuṭṭi kaṇṇan
enkaḷ uḷḷam kavarnta kaḷḷakaṇṇan

Little Krishna of Mother Yashoda, darling Krishna of the gopis! The mischievous Krishna of Vrindavan- the Krishna who has stolen our hearts!

kaṇṇan kaḷḷa kaṇṇan avanai
kaiyyum kaḷavumāy piṭittiṭa vēṇumaṭī kaḷḷa kaṇṇan

mella mella vantē uḷḷattai
sollāmalē koḷḷai koḷkindravan

Krishna, naughty Krishna! We should catch him red-handed... He will come slowly and steal our hearts without a warning.

ennē azhaku enpān – vekkattil
kaṇkaḷai mūṭum oru kaṇattinilē
kannam kiḷḷi celvān
peṇṇē un vīṭṭukkuḷḷē uriyil vaittirukkum
veṇṇaippānaiyinai tiṇṇam tiruṭi celvān

Lord Krishna will praise Your beauty and when you blush and close your eyes, He will pinch your cheeks and run away! O Gopi, He will surely steal all the butter pots from your house and run away!

rādhe rādhe kṛṣṇa kṛṣṇa rādhe govinda bhajo
rādhe gopāla bhajo rādhe kṛṣṇa

O Radha Krishna, Krishna! Sing the divine names of Radha and Govinda!

enna piḷḷai peṭrāy yaśoda
maṇṇum viṇṇum munnar kāṇāta
aṭṭahāsam tānkavillai
kaṭṭikarambu avan cuṭṭittanankaḷellām
muṭrum sahikkavillai tiṭṭa manam varavum illai
rādhe rādhe rādhe rādhe kṛṣṇa

O Yashoda, what a naughty son you have- His mischief is intolerable, unparalleled in the entire universe! Even though the sweet little One's mischief is hard to endure, the heart refuses to rebuke him!

Kaṇṇeḍuttu pārammā (Tamil)

kaṇṇeḍuttu pārammā, piḷḷai idu unadammā

sevi koḍuttu kēḷammā, tāy nī enadammā
bandhuvenḍru sondamenḍru vērevarum vēṇḍāmammā
tuṇaiyāka tāyē nīyē ennuḍen iruppāyammā

O Mother, look at me. I am Your child. Please listen to me. I am Your very own. I don't want any other kith or kin. O Mother, it will be enough if You remain with me.

pārvatiyē paripūraṇiyē śankariyē sarvēśvariyē

O Mother Parvati, Shankari, Goddess of all!

arivillai aramum illai pūjai tavam eduvum illai
sukhabhōga sindanaiyil un ninaivēdum vandadumillai
nal vākku sollittandu nal vazhi kāṭṭittandu
kai koḍuttammā nī enḍrumē kāttiḍuvāy

I have neither the wealth of wisdom nor good deeds. Mired in pleasure, I don't think of You. With kind words, please guide me, holding my hand, and protect me for all times.

pārvatiyē paripūraṇiyē śankariyē sarvēśvariyē

O Mother Parvati, Shankari, Goddess of all!

ennaiyē tandēn ammā unnaiyē taruvāy ammā
nān unnai aṭaiyum nāḷum eppōdu varumammā?
uyir veḍiyum vēḷai tāyē un darisanamē taruka
piravillā nilai tandu karai sēra varum taruka

I offer myself to You. Please give Yourself to me. When will we become one? In my last living moment, please grant me Your vision. Bless me with the boon of spiritual liberation so that I am never reborn.

pārvatiyē paripūraṇiyē śankariyē sarvēśvariyē

O Mother Parvati, Shankari, Goddess of all!

Kaṇṇē kalankātē (Tamil)

kaṇṇē kalankātē
kaṇṇanindra nammun varuvānē
kaṇṇan vantāl tan arulmazhaiyālē
nammai nanaippānē

O dear one, don't be sad. Kanna will certainly appear before us today. When He comes, He will soak us with the showers of His grace.

yanumai nadiyin karaikaḷiranḍum
viragattaṇalin vēdanaiyālē
karugavē viṭuvānō
kaṇṇan indra nammun varuvānō
kaṇṇā kaṇṇā kaṇṇā kaṇṇā

Will our Beloved Kanna let the banks of river Yamuna writhe in the pain and agony due to the heat of separation? Will Lord Kanna appear before us today? O Kanna...

gōkulam gōpiyar gōvarddhanamalai
bṛndāvanattil taḷirviṭum ālilai
ellām marappānō
allāl kaṇṇan nammun varuvānō
kaṇṇā kaṇṇā kaṇṇā kaṇṇā

Will Krishna forget Gokul, the gopis, the Govardhana Mountain and the sprouting banyan leaf in Vrindavan? Will He forget everything? Or will Kanna appear before us? O Kanna.

kaṇṇan palappala līlaikaḷ purintiṭa
mayankiyē irundōm mati marantiruntōm
akantai aravē akandriṭum vēḷaiyil
akattil varuvānō kaṇṇanindru akattil varuvānō
kaṇṇā kaṇṇā kaṇṇā kaṇṇā

We were in a stupor, forgetting ourselves, enchanted by the many charming games of Krishna. When we completely get rid of our individual 'I' (ego), will Krishna enter our hearts? Today will Krishna enter our hearts?

Kaṇṇinakattoru (Malayalam)

kaṇṇinakattoru kaṇṇuṇḍē – atu
kaṇṇaneyariyum kaṇṇāṇē
manassinakattoru pāṭṭuṇḍē – atu
kaṇṇane vāzhttum pāṭṭāṇē
hṛdayamatinnoru pūvāṇē – atu
kaṇṇanucūṭān karutunnē
karaḷiliruppatu collaṭṭē – atu
kaṇṇaneyorkkum vyathayāṇē

There is an eye within my eye - the eye that knows Krishna. There is a song within my mind - it is a song in praise of Krishna. My heart has become a flower today - I keep it safely for Krishna to wear. Let me tell you what is inside of me - memories of Krishna and a deep longing for Him.

pīlittalamuṭi kāṇaṭṭē – atu
kaṇṇāl kāṇān kotiyāṇē
ōṭakkuzhalatumīṭṭaṭṭē – atu
kēṭṭāl manamitunirayunnē
pītāmbaram atucūṭaṭṭē – atu
matiyilaṇakkyān kotiyāṇē
karaḷiliruppatu collaṭṭē – atu
kaṇṇaneyorkkum vyathayāṇē

Let me see Him with peacock feathers and music - I long to see this with my own eyes. Let me hear the melody of his flute - my mind will brim over with happiness. Let him be adorned in yellow robes - I long to put Him on my lap. Let me tell you what is inside of me - memories of Krishna and a deep longing for Him.

karaḷituninnutuṭikkunnē – atu
kaṇṇā ninnuṭecuvaṭāṇē
manamitu satatam aṇakkyunnē – atu
kaṇṇā ninnuṭe kaviḷāṇē
kanalukaḷ karaḷilanakkyunnē – atu
kaṇṇā ninnuṭe smṛtiyāṇē
karaḷiliruppatu collaṭṭē – atu
kaṇṇaneyorkkum vyathayāṇē

My heart beats in rhythm to your footsteps, Krishna. My heart is constantly petting my Krishna's soft baby face. My heart is becoming a glowing ember in Your memory, Krishna. Let me tell you what is inside of me - memories of Krishna and a deep longing for Him.

Kaṇṇirāl kaṇṇā (Malayalam)

kaṇṇirāl kaṇṇā ! kalarnnuninnīṭunno-
rōrmmakaḷ ninne valamvechozhuki
allum pakalum paravaśamākkume-
nnuḷḷam nirāśayilāzhān viṭolle

My memories of You, mixed with tears, flow constantly around my mind, make me dizzy day and night. Please do not let my mind drown in hopelessness.

nī marannīṭilum ñān marannīṭumō
ī muḷantaṇḍindeyīṇam
kāvalāyeppōzhum ñānirunnīṭumboḷ
dūrasthanallennu tōnnum – kaṇṇan
bāhyasthanallennu tonnum

Even if You forget, will I ever forget the tune of this flute? Kanna! You don't appear to be far away. You don't seem like a stranger.

entō marannuvechennapolannu nī
cintichu mandam kaṭannupoyi
prāṇanō? pāzhmuḷantaṇḍō ? maravicha
cintayil cāri ñān ninnupōyi

You walked away slowly, as if You were forgetting something. Was it my life breath that You forgot, or the bamboo flute? I stood there, frozen in thought.

annutoṭṭinnōḷam kaṇṇan kaḷavēṇu
ūtiyiṭṭillennu kēṭṭu
enkilum kēḷkkāmenikkā manōjñāmam
sangītadhārayonninnum

I heard that since that day, Kanna has not played his flute, but I still hear that flow of music in my mind.

Kaṇṇīruṇangātta (Malayalam)

kaṇṇīruṇangātta kaṇṇumāy nin kazhal
neñcakam nīri ninachirippū
mandahāsattinde pontariveṭṭattāl
añcitamākkukenn-antarangam

I sit here with tear-filled eyes. The thought of Your feet burns inside my chest. Please light up my heart with a flash of Your gentle smile.

cintayil cēru puraḷāte tāraka
puñciri śōbhayāl śuddhiceyyū
centāraṭikaḷil vīṇu namikkuvōr -
-kkantarangattil amṛtavarṣam

The hearts of those who keep their thoughts pure and focused only on the light of Your smile, and surrendered at Your lotus feet, are showered with the nectar of immortality.

kaṇṇīrezhuttinde kāraṇa srōtassil
kānāmanēka yugānta svapnam!
āśakaḷ āṭṭikkurukkiyēkātmaka –
mākki nin kālkkal ñān kāzhcaveppū!

At the source of these tears, I see the dreams of many past lifetimes! I surrender all my desires at Your feet, made sublime.

antarangattile andhakāram nīkki
bandhurāngi, nīyuṇarnnu velka!
bhaktiyum muktiyum nin kṛpānugraham
citta viśūddhiyum nin kaṭākṣam

O enchanting One, awaken within me and remove the darkness in my heart. Devotion and liberation are but the blessing of Your grace; a glance from Your eyes bestows inner purity.

Karayallē paitalē (Malayalam)

karayallē paitalē karayallē paitalē
tārāṭṭu pāṭuvān ammayillē
sandigdham mākumen antarāḷattilum
sangītamēkuvān ammayillē ammayillē

Don't cry, little one, don't cry - isn't Mother here to sing a lullaby? In my confused mind, isn't Mother here to bestow the music?

nanayallē mizhikaḷe nanayallē mizhikaḷe
kaṇṇīr tuṭaykkuvān ammayillē
śōkamī jīvita pātayilennennum
āśvāsamēkuvān ammayillē ammayillē

Eyes, do not become wet- isn't Mother here to dry your tears? In this sorrowful path of life, isn't Mother always here to console you?

taḷaralē paitalē taḷaralē paitalē
kūṭe naṭakkuvān ammayillē

iṭarunna jīvitapātayilennennum
vazhikāṭṭiyākuvān ammayillē ammayillē

Little one, do not become tired, do not be weary. Isn't Mother walking alongside you? In this unsteady path of life, isn't Mother always here to show the way?

Karumaiyilē (Tamil)

karumaiyilē putumai kaṇṭēn kāḷī - untan
kaṇkaḷilē kanivu kaṇṭēn dēvī
perumaiyinai pāṭiṭavē kāḷī - sollin
varumaiyilē vāṭi ninṭrēn dēvī
kāḷiyamma durgā dēviyamma

O Kali ! In the blackness of Your hue, I saw newness. In Your eyes, I saw compassion. O Devi, I have no words to describe your greatness. O Mother Kali, divine Mother Durga.

karuvaraiyil unaturuvam kaṇṭēn - daiva
tiruvazhakil manamuruki ninṭrēn
varuvatōṭ cenṭrarellām nīnki - nikazhum
oru gaṇattil vāzhum pēr koṇṭēn
kāḷiyamma durgā dēviyamma

I came to the sanctum, and Your beauty melted my heart. Leaving past and future behind, I have the fortune to live in the present.

irumaiyilē kāṇumpōt nānum - untan
aṭimai enṭrē perumaiyōṭ vāzhvēn
orumaiyilē onṭrum pōt nāmum - āzha
kaṭalum atan alaiyum pōla vanṭrō
kāḷiyamma durgā deviyamma

Seeing the dual aspect, I will become Your slave. In the advaita aspect (oneness), like the wave and the sea, will You and I become one ? O Mother Kali, divine Mother Durga.

Karuṇaiyil pirandu (Tamil)

karuṇaiyil pirandu karuṇaiyil vaḷarndu
karuṇaiyil niraivadu ānmīkam
kalmanam kasindu kadavukaḷ tirandu
uḷḷoḷi kāṇbadu ānmīkam

Spirituality is born out of compassion, nourished by compassion, and blossoms as a result of compassion. It also melts the stony heart and opens the doors of the heart to reveal the inner light.

kānbadil ellām kaṭavuḷaikkaṇḍu
sēvaikaḷ seyvadu bhaktivazhi
kaṭavuḷin karuṇai mazhaiyinil nanaiya
sēvayallādu ēdu vazhi

The path of devotion is beholding God everywhere and serving others with that vision. Without serving others, how else can one become drenched in the shower of divine grace?

kāṇbadai ellām tānāy kaṇḍu
sēvaikaḷ seyvadu jñāna vazhi
kaṇṇukaḷ vizhunda tukaḷinai akattra
kaivaruvadu pōl inda vazhi

The path of knowledge is seeing one's own Self everywhere and serving others with that vision. It is akin to removing the speck from one's own eye.

tanniṭam kāṭṭum karuṇaiyil piraikkum
pirariṭam kāṭṭum karuṇaiyil vaḷarum
inidāy vaḷarum ānmīkam – adu
iraiyaruḷālē niraivākum

The compassion we have for ourselves gives rise to spirituality. It is nourished when we show compassion to others. Thus, one makes spiritual progress. Spirituality becomes complete only through God's grace.

Kāruṇya murtte (Kannada version)

kāruṇya mūrtti śyāmala varṇṇā
kaṇṇu tereyō kṛṣṇā
duḥkhanivāraka nallave nī - ena
tāpava kaḷē kṛṣṇā

namagellā āśraya nīne
candāvare nayana śrīkṛṣṇa
pūjege anudina kambani haniyē
puṣpāñjalī ō kṛṣṇā
tāpava kaḷē kṛṣṇā

iruḷali baḷalide nānu
mānasamōhana gōpāla
īrēḷu lōkava āḷuva śrīdhara
kaṇṇu tereyō kṛṣṇā
tāpava kaḷē kṛṣṇā

Kārunya rupiṇi (Malayalam)

kārunya rupiṇi ammē, kāḷukayāṇende cittam
ninneyōrttalppavum kēzhān
prēmattin nīruravilla

O Mother, embodiment of compassion! My heart is craving to cry out in longing for You, but there are no flowing streams of love within me.

ērunnu mōhamitennum
śuddhasnēhamē ninne ariyān
māya tan mūṭupaṭam nī mātti
ennil teḷiyunnatennō?

The desire to know the pure love that is You is growing inside. When will You remove the veil of illusion and shine clearly within me?

śuddhasaundaryamē ninne kaṇḍu
uḷḷam kuḷirkkunnatennō?
ā maṭittaṭṭilī kuññu
viśramam koḷḷunnatennō?

O pure and beautiful form, when will my heart rejuvenate at Your sight? When will You allow this child of Yours to take rest in Your lap?

Kaṭaikkaṇ pārvai (Tamil)

kaṭaikkaṇ pārvai ondrē pōtum
ammā untan aruḷ vizhiyāl
kanimozhi ondrē pōtumammā
kavailakaḷ parantōṭum
kavailakaḷ parantōṭum

A glance from the corner of Your divine eyes is enough, Your sweet words are enough, for our sorrows to vanish.

amma untan aruḷ pārvai
pala mozhi pēsiṭum, un seyalkaḷ ellāmammā
pala poruḷ uṇarttiṭum
pala poruḷ uṇarttiṭum

Mother Your divine glance speaks a lot of words. Mother all Your actions make us understand many truths.

sparisanam ondrē pōtumammā
akamatai kuḷirvittiṭum tiruvaṭi toṭṭa pozhutil
karma vinai parantōṭum
karma vinai parantōṭum

Mother Your touch is enough to cool and pacify our heart. Prostrating at Your divine feet rids us of the burden of our past deeds.

jai jagadīśvari jai bhuvanēśvari
jai paramēśvari jai amṛteśvari

Glory to the Goddess of the universe, glory to the supreme Goddess, glory to the eternal Goddess!

Kāttrāka nān (Tamil)

kāttrāka nān irundāl enna seyvēn - ammā
nī pōkum iṭamellām nānum varuvēn

If I were the breeze, what would I do? O Mother, I would follow You wherever You go.

nilamāka nān irundāl enna seyvēn - ammā
un pādam tāmgikkoṇḍu pūrittiruppēn
neruppāka nān irundāl enna seyvēn - ammā
un kōyil dīpamāka suṭarviṭuvēn

If I were the earth, what would I do? O Mother, I would rejoice in supporting Your feet. If I were fire, what would I do? O Mother, I would glow as the lamp in Your temple.

visumpāka nān irundāl enna seyvēn - unakku
vānavillāl tōraṇam kaṭṭi makizhvēn
nīrāka nān irundāl enna seyvēn - undan
pādābhiṣēkam seyyum pannīr āvēn

If I were the ether, what would I do? O Mother, I would delight in festooning the skies with a rainbow. If I were water, what would I do? O Mother, I would be the rose-water that washes Your feet

pūvāka nān irundāl enna seyvēn - ammā
mālaiyāki un tōḷil sāyndu koḷvēn
kuyilāka nān irundāl enna seyvēn - ammā
unnōṭu bhaktigānam pāṭi makizhvēn

If I were a flower, what would I do? O Mother, I would rest on Your shoulders as a garland. If I were a cuckoo, what would I do? O Mother, I would revel in singing devotional songs with You.

Kāvaṭiyām kāvaṭi (Tamil)

kāvaṭiyām kāvaṭi kantavēlan kāvaṭi
śēvarkoṭi azhakanukku vaṇṇamayil kāvaṭi
vēdanaiyē vāzhkaiyalla bhaktiyatu urutuṇaiyē
vēṇḍutalāy vēlavan sannidhiyil kāvaṭi

Come let us offer kavadi (ceremonial offering) to Lord Murugan. Let us offer the multi-hued peacock kavadi to the beautiful Lord whose flag bears the symbol of a rooster. Life need not be full of sorrows, devotion to the Lord ensures protection. Let us offer kavadi in the divine presence of One who holds the spear.

pālum tēnum pañcāmṛta kāvaṭi
pazhamum śarkkarayum vibhūtiyil kāvaṭi
candana kāvaṭiyum puṣpakāvaṭiyum
ṣaṇmukhan sannidhiyil azhaku kāvaṭi

Let us offer kavadi of milk, honey, and panchamritam. Let us offer kavadi of fruits, jaggery and sacred ash. Let us offer kavadi of sandalwood, kavadi of flowers. Let us offer beautiful kavadi in the divine presence of Lord with six faces!

kāvaṭiyāṭu kandan cēvaṭi tēṭu
kāvaṭiyāṭu kumaran tiruvaṭi nāṭu
karuṇai vēlan ārmukhan malaraṭi tēṭu

Kavadi seeks the holy feet of Lord Kandan (vanquisher of mighty foes). Kavadi seeks the divine feet of Kumaran (eternal youth), the lotus feet of the compassionate Lord Velan with six faces.

tinayum tiraviya pannīrāl kāvaṭi
maccamūm sarppamum iḷanīrāl kāvaṭi

mayūra kāvaṭiyum santāna kāvaṭiyum
śaravaṇan sannidhiyil muttu kāvaṭi

Let us offer kavadi of millets, money and rose water, kavadi of fish, snake and coconut water. Let us offer peacock kavadi and sandalwood kavadi. Let us offer pearl kavadi in the auspicious presence of Lord Muruga!

iṭumbanavan eṭuttānē mutal kāvaṭi
irupuramāy tōḷinilē sumantānē kāvaṭi
śivagiri orupuramum śaktigiri marupuramum
śivaśakti pālanin vēlkāvaṭi

Like the demon devotee Idumba who carried the pearl kavadi, I carry the kavadi on either side of my shoulders. One side represent Shivagiri and the other Shakti giri. Vel (spear) kavadi of the son of Shiva and Shakti!

Kayilaiyilē śivaperumān (Tamil)

kayilaiyilē śivaperumān
uṭanuraiyum umaiyavaḷē
tuyilizhantu entan uḷḷam, vāṭuvatai ariyāyō?

O Goddess Uma with Lord Shiva in Kailash, don't You know that our hearts are becoming parched, foregoing sleep?

mañcaḷilē piṭittuvaitta
piḷḷaiyinau koñcukirāy
añcavaikkum kōpakkāra
kumaranaiyum keñcukirāy
intapiḷḷai iḷayapiḷḷai
eṭuppārtaṁ kaippiḷḷai
nontapōtu vantaṇaikka
tāymanatil īramillai

You adore Lord Ganesha (whose form is moulded using turmeric) and beg hot-headed Lord Subrahmanya not to leave Mount Kailash. Yet when this youngest child is suffering, Mother's heart dries up, You don't come to hug me...

ennainalla piḷḷaiyākka
annaiyāṭum nāṭakamō
erimalaipōl kōlamkāṭṭi
irankuvatum unmanamō
enakkāka vēṇḍavillai
nānarivēn tāymanatai
piṇakkāka nīṭippatu
unperumaikkazhakumillai

Mother is playing this drama to make me a good child. After showing Your form as lava, Your heart comes down. I am not praying for myself I know Mother's heart. It is not good for Your reputation if this dispute continues.

Kazhaliṇayil (Malayalam)

kazhaliṇayil ittiriyiṭam taraṇam ammē
kaṭa-mizhikaḷālonnu tazhukēṇam enne
kazhivillayivan-ennu nīyariyumallō?
azhal-akhilamuṭanē akattīṭukillē?

Please grant me a little space at Your feet. Caress me with Your sidelong glances. You know that I have no talent. Won't You remove all my sorrows?

amṛt-ozhukumamara-nadi pōle nī pāril
kaluṣatakaḷ nīkkiyazhak-eṇgum nirakke
'aha' miti-vicāramalinam mama hṛdantam
oru pozhutu karuṇa-jala-dhārayāl kazhukū!

Like the ambrosial river that flows through the world, removing all sorrows You permeate everything with beauty. My mind is murky with ego. Please purify my mind with the waters of Your compassion.

suratarusamānam bhajippavarkkennum
abhilaṣitam-akhilavumaṇakkunna tāyē
arutarutu tāmasam mama hṛdi vasikkān
pada-kamala-mūnniyoru mṛdunaṭanamāṭān

For those who pray to You, You are like the tree of heaven. O Mother who fulfills all wishes, please don't hesitate to stay in my mind and dance with Your tender lotus feet.

anunimiṣam amba! nin varavu-kāttakamē
niradīpamēnti ñān nilkkunnu nityam
etirēttu ninneyennakamēyiruttān
kotiyōṭe ñān kāttirappatariyillē?

Each moment I am waiting for You with the lamp. Don't You know that I am yearning to welcome You and make You dwell in my mind?

anukambayārnnende abhilāṣamippōḷ
niravētti niravenikkēku! jagadambē
jani-mṛtiyil-uzhalamī jīvan-aviṭutte
smṛtiyilaliyaṭṭe, amṛtāmbudhiyatallō!

Please fulfill my wish with Your compassion and fill it O Mother! This life that wanders through life and death, let it rest in Your memories. Is that not the ambrosial ocean?

Kēḷiraṇṇā (Kannada)

kēḷiraṇṇā kēḷirammā
kalitanada mātonda kēḷirellā
hiriyaru racisida jīvana rīti
pālisi paḍeyonna kīruti

Listen brother, listen mother (traditional way of addressing men and women with respect). Listen to the way of life created for us by our elders. Let us follow it and rise to great heights.

kaḷavaḷisidaru kaḷedu hōguvadu
kaḷedē hōguvadu kēḷu
bāyendu karedaru bhāgyadallilladu
baruvadē illayentu kēḷiraṇṇā
dvēṣavu tānu rāgadanteya
bandhisi biḍuvudu eccara
vairava tōruva nararigu nīnu
nagutali namisibiḍu kēḷiraṇṇā

Though you may struggle to retain your worldly possessions, they will one day be lost to you. What is not destined to be yours will not come to you, no matter how much you yearn for it. O listen brother, beware – often hatred comes in the disguise of sweetness, to ensnare you into bondage. Smile and love even those who show you enmity. O listen brother.

śiva śiva endu śiva nāma japisu
bēgane baruvudu bhakuti
bhavarananannu bēḍutaliddare
dorakuvutallā mukuti kēḷiraṇṇā

Chant the name of the Lord incessantly – it will quickly bring you the treasure of devotion. Begging for worldly things will not take us to liberation. Listen brother...

śiva śiva hara hara
śiva śiva bhava hara

Shiva, the one who takes us across the ocean of transmigration!

Kēśava nāmamu (Telugu)

kēśava nāmamu klēśaharaṇamu
pāḍavē manasā harināmakīrttanam
śrī vēnkaṭēśa hari hari
śrīnivāsa prabhu hari hari

O mind, sing the names of the Lord, which dispel all distress.
O Lord Venkatesa, Srinivasa !

paripari vidhamula bhavarōga mulaku
harināma kīrttanē siddhauṣadham
cittaśāntiki śrīharināmamu pāḍavē manasā
harināma kīrttanam

Singing the Lord's name is the remedy for all diseases of the world.
To attain mental peace, O mind, sing the names of the Lord.

cañcalamanasunu sthirapara cuṭaku
harināma kīrttanē ēkasādhanam
satvalabdhiki śrīhari nāmamu pāḍavē manasā
harināma kīrttanam

Singing the Lord's name is the only instrument to stabilize the unsteady mind. O mind, sing the names of the Lord.

ā padarājīva mula cēruṭaku
harināmakīrttanē rājamārgam
satyasiddhiki śrīharī nāmamu pāḍavē manasā
harināma kīrttanam

Singing the Lord's name is the royal highway to reach His lotus feet. To realize the truth, sing the names of the Lord, O mind.

Kōṭṭaiyenṭrē (Tamil)

kōṭṭaiyenṭrē āṇavamāy kuṭiyiruntālum - itu
ōṭṭai ombatuḷḷa vīṭu ambalavāṇā
vēṭṭayāṭa kālanvantu ninṭriṭum pōtum - ivar
sēṭṭayatu kuraivatillai ambalavāṇā

Thinking that the body is a fort, people live with pride, but in fact it is just a house with nine holes.

māṇḍavarkku azhutiṭuvār ambalavāṇā - tānō
māḷvatillai enṭriruppār ambalavāṇā
vēṇḍumsottu talaimuraikku malaiyaḷavenṭrē
vēṇḍātana seytiṭuvār ambalavāṇā

People lament for the dead, thinking they are never going to die, O Shiva. To accumulate a mountain of wealth for many generations, people commit many undesirable acts, O Lord!

ambalakkuttā ṭuvōnē ambalavāṇā - em
akattil naṭampurivāy ambalavāṇā
ambarattin rahasyattai ambalamākki
ānandamām nilai aruḷvāy ambalavāṇā

O One who performs the cosmic dance in the court of gods, please come and dance in my heart of hearts. Please reveal the supreme secret and grace us with the state of everlasting bliss, O Lord Shiva!

śiva śiva śiva śiva cidambarēśā
hara hara hara hara kanakasabēśā

O Lord Shiva, Lord of Chidambaram, destroyer of evils, the Lord of the golden assembly!

Kṛṣṇa kanaiyyā (Malayalam)

nāhaṁ vasāmi vaikuṇṭhe
yogināṁ hṛdaye na ca
mad bhaktā yatra gāyanti
tatra tiṣṭhāmi nārada, tatra tiṣṭhāmi nārada

'I dwell neither in Vaikuntha nor in the hearts of the yogins, but I dwell where my devotees sing my name, O Narada.'

kṛṣṇa kanaiyyā sundarabālā
vṛndāvana candrā vā, nīlamegha varṇṇā vā
nandakiśorā karmukil varṇṇā
rādhikalolā vā, rādhikālolā vā

O Krishna, beautiful boy, moon of Vrindavan, with the complexion of a blue cloud, come! Son of Nanda, dark-hued like a rain-cloud, Radha's delight, come!

bhaktacitta corā yaśodabālā
navanītacorā vā, kṛṣṇa navanītacorā vā
gopakumārā kāḷiyadamanā
sundara rūpā vā, sūndara rūpā vā

Stealer of the hearts of the devotees, child of Yashoda, butter thief, Krishna, come! Young cowherd boy, subduer of the serpent Kaliya, one with a beautiful form, come!

vaṁśīdhārī dvārakanāthā
muraḷīmanoharā vā, kṛṣṇa muraḷīmanoharā vā
sajjana sevita madanagopālā
govarddhana giridhārī govarddhana giridhārī

Bearer of the flute, Lord of Dvaraka, most enchanting flute player, come! You are served by good people, O delightful cowherd boy, and you lifted the Govardhana Mountain!

Kṛṣṇā ninnā bāla līle (Kannada)

kṛṣṇa nanna kṛṣṇā!
bālakṛṣṇa bāla kṛṣṇā!

O Krishna, my Krishna, O little Krishna!

kṛṣṇā ninnā bāla līle
kaṇṇi geṣṭānanda
ninna jōḍi āṭuvudēnō
ānanda apāra

O Krishna, how pleasing are Your childhood games. Playing with you brings me immense joy.

kṛṣṇā bālakṛṣṇā
nīla kṛṣṇā nanna kṛṣṇā

O Krishna, little Krishna, O blue Krishna, my Krishna!

nīli tāvare mogadali miñcide
beṇṇe kaḷḷana nōṭṭa
edeyali eddide prēma pūra
hebbale ārbhaṭā

The butter thief's sidelong glances flash in his blue lotus face. A flood of love rises in my heart, the rumbling of huge tidal waves.

giridhara ninna kiruberaḷāṭa
muraḷī gānavō
munkurulāṭa gōpiraka hṛdayadī
prēma sañcārā

O He who lifted the mountain, the play of Your little finger creates tunes on the flute. The play of Your curls inspires reverberations of love in the hearts of the gopis.

kinkiṇi kilikili nūpura jaṇajaṇa
sṛṣṭi spandanā

muttina adhara sparśadi nīṭu
viśvadarśanā

The jingling of the ornaments around Your waist and Your ankles are truly the vibrations of creation. Grant me the universal vision with the touch of Your lips in a kiss.

Kṣaṇakṣaṇavu (Kannada)

kṣaṇakṣaṇavu anukṣaṇavu
makkaḷa smaraṇe māḍuva
makkaḷigāgi bāḷuva dēviya
kaṇḍīdirā... kēḷīdirā – ō nōḍīdirā

Do you know of a Goddess who is always thinking of her children and is living a life for the sake of her children? Have you heard of such a One, have you seen such a One?

mantrarūpiṇi ātmarūpiṇi
caitanyarūpiṇi dēviya
ānandarūpiṇi śaktiya ammana
kaṇḍīdirā... kēḷīdirā – ō nōḍīdirā

She is the form of mantra, the embodiment of the Self. She is in the form of consciousness, She is Mother. Have you heard of such a One, have you seen such a One?

śvāsaniśvāsavu nisvārtthadegāgi
mī... saliṭṭiha dēviya
ellarigāgi bāḷuva tāyiya
kaṇḍīdirā... kēḷīdirā – ō nōḍīdirā

Have you come across such a Goddess who has devoted Her every breath for selflessness, and is living for the sake of everybody? Have you heard of such a One, have you seen such a One?

Kuraiyellām nīkki namma (Tamil)

pōṭṭadellām ponnākkum
inda bhūmi enkaḷ daivamamma
pozhutellām pon tūvum
anda sūriyanum daivamamma
vānattilē mazhai mēgham
indiranum daivamamma
varappellām nīr niraikkum
anda varuṇanum daivamamma

Whatever you plant in the earth is offered back as gold. Mother Earth is our God. During the day there is sunshine, that sun is our God. Indra, Lord of the sky and clouds, and Varuna, Lord of the rain, raining on the crops - all are our Gods.

kuraiyellām nīkki namma kulamellām tazhaittōnga
kuru vaṭivāy vandinkē koluvirukkum māriyammā
karuṇaiyōṭu kāttiṭuvāy inda kāḷīyammā
varumaiyellām pōkki vazhi kāṭṭiṭuvāḷ māriyammā

Remove all our limitations and bestow prosperity upon our families. Mariamma is sitting here in the form of Guru. Remove all kinds of poverty and guide us to prosperity. Mariamma showers Her grace as Mother Kali.

ammā avaḷ aruḷmazhayāl aruvaṭaiyum perukiṭavē
kanalēnti bhaktiyuṭan pāṭi vantōmmā
āvalōṭu unnazhaku mukham kāṇa tiruvaṭi tēṭi vantōmā
anpu daivam unnai tānē anudinamum tudippōmā

Mother please shower Your grace for a good harvest. We came singing with devotion, holding up lamps. We came to see Your beautiful face and to prostrate at Your lotus feet. You are our loving God whom we worship everyday.

aḷḷittanda āttāḷukku aruvaṭaiyai paṭayal vaikka

aḷḷittanda āttāḷukku aruvaṭaiyai paṭayal vaikka
tuḷḷikkudittu ponkal vaittōm tūyavaḷē unnai azhaittōm
kāḷī triśūli ammā kanivuṭanē vantiranki
māri makamāyi tāyē makizhvuṭanē ēttrukoḷvāy

We offer our harvest to the Mother who has given abundantly. We offer pongal (sweet pudding) and call out to the Mother of purity, Mother Kali, bearer of the trident! Please come compassionately and accept our offerings with joy.

māryammā ava aruḷiruntāl
makkaḷellām makizhvaṭaivār
manattērilammā ēri nindru māsellām pōkkiṭuvāy

Mariamma, all Your children will be happy if Your grace is there. Please enter the chariot of my mind and purify the impurities!

Kurumbukkāra (Tamil)

kurumbukkāra kaṇṇan līlai kēṭka kēṭka inikkumē
karumbu pōla inikkum atai ninaikka uḷḷam makizhumē
arumai mukham kāṇachentrāl kaṭamaikkuppō embān
kaṭamayilē mūzhkiviṭṭāl marandanaiyō embān
kurumbukkārā...

Kanna, O mischievous One, hearing about Your divine play brings me more and more joy. Contemplating Your divine play, sweet as sugarcane, gladdens my heart. When we come closer to look at His beautiful face, He bids us to our work (duty). When we become immersed in work, He says we have forgotten Him. O mischievous One . . .

toṭṭuppēsa oṭṭinintrāl taṭṭiviṭṭu selvān
eṭṭanirkkum gōpiyarai kiṭṭacenṭraṇaippān
maṭṭam taṭṭi piraretiril kēli seytu makizhvān
tiṭṭam pōṭṭu namataiyellām tiruṭichenṭru maraivān
tiruṭichenṭru maraivān

If we sidle up to him, he pushes us away, goes to the gopi standing far away, and hugs her. He takes delight in poking fun at us. He schemes to steal everything that belongs to us, and then hides Himself.

tanakketuvum teriyātena mandiram pōl solvān
vāyu tirandāl aṇḍāmellām namakkutteriya seyvān
tanakketuvum vēṇḍāmena eppozhutum solvān
uṭal poruḷōṭāviyellām sontamākki koḷvān
sontamākki koḷvān

He repeatedly says that he knows nothing, but when He opens His mouth, He reveals the whole universe. He says always that He needs nothing; He captures us, heart and soul.

gōpiyarin mannavanai gōpālabāla
rādhaikkoru mādhavanē rādhāvilōlā

O cowherd boy, Lord of the gopis. O consort of Radha, Her joy and delight!

Kuzhandaiyena (Tamil)

kuzhandaiyena umayē unai pārāṭṭavā
āruyirē mārbil unai tālāṭṭavā
bālāmbikai dēvi tripurasundari
bālādēvi śrī śōḍaśi

O Bala Devi, Sri Shodashi, soul of my soul, shall I worship You as the 'little Goddess'? Shall I sing You a lullaby, holding You close to me?

makaranta maṇamsērttu pūñcōlai koṇarntu
muttē nān pūcchūṭṭi koṇḍāṭavā
kapaṭamillāmal nī kulunki sirittāy
kaṇpaṭṭiṭum kannattil poṭṭu vaikkavā
kaṇpaṭṭiṭum kannattil poṭṭu vaikkavā

Along with the perfumed jasmine, shall I fetch colorful flowers to decorate Your tresses?! Seeing Your innocent laughter, the evil eye may fall upon You- shall I keep You safe from harm by putting a black kohl dot on Your chin? (Indian tradition)

ponnāna pādaṅkaḷ puṇṇākiṭāmal
en kaikaḷ nilam vaittu vazhi amaikkavā
koñcum calankaikaḷ isaiyil nī mayanki
ōṭātē kaṇṇē urankiṭavā
ōṭātē kaṇṇē urankiṭavā

Walking on the bare ground Your golden feet may get hurt; shall I lay a path with my palms for You to walk on? Wanting to hear the jingling of Your anklets, You are running hither and thither; please come back and rest!

Lālāli lālalē (Malayalam)

lālāli lālalē lēlēli lēlalē
lālāli ūla lēlēli lēlalē
lālāli lālalē lēlēli lēlalē
lālāli ūla lēlēli lēlalē

tāru viriññatupōloru paital
tāne kiṭannu cirikkunnu
kaṇṇu marachuḷḷa kaḷḷiyarakkaññi
kaiyukaḷ nīṭṭiyaṭuttetti
kayyālaṅgārnneṭī mārōṭe cērnneṭī
neñcinkal koṭum nañcūrum pāleṭī

Baby Krishna, tender as a freshly blossomed flower, lay there by himself, smiling. The demoness Putana, full of deceit, came stretching out her arms to him. She took the baby in her arms, held the baby to her bosom - in her breasts was poisoned milk.

pūvitaḷ pōluḷḷa cuṇḍumukarnnatu
pūtana taṇṇuṭe prāṇanāṇallō
kāḷāya rūpatte pūṇḍuḷḷa pūtam
kallumalapōle vīṇoṭuṅgi
meyyārnnaṅgāṭeṭī mēḷattil pāṭeṭī
kaṇṇande līla ōrttōrttu pāṭeṭī

Those lips, tender as flower petals, sucked out the prana (life-force) of Putana. Girls, sway and dance, sing in rhythm! Sing remembering the lilas of Krishna over and over again.

ōrō dinattinde cāṭurumbōḷ
cāṭāyi vannuḷḷa mallanumappōḷ
tāmarattuṇḍu pōluḷḷoru kālāl
tāvum taviṭu pōlākechitari aṅgane
meyyārnnaṅgāṭeṭī mēḷattil pāṭeṭī
kaṇṇande līla ōrttōrttu pāṭeṭī

As days passed, the demon Shakadasura came assuming the form of a wheel. Krishna's lotus-like feet powdered him to sawdust and scattered him to the winds. Girls, sway and dance, sing in rhythm! Sing remembering the lilas of Krishna over and over again.

kāḷindi tanneyaṭakki vāṇīṭunna
kāḷiya sarppat tekkaṇḍīllēṭī
vāya piḷartti vizhuṅgumeṭī
vālināl cuttivalikkumeṭī
kārikālan pāmbeṭī kākōḷakkayareṭī
paṭūkūttan paṭam ōrōnnāykkāṇeṭī

Do you see the serpent Kaliya, who rules the waters of the Kalindi River? With his large mouth, he will swallow you up; his tail will circle tight around you and pull you to him. He is fiercely venomous; see his gigantic, flaring hoods one by one.

kāñciyum mālayumākeyulachum
kāttupōl aṅgōṭṭum iṅgoṭṭu māññum
kāḷiyan pāmbindeyāḷum phaṇaṅgaḷ
tāṇatu ceñcōra kunkumamārnnē
centāril cēvaṭī onnonnāy vechaṭī
kaṇṇande nṛttam ellārum kāṇeṭī

Krishna dances like the wind, ornaments swaying from side to side. The serpent Kaliya's hoods are trampled down one by one until they are red with blood. See Krishna dance with ease, stepping on them one by one, as though on tender red flowers.

māripeytiṅgu mānam muriññē
mānitam-onnāyiyāke valaññē
tanniṭam kaiyyilāy māmalayēnti
tannōṭu cērttē gōkulattē
meyyārnnaṅgāṭeṭī mēḷattil pāṭeṭī
kaṇṇande līla ōrttōrttu pāṭeṭī

The sky splits with thundering showers; the entire world is in distress. Carrying the Govardhana Mountain in his left hand, the Lord holds the people of Gokula close to him. Girls, sway and dance, sing in rhythm! Sing remembering the lilas of Krishna over and over again.

pālitu kaṭṭukuṭikkum kurumbane
pārichuralilāy keṭṭiyiṭṭē
muttatte māmaram tettiyiṭṭē
muttum ciriyōṭe ninniṭunnē
tāḷattil colleṭi covārnnaṅgōteṭī
kaṇṇande līla ōrttōrttu pāṭeṭī

The mischievous Krishna is tied up to a mortar for stealing milk. Dragging the heavy mortar, he pulls down the giant trees and stands with a smile on his face. Girls, sway and dance, sing in rhythm! Sing remembering the lilas of Krishna over and over again.

pīlipūvukaḷ vaṇḍaṇimāla
ōṭattaṇḍatumōmanachuṇḍil
ottulayunna ponnarayāṇam
kaḷḷakkaṇṇanekkāṇeṭī peṇṇē
meyyārnnaṅgāṭeṭī mēḷattil pāṭeṭī
kaṇṇande cuttum āṭānāy kūṭeṭī

Wearing the peacock feather in His hair, and a fragrant garland towards which bees swarm; lips pressed to His flute, His golden waistband moving gracefully with every movement. Come, join us, girls, let us dance around Kanna!

Lallē lallē (Malayalam)

lallē lallē lālē ā lallē lallē lālē ā
lallē lallē lālē lallē lallē lallē lālē

pīlitirukiveccā koṇḍalkeṭṭatukaṇḍō ā
muttum mālēm kaṇḍō ā
muttum mālēm cinnam cinnam
uṇṇikaṇṇā āṭū ā uṇṇikaṇṇā āṭū

Did you see the crown adorning the head of the One with the peacock feather? Did you see the pearl and necklace? Beautiful! Dance little Krishna, O little Krishna, dance!

kāyalmīnē tennumbōle
nīlakkaṇṇatukaṇḍō ā
ōmal puñciri kaṇḍō
ā ōmal puñciri minniminni
uṇṇikaṇṇā āṭū ā uṇṇikaṇṇā āṭū

Did you see the enchanting smile of the blue Krishna, like a fish jumping in the backwaters? Little Krishna dance, dance with Your glittering, enchanting smile!

māratte mālakkeṭṭinu
vāṭāmalaruṇḍō ā
cūṭān malaruṇḍō ā
cūṭum malarukaḷ piñci piñci
uṇṇikaṇṇā āṭū ā uṇṇikaṇṇā āṭū

Are there any unwithered flowers to make a garland to adorn his chest? Dance, O little Krishna, dance, letting the flowers fall from the garland.

maññāpizhiññānalla
kōṭippaṭṭatukaṇḍō ā
ponnarayāṇam kaṇḍō ā
ponnarayāṇam cillam cillam
uṇṇikaṇṇā āṭū ā uṇṇikaṇṇā āṭū

Did you see the yellow silk cloth? Did you see the golden waistband? The beautiful, beautiful golden waistband, O little Krishna dance, little Krishna dance!

ōmal coṭiyil muttum
ōṭattaṇḍatu kaṇḍō ā
ponnin kaivaḷa kaṇḍō
ponnin kaivaḷa cinnam cinnam
uṇṇikaṇṇā āṭū ā uṇṇikaṇṇā āṭū

Did you see the bamboo flute kissing His lips? Did you see the golden bracelets of Krishna? The golden bracelets are beautiful! Dance little Krishna, O little Krishna dance!

kālilaṇiññānallā
kiṅgiṇikālttaḷakaṇḍō ā
muttaṇi kiṅgiṇi kaṇḍō ā
muttaṇi kiṅgiṇi cillam cillam
uṇṇikaṇṇā āṭū ā uṇṇikaṇṇā āṭū

Did you see the anklets that adorned His feet? Did you see the pearl bell? That pearl bell! Beautiful, beautiful! Little Krishna dance!

nīlakkaṭambin mītē nīlakkāraṇi kaṇḍō ā
pāṭum pāṭṭukaḷ kēṭṭō ā
pāṭum pāṭṭukaḷ koñci koñci
uṇṇikaṇṇā āṭū ā uṇṇikaṇṇā āṭū

Did you see the blue One who dances near the blue Kadamba tree? Did you hear the song? Little Krishna dance!

cembaññiñcāraṇi pādam
cēlil veykkaṇa kaṇḍō ā
ā cuvaṭukaḷ vaykkū tañci tañci
uṇṇikaṇṇā āṭū ā uṇṇikaṇṇā āṭū

Did you see the soft feet beautifully dancing? Keeping those feet in rhythmic steps, Little Krishna- dance, O Little Krishna dance!

veṇṇakkāy nīṭṭum kayyukaḷ
tiṇṇameṭuppatu kaṇḍō ā
kaṇṇukaḷ cimmaṇa kaṇḍō ā
kaṇṇukaḷ cimmi cimmi cimmi
uṇṇikaṇṇā āṭū ā uṇṇikaṇṇā āṭū

Did you see the blinking eyes – eyes that are blinking, blinking! O did you see the hands stretching out for butter and taking their fill? Little Krishna dance!

mullappum pallukaḷ kāṭṭi
ottu cirippatu kaṇḍō ā
tatti naṭakkaṇa kaṇḍō ā
tatti naṭannu pinnēm pinnēm
uṇṇikaṇṇā āṭū ā uṇṇikaṇṇā āṭū

Did you see the smile showing his jasmine-like teeth? Did you see the toddlers steps? Walking again and again, dance, O little Krishna dance!

Lemmu nara kiṣōramā (Telugu)

uddharēd ātmanātmānam nātmānam avasādayēt

Let one uplift oneself by one's self alone.

lemmu nara kiṣōramā mēlukō
nīvē ātmavani telusukō
gamyam cēruvaraku āgaku
ātmavu! ātmavu nīvu! nīvē ātmavu!

May one not debase oneself. Arise and awake, O mortal lion! Know that you are the Atman, the Self. Stop not till you reach the goal. Atman, Atman! You are the Atman!

māyā pañjaramu viraci garjiñcu
hṛdayadaurbalyamu vīḍi ghōṣiñcu
nī anantaśaktini bāhyaparici cūpiñcu
viśvamu nīvēnani erukato jīviñcu
ātmavu nīvē ātmavu!

Break free from the cage of illusion and roar! Overcome weak heartedness and proclaim the truth. Manifest the infinite energy within you! 'You are verily the Universe'– live with this awareness! You are the Atman!

dēhamu nīvukādu ātmavi nīvu
bandhamu nīkulēdu ātmavi nīvu
ahamunu vīḍicūdu sākṣivi nīvu
ānandasvarūpuḍavu amṛtaputruḍavu
ātmavu nīvē ātmavu!

You are not the body, but the atman! You are not bound; you are the Atman! Renounce the ego and know yourself to be the witness. You are the embodiment of bliss and the heir to immortality. You are the Atman!

Madhura mohanam (Sanskrit)

madhura mohanam manojña sundaram
vimala vigraham vibudha vanditam
hṛdi tamoharam cāru cinmayam
jagannātha he yacha darśanam

Sweet and enchanting, of captivating beauty, of pure form, and worshipped by the wise, dispeller of the heart's darkness, and who is the nature of consciousness, O Lord of the universe, bless me with Your vision.

vṛṣakulē vibhūm gopa raṇjanam
divya bhūṣaṇam pītāmbaram
sahaja śobhitam parama pūjitam
bhajati mānasam tava padāmbujam
jagannātha he yacha darśanam

Chief of the cowherd clan, in whose presence the cowherds revel, You are adorned by celestial ornaments and yellow robes. Naturally resplendent, and worthy of the highest worship, my heart worships Your lotus feet. O Lord of the universe, bless me with Your vision.

śrī kṛṣṇā muraḷīdharā veṇugopālā
jagadīśā janārdanā jaganmohanā

Lord Krishna, bearer of the flute, O cowherd, Lord of the universe, Janardana, You enchant the entire universe.

khala vidūṣaṇam doṣa vāraṇam
punita pāvanam bhava vimocanam
bhakta mānase śīghra gāminam
bhajati mānasam tava padāmbujam
jagannātha he yacha darśanam

Annihilator of evil-doers and negativities, of utmost sanctity, You grant liberation from sorrowful existence. You rush to the hearts of the devoted. My heart worships Your lotus feet.

Mādhuri (Gujarati)

mādhuri mādhuri kānā, mādhuri mādhuri kānā
mādhuri mādhuri tāri vāsalaḍi
mādhuri mādhuri kānā mādhūri mādhuri kānā
mādhuri lilā tāri vṛjavāsi
mādhurī lilā tāri mādhuri

O Krishna, the sweet One! Your flute is also sweet, O Krishna, You who are so sweet! Your lilas (divine plays), they too are so very sweet.

eri yaśodā, bhari bajārmā
phoḍi teṇe maṭki māri
chāśathi nahāy rahi hu gavālaṇ
māvalaḍi ō māvalaḍi

A cowherd woman complains to Krishna's mother, "Hey Yashoda! He broke my pot in the middle of the crowded market place. I got bathed with butter milk!"

maṭki phoḍine āve
mākhaṇ corine khāve
chatā na hāthāve nandano lālo
tophān kānānā sūṇi
bāvari yaśodā bani
māvalaḍi ō māvalaḍi
mādhūri lilā tāri mādhuri

"He breaks pots, steals, and eats butter, yet that son of Nanda never gets caught." Listening the list of Krishna's pranks drives Yashoda crazy. O Krishna, sweetest One, Your lilas are so sweet.

suṇ ō maiyā, dhenu carāvi
hu hamṇā te āvyo
kyāre phoḍi me maṭki teni
māvalaḍi ō māvalaḍi

Krishna replies, "O dear Mother, listen to me! I just returned from grazing the cows. When did I break her pot, dear Mother?"

tu māri maiyā, hu tāro lālo
nāno bhoḷo ne bhāḷo
kānāni vātmā mohāy yaśodā
māvalaḍi ō māvalaḍi
mādhūri lilā tāri mādhuri

"You are my dear Mother. I am Your darling child. I am so small and innocent." Yashoda is won over by little Krishna's baby talk.

ḍhoḷ bāje ḍhoḷ bhāje, ḍhōḷ bhaje ḍhōḷ
govāḷiyāni manḍaḷimā koṇ macāve śor
mākhaṇ cor te nandakiśor te, yaśodāno lāl

The drums are playing. Amongst the cowherd boys, who is the most mischievous of all? It is the one who steals butter, that son of Nanda.

rādhānā śyāmni
nandanā kūmārni
yaśodānā lālni jai
he mirānā nāthni
giridhar gopālni
raṇchoḍarāyni jai

Victory to Radha's Shyam, to Nanda's son, to the darling of Mother Yashoda! Victory to Meera's Lord, to the One who held the Govardhan hill aloft. Victory to Lord Ranchodrai, the One who abandoned the battle field!

Māhā nāṭakam (Telugu)

māhā nāṭakam, māyā nāṭakam
māhāmāyi āṭe jagannāṭakam

The grand play, the illusionary play, the universal play enacted by the Mother of Illusion!

vividha pātralu sṛṣṭiñci
triguṇa mulatō āṭe nāṭakam
evari pātrayento yentakālamō
antu teliyani vicitra nāṭakam

Creating different roles, playing through the three gunas. How much is our involvement and how long, O fathomless, wonderful play?

jīvitam lō natiñci, nāṭakam lō jīviñci
amma manato āṭu nāṭakam
manapātrakku jīvampōsi manalanu
māyā bhrāntulanu cēsina nāṭakam

Playing in the life and living in the play; the play in which Mother plays with us. Giving life to our roles, playing with us, making us confused!

Māi bhavānī (Marathi)

māi bhavānī premasvarūpiṇi ude g ambe ā-ī
āsura mardini amṛtavarṣiṇi ude g ambē ā-ī

O Bhavani, consort of Shiva, whose true nature is love. Awaken Mother, slayer of the asuras. You constantly shower the nectar of love on us. Awaken, O Mother!

ādi śakti ambābāyīcā jāgar karto āmhī
jñāna bhaktīce de vardān lekar tujhī āmhī
tuljhā bhavāni śambhu mohinī mahādevī māte
sukhdāyiṇī jagadambe tū yogeśvarī māte

Mother, we invoke the primeval power that is You. Please bestow upon us the boons of knowledge and devotion. O Goddess Bhavani of Tuljhapur, who charms Lord Shiva, great Goddess, Mother, giver of all happiness, O Mother of all the worlds, Goddess Durga, our object of worship.

udē g ambē udē g ambē udē g ambē bāyī

Awaken, O Mother!

abhīṣṭadāyini ariṣṭanāśini mahālakṣmī māte
jñāna śakti tū sattva svarūpiṇī śārade māte
ānandadāyini hṛdaya nivāsini reṇuke māte
prāṇadāyini muktipradāyini mahākālī māte

Mother Lakshmi, You fulfill all our desires and destroy all evils. Mother Saraswati, You are the power of knowledge and the embodiment of purity and wisdom; Mother Renuka, You give happiness and reside in our hearts. Mother Kali, You are the life-giving force and You grant liberation.

udē g ambē udē g ambēudē g ambē bāyī

Awaken, O Mother!

Mā jai jai mā (Hindi)

mā... jai mā... jai jai mā...
jai jai mā...
jai jai mā...
jai mā... jai mā...

Victory to Mother!

mā darśan de
tū he jagadīśvarī
mamatāmayi parameśvarī

Give me darshan, O Mother of the universe, compassionate, supreme Goddess.

hṛdayēśvarī tū hai bhayahāriṇī
varadāyinī bhavatāriṇī

You reside in the heart, and alleviate all fears. You bestow boons and take us across the ocean of life.

tū dil me ākē bas jānā mā
haskē cāndni barsānā mā

Come and dwell in my heart, Mother. Smile and shower us with moonlight, Mother.

bhīge tanman śītal hō mā
merā jīvan dhanya bane mā

O Mother, cool the heat of this worldly life and make this human birth worthwhile.

karuṇā se mujhe
nehalānā mā
man kā jalan miṭā denā mā

Bathe me with Your compassion, Mother, and rid me of the burning of my heart.

simirū har pal tujh
kō hī mā
esā var mujhe dēnā maiyā

Bless me that I may think of You every moment, O Mother.

Manakkōyil (Tamil)

mārukinḍra ulakil mārātavaḷ māriyammā
tēḍukinḍra manatil tōnḍriḍuvāḷ māriyammā
vēṇḍukinḍra varangaḷ tandiḍuvāy māriyammā
pāḍukinḍra pāḍalil maraindiruppaḷ māriyammā

In this changing world, the only constant is the divine Mother Mariyamma. She dawns in the hearts of those who seek Her.

She bestows the boons that we seek. She is veiled in the songs we sing.

manakkōyil tirandu vaittēn māriyammā - atil
dinantōrum ezhundaruḷvāy māriyammā

O Mariyamma, the doors of my inner shrine are open. Please dawn within daily.

tirisūlam kaiyil ēndum sūliyammā - undan
tirupādam tozha vandēn māriyammā
māviḷakkai ēndi vandēn nīliyammā - endan
mana azhukkai nīkkiṭuvāy māriyammā

O Mariyamma, Mother who wields the trident, I have come to worship Your feet. I have come with some sweet pudding for You. Please remove the impurities from my mind.

māriyammā muttu māriyammā
māriyammā muttu māriyammā

Mariyamma, darling Mariyamma!

karumbu villai tānkum karumāriyammā undan
karuṇaikku ellai illai māriyammā
ponkal pānai ēttri vaittēn dēviyammā - undan
tunnai veṇḍi ēnkukirēn māriyammā

O dark-hued Mother who holds the sugarcane bow, Your compassion is boundless. O Goddess, I have come with a pot of pongal (pudding). I yearn for Your divine grace.

nōy noṭikaḷ tīrkkum muttu māriyammā - undan
sēy unnai azhaikkumbōdu vārum ammā
vēppilaiyai eṭuttu vandēn kāḷiyammā - vērā-
-rumillai enai kākka māriyammā

O sweet Mariyamma who heals all diseases, You come running when Your child calls. O Mother Kali, I have brought some neem leaves for You. There is no one else who can protect me.

Manamenḍrum undan vīdu (Tamil)

manamenḍrum undan vīdu
marundu enḍrum untiru nīru
idamāna mozhikalai kūru
iduvandro perum pēru

My mind is ever Your abode. Your sacred ash is the medicine. Is it not my good fortune to listen to Your soothing words?

anpāi nī kaḍaikan pārtu
arulāl enai karayil sērtu
vemmāya piṇitanai tīrtu
vidi tannai nalamāy māṭru

Give me a loving glance. With Your grace, take me across the water. Remove the disease of illusion. Change my fate to goodness.

eduvellām enakiḍayūr
adan kūṭrāy aran nī māru
nīyinḍri gatiyār vēru
nī tāne kanivin mēru

You change the aspect of whatever obstacle comes to me. Without You there is no refuge. You are the mountain of compassion.

hara hara hara hara shankara
shiva shiva shiva shiva sada shiva
shambho shankara sarvesha
sharanam sharanam samba shiva

I take refuge in Hara, Shankara, Shiva, Shambho (all names of Lord Shiva)!

Manamirukka ahankāram (Tamil)

manamirukka ahankāram nānirukkutu
nānirukka daivam vēru āgi nirkkutu
vēru āgi nirkkum daivam svayam jvalippatu
svayam jvalikkum daivamakam svayam nuzhaivatu

The mind is the seat of the ego known as 'I.' Where there is the sense of 'I,' God remains seemingly distinct. The distinct God is self-effulgent. The self-effulgent one enters the heart of its own accord.

svayam nuzhainta daivattāl dharmmam nirkkutu
dharmmam tazhaippatāle maṭṭum dayai viḷankutu
dayai viḷanka anpu ōnki kulam sirakkutu
kulam sirantu paramabhaktiyāl niraikkutu

There is righteousness because of the self-entered God. Because there is righteousness, there is compassion. Because there is compassion, love is predominant, resulting in goodness. Because there is goodness, there is supreme devotion everywhere.

paramabhaktiyin tarangam amaidi sērkkutu
amaidi sēra sēra sēra manamoṭunkutu
manamoṭunkum nēram ahankāram tōrkkutu
ahankāram tōrkka marai daivam teriyutu

The vibration of supreme devotion brings about peace. As peace deepens, the mind sinks back to its source. When the mind sinks, the ego fails miserably. When the ego is defeated, God manifests himself.

Manan karo man (Hindi)

manan karo man yatn karo man
ahankār ko dūr karo

Introspect, O mind! Remember, O mind: distance yourself from pride.

guru caraṇan kā smaraṇ karo man
guru vacanan kā dhyān dharo
hṛday me prem aur bhakti bharo man
bhav sāgar kā pār karo

Immerse yourself in the lotus feet of the Guru. Meditate on the words of the Guru, fill your heart with love and devotion, and cross the ocean of samsara.

bacpan khelat sovat khoyā
yauvan māyā moh me ḍuboyā
arth kām aur yaś ke lobhī
vṛddh bhayo api sudhi nahi pāyā

Childhood is thrown away in sleep and play. Youth is drowned in illusionary desires. We have become old in the race for money, name, and fame. We have not yet realized the truth.

vyarth gavāyā jīvan sārā
ahankār kā bhār baḍhāyā
nām prabhu kā smaraṇ na āyā
ab to jāgo manvā morā

Our whole life has remained meaningless. We have become blown up with pride. We never remember the name of the Lord. At least now, awaken, O mind of mine!

guru caraṇan kā smaraṇ karo man
guru vacanan kā dhyān dharo

Immerse yourself in the lotus feet of the Guru, meditate on the words of the Guru.

Manasavāca karmaṇā (Kannada)

āgalī vivēka sūryana udaya
araḷali hṛdaya kamala vimala

May the sun of discrimination dawn. May the pure flower of the heart blossom.

manasavāca karmaṇā śaraṇembenu
nina ichage śaraṇu sankalpake śaraṇu

I surrender to You, O Mother, by thought, word and deed. I surrender to Your wish, and to Your will.

śaraṇembenu kṛpārāśiyē
śaraṇembenu kṛpārāśiyē

Overflowing grace, Mother, I surrender . . .

attitta nōḍadantē andhēyāgisammā
nina sānnidhyadi manava nillisu
bērellu aleyadantē bandhiyāgisammā
nina sēve mātradi tanuva nillisu

Make me blind that I won't see here and there. May my mind dwell only in Your presence. Imprison me, that I will not roam about here and there. May my body be ever engaged in Your service.

nānu nānendu nuḍidare dēvī
'nina pāda' vendu tiddi nuḍisu
nānu māḍide nendare dēvī
'ninna prasāda' vadendu nuḍisu

If I say, "I, I," correct me into saying, "Your feet." If I say "I did it", correct me into saying "it's Your prasad."

Mānasavīṇiya (Telugu)

mānasavīṇiya mrōgiñcavā prabhu
mañjuḷa gānamu ravaḷiñcagā
tegina tantrulanu atikiñcavā prabhu
tīyaṇi nādamu noḷikiñcagā

O Lord, play the veena of my heart. Let the beautiful music of bliss be heard. O Lord, mend the broken strings of the instrument, may only melodious sounds emanate.

apaśrutulanni tolagiñcavā prabhu
susvaram mulanu paḷikiñcagā
mauna bhāvālakadaliñcavā prabhu
madhurarāgāla śrutiyiñcagā

Eliminate all the incorrect notes, O Lord. Let only the right tunes be heard. Lord, awaken the unvoiced inner feelings, that the enchanting ragas may be created.

amṛta dhārāla kuripiñcavā prabhu
ānanda vāhini nōlalāḍagā
niratamu nīpada sankīrttanammuna
satatamu nīrūpa sandarśanammuna

O Lord, shower the nectar of Your grace. Let me be engulfed in the stream of divine happiness. Bless me that I may always sing in praise of Your lotus feet. Bless me with the uninterrupted vision of Your enchanting form.

madhurima poṅgulu vāru ṭendamuna
praṇavamu jummani rēgu candamuna

Bless me that my heart may overflow with bliss and that the sacred syllable 'Om' may resonate in my whole being.

Manasē kēḷū (Kannada)

manasē kēḷū bēgane mane sēru

Listen O mind, get home quickly.

kāla saridide dāri uḷidide
bēga bēgane naṭemunde

Time is passing by, but the path remains to be covered. Walk fast, walk forward.

rāgadvēṣa gaḷali kāla kaḷeya bēḍa
iṣṭāniṣṭā gaḷali dinava dūḍa bēḍa
māyeyoḍḍuva belage kālu toṭaradante
nāma smaraṇe baladi munda mundake naṭe

Do not waste time in attachment and aversion. Do not squander days in likes and dislikes. Do not let yourself trip before the obstacle of maya. With the strength of the remembrance of the name of God, keep on going forward.

amma iruvaḷalli bā
entu karaytihaḷu. . .
māte maṭilu tāne
namagella nijada maneyū
manasē . . . ō manasē . . .

There is Mother. She is calling you. Isn't Mother's lap our real home? Mind, O mind.

Manassil nīla sarasil (Malayalam)

manassil nīla sarasil
oru sarasīrūham viriññu
azhakil bhāva niravil
oru sarasijānanam teḷiññu !

In the stillness of my mind, a beautiful lotus bloomed. In the beauty of that flower, I saw Your enchanting face.

amaratvakānti vitarunna - jñāna
varadāna rūpavadanam
teḷivuttu kaṇḍu nirabhakti pūṇḍu
nanavārnniṭunna nayanam

When I saw Your everlasting beauty, devotion welled up inside of me, and I began to cry.

akaneññu nīri asidhāra-yāya
vazhi-yetra tāṇḍi-yoṭuvil
abhivandyarāya ṛṣivṛndamātma
mizhiyālariñña poruḷ, nī

After so much desperate searching, all the great sages came to know You through the inner Self.

Mangaḷa nāyaki (Tamil)

mangaḷa nāyaki ādiparāśakti
mangaḷam ponkavīttriruntāḷ
marakata uru mayil naṭai azhakil
yāzhisaiyuṭan iyarkaiyin ezhilil
innisaiyōṭu narttanamāṭi
mandiram mozhintu neñcam pukuntāḷ

Adiparashakti, the auspicious One is seated auspiciously on Her throne. Her form shines like a diamond, Her gait is like that of a peacock. Accompanied by the sound of the divine veena and the beauty of nature, She comes into my heart, chanting a mantra.

nadiyōram kuḷirtēntral inimai
maṇamiraikka malarvanam atilāṭum

mayilāṭa kuyil kūvum kārmēgham
malarmaṇḍapattil alankāram koṇḍāṭṭam tiruvizhā

A cool breeze can be felt on the banks of the river. The flower garden, exuding a sweet fragrance, dances to its tune. The dancing peacock is a blissful sight to behold, along with the singing bird. The hall is decorated grandly, as if for a festival.

kalaikaṇkaḷ naṭanam puriyum
tiruviḷakkin oḷisintum sānnidhyam
pūmālai tōraṇangaḷ āṭivarum
meymarantu kāṇbōrkku daivīkadarśanam

Devi's beautiful eyes move about as if dancing. The divine lamp spreads the light of peace and tranquillity; it's flame sways to and fro. Forgetting themselves, those who witness it enjoy the divine vision.

jai jai gāyatri śrīvidyai śankari
jai jai jñānasvarūpiṇi vāṇi
jai jai vēdanāyaki vittaki
jai jai cāmuṇḍēśvari māyi

Glory to Gayatri, Sri Vidya and Shankari! Hail to Sarasvati, the Goddess of knowledge! Glory to She who leads the Vedas, victory to the slayer of Chanda and Munda!

Mangal vadana (Hindi)

mangal vadana karuṇā mandir
sundar sur vandit tū
sakal varad kavitādāyak
sankaṭ gaṇ bhañjak tū

You have an auspicious face, You are a temple of compassion and the gods worship Your beautiful feet. You bestow all boons and poetry, and remove our many problems!

gaṇanātha... śubhadāta... śivabāla... natapāla...
jitakāma deva... bālarūpa... vedasannuta
gaṇanātha... śubhadāta... śivabāla... natapāla...
jitakāma deva... bālarūpa... vedasannuta

O Lord of the Ganas, giver of auspiciousness, son of Shiva, preserver of dance, vanquisher of Kama - Your form is like that of a child and You are praised in the Vedas!

amṛt kalaś kar me sohe
ankuś nav modak bhī
akhil vimal guṇ kīmūrat
rañjit raṇ vijayī

In Your hands You hold a pot containing the nectar of immortality, the elephant goad and sweet laddus. You symbolise the universal qualities of purity and goodness, and are victorious in war.

caraṇ śaraṇ var de bārak
kinkar hamre cākar
kalabh vadan dikhalā gaṇanāthā
mangal bikhare jagme

Please grant the boon that we may take refuge at Your feet. Thus our minds' demons will become our servants. Please show us Your divine form, Lord of the Ganas, that happiness and joy may spread in this world!

Manitā iraivan (Tamil)

manitā iraivan tān inbavūttru - atai
nī arintu endrum pōttru

O human being! The supreme is the actual source of bliss. Recognize this and praise the supreme.

maraikaḷ nāngum itarkku sāndru
atai nī arintu karai akattru
manatil māsennum karai akattru
itanālē uṇaralāmē inba ūttru

The four Vedas are evidence to this fact. Understand that and try to remove the impurities from your mind. Through this you can realize the actual source of bliss.

orupōdum utavātun ulaka pattru
itai nī arintu appattrakattru

None of your worldly possessions will actually benefit you. Understand this and cultivate the attitude of detachment.

unnuḷḷil uraikintra irai uṇarttu
itanālē uṇaralāmē inba ūttru

Invoke the Supreme that dwells right within you. Through this you can realize the actual source of bliss.

Mano nā visāri (Punjabi)

mano nā visāri tere dar te āye hā
mātā merā kaun sahārā tere sivā

Please let me remain in Your heart; I have come to Your abode. O Mother, who else is there for me other than You?

meri bigaḍi banāye kaun (tū hi banāye mā)
mere dard miṭāye kaun (tū hi miṭāye mā)
merā kaṣṭ haṭāye kaun (tū hi haṭāye mā)
mainu apnā banāye kaun (tū hi banāye mā)
merā viṣay vikār haṭāye merī mā
tū meri mā (jai devi mā)

Who resolves all my problems? You alone, Mother. Who removes my pain and sorrows? You alone, Mother.Who removes my worries and problems? You alone, Mother. Who makes me Her own? You alone, Mother. You alone remove my worldly attachments.

banke tārā camko akkhā vich
dūr hove māyā dā kohrā
dekh tanū akhā bhar āyiyā
caraṇ pivā mai tere to to maiyyā
caraṇ pivā mai tere to to maiyyā

Like a beautiful star, please shine in my eyes. The fog of delusion disappears. Just looking at You, my eyes fill with tears. Washing Your feet thus, I want to drink divine nectar.

ik tū hī is duniyā vich, samjhe dil dī bolī
bākī sāre matlab de, riśtte nāte cūṭhe
mainū apṇe caraṇā vich biṭhāle hun māyiye
mainū apṇe dil vich, chipāle hun māyiye
mainū apṇe dil me, chipāle hun māyiye

You are the only one who understands the language of my heart. The rest are all selfish minded, and worldly relations are unreal. Give me refuge at Your divine feet, Mother. Hide me in Your heart, O Mother!

Manujkāy hāthī (Hindi)

manujkāy hāthī sirvālā
śok moh nāśak śiv bālā
ādidev vancit varadātā
dīn nāth vande gaṇarāyā

One with the body of a human, and the head of an elephant, son of Shiva, the destroyer of sorrow and attachment. O supreme Lord, giver of boons, protector of the destitute, we bow to You, Lord of the elephants.

śaraṇam śaraṇam śaraṇam śaraṇam śaraṇam
śaraṇam śaraṇam śaraṇam śaraṇam śaraṇam
śaraṇam śaraṇam śaraṇam śaraṇam śaraṇam
ganeśa śaraṇam

O Ganesh, we take refuge in You!

cāra ved terī guṇ gāthā
tīn lōk vyāpit tavakāyā
dān bhāv mere man jāge
bār bār vande pad terā

Your praises are sung in the four Vedas and in the three worlds. O Lord who awakens the attitude of giving in me, I bow to Your feet again and again.

gyān dān denā tum devā
nāc gān rasikā sukumārā
yōgirāja jaya dīnadayālā
dījiye caraṇa dāsya hamēśā

O God bless me with knowledge, Lord who revels in the beauty of music. O King of all yogis, victory to You, compassionate One. Please bless me that I may ever be the servant of Your feet!

Mā o mā (Gujarati)

mā o mā mārī mā
tārā sivā kōṇ mārū
tārā sivā mane
nā jōve kōyī bījū

Mother, I have no one other than You. I also don't want anyone besides You.

tu mārī sāthī tu sangāthī
tu mārā śvāsōnā śvāsō śvās

rōm rōm mā tārō vās
kyārē samāviś mujnē tuj mā

You are my friend, You are my companion, You dwell in each breath I take; when will You merge me in You?

tu mārī pāsē chatā hun tārāthī dūr
tāru māru kēvu ā bandhan
hu ātmā tun paramātmā
kyārē samāviś mujne tuj mā

What sort of relationship is this? You are always by my side, yet I am so far from You. I am the atma (self), You are Paramatma (supreme Self); when will You merge me in You?

tu mārī dēvī ā jagnī tu jananī
tārā caraṇoma cārō lōk
hu ā jagmā ā jag tuj mā
kyārē samāviś mujnē tuj mā
mā ō mā...

You are my Goddess, You are the Mother of this world, the four worlds are at Your feet. I am of this world, and this world remains in You; when will You merge me in You?

Māriyamma māriyamma (Tamil)

samayapurattāḷē sankaṭankaḷ nīkkiṭamma
kaṇṇpurattāḷē kavalaikaḷ pōkkiṭamma
āyi mahāmāyi aruḷkaṇṇai kāṭṭiṭamma
kāḷi triśūli kaṇ tirantu pārttiṭamma

O Mother who resides in Samayapuram, please remove obstacles. O Mother who resides in Kannapuram (place names), please remove all worries. O great Mother, see with Your compassionate eyes. O Kali who holds the trident, open Your eyes and look at us!

māriyamma māriyamma śankarittāyē
āyiram kaṇ koṇḍavaḷē
tūya uḷḷam pūṇḍavaḷē māriyammā
tumbattai nī tuṭaittiṭa vā vā
vēppilai vīsiyē vā vā
nōyivēdanaikaḷ ellām tīra
karankaḷil tīccaṭṭi ēntivantōm
enkaḷuḷḷam kuḷirntiṭa nī vā

O Mother Shankari, Mariyamma, You have a thousand eyes. O Mariyamma, You have a pure heart, and hold neem leaves. Please come and rid us of our worries! We come with fire pots in hand. Please make us happy by relieving the pains of our diseases.

kāttrāki nīkkamara enkum niraintavalē
ārāki pāvavinai tīrkka pirantavaḷē
aruvāki uruvāki karuvāki tiruvāki
pattrarukkum paruporuḷē māriyammā
sundari antari purantari bhayankari

You are all-pervading like the wind. You come as a river to wash away our sins. You are form and formless, the primordial cause and real wealth. Giver of auspiciousness and prosperity, remover of fear, great Mother!

jagam pukazh puṇyavati akamalarum pankajākṣi
akamanatil iruḷakattrum kāmini kāmākṣi
kavipāṭa kaḷiyāṭa manamāṭa uraintāṭa
kanakāngi karumāri māriyammā
sundari antari purantari bhayankari

O meritorious One, You are praised by the whole world. Lotus-eyed One, You bloom in our hearts. O giver of desired boons, please remove the darkness in our hearts. We invite You wholeheartedly by singing and dancing, O golden-hued Karumari, Mariyamma. Giver of auspiciousness and prosperity, remover of fear, great Mother!

matiyōṭu manam makizhum pārin paramporuḷē
matimōha māyainīkkum māyā svarūpiṇiyē
matiyil nin tirunāmam uraintiṭa vēṇḍumammā
matillōka iṭarillāmal kāttiṭum māriyamma
sundari antari purantari bhayankari

O most supreme One in the universe, You make our minds and intellects happy. You are the source of Maya. Please remove our delusion. Your name should be established in our hearts. O Mariyamma please save us from the obstacles of the world. Giver of auspiciousness and prosperity, remover of fear, great Mother!

sundari antari purantari bhayankari
śankari śrīkari śivankari abhayankari
āyi mahāmāyi karumāri triśūli
kāḷi ankāḷi pozhivāyē aruḷmāri

Giver of auspiciousness and prosperity, remover of fear, great Mother! Bearer of the trident, Kali, Angali, kindly shower Your grace!

Māya lōniki neṭṭak-amma (Telugu)

māya lōniki neṭṭak-amma!
ō mahāmāyi
daya cūpi kanipeṭṭ-ammā!
nī biḍḍan-ammā

Don't push me into this illusion, O great deluder. Protect Your child with Your compassion!

māya bommala madhya dimpiti-vammā
māyalāṭal-āḍamanṭi-vammā

O Mother, You put me in the midst of illusory toys and allowed me to play these illusory games.

āṭalalō lāgabaṭi ninnu maracitin-amma!
āṭanē nijam-anukoni bratikitin-amma

Immersed in these games, I forgot You. I lived all these years assuming this to be the reality.

bommalāṭalō alasi pilicitin-ammā
kottabommalu kuni ichitiv-ammā !

When I got tired of these toys, I called out for You and You gave me new toys to play with.

ninnu maraci āṭalāḍi visigitin-amma
āṭalō yēmunnati ani telisinat-amma

I am tired of playing these games– forgetting You. I understand that there is nothing in these games.

ī bommalu nākoddu
ī āṭalu nākoddu!
manic-ceḍalu nākoddu
bhava bandhālu nākoddu!

I don't want these toys! I don't want these games! I don't want good or bad! I don't want these worldly bonds!

māyā prapancam nākoddu!
janma maraṇālu nākoddu!
amma kāvāli! nāk-amma kāvāli!
amma kāvāli! amma prēma kāvāli

I don't want this illusory world! I don't want birth and death! I want Mother! I want Mother's love! I want Mother!

Māyā ulagam (Tamil)

māyā ulagam kaliyuga māyā mayakkam
meytanai marantu pōytanai nāṭum māyā ulagam
sattiyattai tēṭi tēṭi enkenkō alaikirāy
kaṇmunnē iruppatai kāṇātēverukkirāy
iyarkkayōṭu iṇakkamindri vilaki vilaki nī selkirāy
poyyāna mukham kāṭṭi pōliyāka sirikkirāy

The unreal world is the illusion of Kali Yuga, the age of vice and demonic tendencies. You are wandering in search of truth, but you are not seeing it right in front of your eyes. You are moving away from the harmony of nature, and showing a false face and a fake smile.

ādaravāy anpozhuka pēsa nīyum marukkirāy
ādhāramām iraipōruḷai teṭa maṭṭum ninaikkirāy
bandhapāśam nān enatu endrē tān uzhalkirāy
poyyāna ulakamendru kuraikūri alaikirāy

You are preventing yourself from speaking lovingly and consolingly, even as you desire to search for the true source. You are living for your relations, ego and attachments. You are wandering - blaming the world for your problems.

nalvazhi kāṭṭinālum ērkkāmal suzhalkirāy
nittiyamāy unnil unnai kāṇāmal tavikkirāy
nalintōrkku sēvai seytu nallulakam nāṭalām
anpāna vāzhvinilē meyyulakam kāṇalām

You are going around without accepting the good path shown to you. You are suffering without knowing your eternal essence. You can serve under-served people and seek the good world! You can see the real world by living a life with love.

Mayilirakaṇi mādhavanē (Tamil)

mayilirakaṇi mādhavanē
vēnkuzhal ūtiḍum nāyakanē
untan ninaivil anudinamum
enkaḷ manatil urutipera
untan aruḷai nāḍukirēn kaṇṇā

O Madhava, adorned with a peacock feather! The Lord who plays the flute! Krishna, I pray daily that my mind may remain steeped in thoughts of You.

veḷḷai uḷḷa kaḷvā veṇṇai uṇṇa vārāi
yārum kāṇum munnē kaṇ maraintu selvāi

Thief with an immaculate mind, please come to eat some butter. But You must disappear before anyone sees You!

kaṇkaḷum nīyē kāṭciyum nīyē
kāṇpavanum kaṇṇā nīyē

O Krishna, You are the eyes that see, the object that is seen and the seer.

kaṇṇanindri inkē kāṇayārumuṇḍō?
kaṇṇan seyyum līlai kaṇkaḷ ariyumuṇḍō?

What else is there to see but Krishna? In His divine play, is there anything different from him that can be seen through our eyes?

Merā mujh main (Punjabi)

merā mujh main kuch nahi maiyyā
jō kuch hai ō tū hī maiyyā
terā tujhkō saupkke maiyyā. . .
meri maiyyā . . . ō meri maiyā . . . main
tere vich racadā jāvā me jay mātādi gāvā

I have nothing in me that is mine, all that I have belongs to You. May I surrender everything to You and merge in You.

jithe dekhā tūhī dissdā, har dil de vich tūhi
teri ḍōr vich har dil nū mai, ek dil kardā jāvā
sukh vī terā dukh vī terā, sab racanā hai teri maiyā
terā terā kardā hī mai, tere vich racadā jāvā – main
tere vich racadā jāvā

Wherever I look, I see only You; You are in every heart. May we join all hearts together with the thread that leads to Your heart. Happiness, sorrow, the entire creation is Yours. May we see everything as Your grace and merge in You.

śerāvāli jōttāvāli lāṭhāvāli
mehrāvāli pahadavāli polipāli maiya
tere vich racadā jāvā, me jay mātādi gāvā

kar kirpā kī isa sevakkdī ichā hūve pūri
mangā nā kuch tere tō mai
dhan dhan kardā jāvā
kehende sadguru kaḷḷā nahi tū
teynū pal pal cukkdā jāvā
ik kadamu tū mereval cukkdā dassa kadama mai āvā
dassa kadamu mē āvā

Bestow Your blessings on this servant so that his desire is fulfilled; I don't ask for anything but just want to thank You. The Satguru says, 'You are not alone in this world, I am always carrying you along When you take one step towards me, I take ten steps towards you.'

gajj ke gāvō. . . jay mātādi
phatē bulāvō. . . jay mātādi
mai nahi suṇēyā. . . jay mātādi
ral mil gāvō. . . jay mātādi

Sing with all your might: Victory to Mother! Call out for victory! Sing louder, I can't hear you! Let us all sing together: Victory to Mother!

Mere guruvāṅ di vāṇi (Punjabi)

mere guruvāṅ di vāṇi sun lo – mere
guruvādi vāṇī sun lo
e hegī – cāṣnī nālon mīṭhī
e hegī - pānī nālon patlī
e hegī - sāre jagtī nyārī

Listen to the words of my great masters! These words are sweeter than concentrated sugar syrup and at the same time, thinner than water - these words are out of this world!

o bande tū hī karle, is dā simraṇ
savār le pāgānū sunkar kare vacan
lagjā pār tū muṣkilānū lāng kar
tarjā tū is jahāz te caṭkar - o

O Man, you too learn and chant these words. Pamper your fortune by listening to these true words. You can cross the ocean of transmigration by listening and adhering to these words!

is vāṇī vich pariyā amarat
is dī rāh jo chalyā, o sokhā
nā rahe terā paisā mān dē śarīr
na pucche chūṭṭe sambandhi te śarīkh

These words are full of spiritual nectar, whoever followed these words made their life easy! None of your wealth, name or body will remain, even your friends & family will not be with you!

Mizhinīrilāzhnna (Malayalam)

mizhinīrilāzhnna manatārilinnu
madhuvillayende jananī
tazhayāteyonnu tuṇayāyivannu
tazhukīṭukenne sadayam

O Mother, there is no honey in the flower of my heart, which is wilting in tears. Forsake me not, come to my aid, and caress me compassionately.

verute viriññа vanasūnamoṭṭu
niramārnnatalla vanajē
padatārilēykku patiyānorittu
kanivēkiyamba kaniyū

O Vanaja (a name of the divine Mother), the wildflowers of my heart, which blossomed haphazardly, are not very colorful. Deign to show just a little mercy so that I may offer this heart-flower at Your lotus feet.

iruḷārnna neññiloḷiyāyirunnu
gatiyēkiṭunna jananī
karuṇākaṭākṣam aṭiyannu nalki
arivēkiyennilamarū

O Mother, shed some light in this benighted heart and lead me to a better destiny. By directing Your compassionate gaze on this lowly one, awaken knowledge in me and enshrine Yourself in my heart.

tava pādarēṇuvaṇiyān enikkyu
varadānamēku varadē
bhavasāgarattil alayunnorende
azhal nīkkiyennil aṇayū

O Varada (bestower of boons), bless me so that I can smear myself with the dust of Your feet. Remove the sorrow of this child, drifting in the ocean of samsara (cycle of births and deaths), and make me one with You.

Mōkēda ammanu (Tulu)

mōkēda ammanu bāle oñji leppuṇḍu
taḍamalpande amma kare korule
ammanu leppare bāle guñji gottuṇḍu
puggelḍu jeppuḍādu mānālē amma

One small child is calling for his most dear mother. Don't delay Mother! Consider the call! The child only knows to call his mother. Put the child to sleep in Your arms and console him, Mother.

malpunā bēleḍu unpinā nuppuḍu
pratiyoñji karmogu ammanu nenetondu
usir usirḍu ammanā anugraha
anubhavisuvuna bhāgyā olipāle

The child is remembering the mother in everything he does, in all his work and the food he eats. Please grant the luck that this child may experience Mother's blessings in every single breath.

koḍacādri giriṭu īre, nandininā taṭōṭu īre
barsadā panipaniṭu īre bhagavati
sṛṣṭida anu anu bērtu sāgunā ammā
darśana korlē enklēgu manada cāvaḍiḍu

Goddess Mookambika, You reside in the hills of Kodachadri and on the banks of the River Nandini. Every single raindrop is You, Bhagavati. You are in every atom of creation, Mother, You are the absolute with attributes. Please grant us Your vision in our minds.

hṛdayēśvari ammā
paramēśvari ammā
jagadīśvari janani
akhilāṇḍēśvari

Mother, Goddess of our heart, Supreme Mother Durga, universal Mother, most intelligent Goddess!

Mother nature (English)

nature is our home
god in another form
let's love and protect, care and respect
the wonder of this world

mother nature,
may our hearts rise
in the beauty of creation

seeing god in one another
in the wind, the trees, the water

every bird that sings
all living things
are nothing else but you

as part of the whole
we have to play our role
learning to feel, striving to heal
the wounds of this world

nature only gives
sustaining all that lives
for us to survive we need to strive
to care for all of life

Muraḷīgānamutirkkunnu (Malayalam)

muraḷīgānamutirkkunnu hari
vṛndāraṇya-nikuñjē
navarasamadhurima rūkum nava nava-
madhumaya rāgamanōjñam

Krishna is playing his flute in the Vrindavan garden, and His divine music can be heard everywhere, bringing joy to all.

jalavum dharaṇiyum-anilanumoppam
sakalacarācaravṛndam
madhuramanōhara vamśīninadam
pakarum madhu nukarunnu

The water, earth, wind and all of creation on Earth are in ecstasy listening to the Lord's music.

gopavadhū janavṛndam mādhava-
savidham-aṇaññatiramyam
rāsarāsotsava lahariyilāzhān
lāsyachuvaṭukaḷ veypū

All of the gopis and gopas of Vrindavan gather round Krishna and join in the rasa lila dance.

mama hṛdayattilum-amṛtam peyyum
naṭanam ceyyu ! mukundā
mama janmatteyum-alivinnuravāl
amṛtātmakamākku nī

O Krishna! Please come and dance in my heart so that I too will become blissful. With Your compassion, please make my life meaningful by granting me immortality.

Muraḷī manohar (Hindi)

muraḷī manohara, mādhava
yadu rāja nandan sundarā
karuṇādramānas mohanā
vraja lokanāyak nandanā

O Madhava, Krishna, player of the flute, O beautiful son of the Yadu King of Vraj, compassionate One!

bolo mādhav gāvo keśav
yādavā madhusūdanā brajnandanā
rādhākṛṣṇā gopīkṛṣṇā jay jay muraḷīkṛṣṇa

Chant the names of Madhava, sing the names of Krishna. O Radha Krishna, Gopi Krishna, victory to Krishna!

vanamālabhūṣaṇ bhūte
śiśūpālsūdan śrīpate
paśūpālbālak śyāmaḷā
madhurāpurādhipa mangaḷā

The One with the beautiful garland, consort of Lakshmi, You put an end to the evil Sishupala. O dark-hued cowherd boy, auspicious One of Mathura!

Murugā vēlmurugā (Tamil)

kaṇmaṇi murugā karuṇāsāgarā murugā murugā
vēlavā vaṭivēlavā vinaiyarukkum māl marugā
vēl vizhiyāl bālakā daṇḍāyudhapāṇiyē

O precious Muruga, ocean of compassion. The little child of Uma, You have piercing eyes and bear a wooden staff as Your weapon.

murugā vēlmurugā vettrivēlazhakā
kumarā skandā vēlā mālmarukā
vēlavā vaṭivēlavā vinaiyarukkum mālmurugā
vēlvizhiyāl bālakā daṇḍāyudhapāṇiyē

O Muruga, holder of the spear, handsome nephew of Lord Vishnu, slayer of past life karma. The little child of Uma, You have piercing eyes and bear a wooden staff as Your weapon.

sinkāravēlavā śivaśakti bālakā
sinkārakāvaṭiyai eṭuttu vantōmē
sinkārakāvaṭiyil tēnum tinaiyum vaittu
sinkārakāvaṭiyai arppaṇittōm

The bearer of a highly decorated and most beautiful spear, the child of Lord Siva and Parvati, we carry the beautiful wooden arch, we have put honey and millet in that arch, we humbly offer this to You O Lord!

suṭṭa veṇṇīr pūsi azhakanāy vantāy
suṭṭapazham tantu pāṭṭiyin tamizh keṭṭāy
jñānappazhamē nīyē kōpamkoṇḍu āṇḍiyānāy
jñānacuṭarē navamaruntē anpānāy

Adorned with pure white ash, O handsome One, You played with the 'Tamil Grandma' by offering 'hot' fruits (fruit of knowledge). O embodiment of knowledge, out of anger, You took the form of a total renunciate. Flame of knowledge, panacea for all diseases (as the form of the nine medicinal herbs). You are love.

sūravadham seytu taivānai maṇamuṭittāy
kizhavanāka urumāri kuravaḷḷi karampiṭittāy
tantaikku praṇavamōti satguruvāy ninṭrāy
sēytanai kāttiṭuvāy tirumurugā

You killed the demon Surapadman and married Theivanai. Disguised as an old man You took the hand of the gypsy girl Valli in marriage. You revealed the meaning of the pranava mantra 'om' to Your father and stood tall among Satgurus. Auspicious Lord Muruga, please protect this child!

Muttu mūkkutti (Tamil)

muttu mūkkutti mukhattil minna nī muttam koṭukkaiyilē
anpu muttam manam kavarum ennai nī aṇaikkaiyilē
kavalaiyāl kalankum nān tiruppādam tozhutiṭavē
apalai nān enai marantē kaṇṇīrāl nanaittiṭuvēn

As You embrace me and bestow Your loving kiss, Your pearl nose-ring shines, and my mind is engulfed! Gripped with sorrow I bow down at Your divine feet; helpless I forget myself and drown in my tears.

muttamiṭṭu ivvulakai pūnkāvanamākkukirāy
anpu tantu tuyarakatti ezhilpūmiyākkukirāy
nīrōṭum nadiyinaiyum tīrtthamāka māttukindrāy
nī varaṇḍa idayattai gangayāka māttukindrāy

With Your love You transform the world into a garden. With Your love You remove all sorrow and make this world beautiful. You transform the flowing waters of the river into holy water. You transform the dry mind into the Ganges River.

vinaippayan kaṭantu mukti padam kāṭṭiṭavē
viyanulakil anpāna tāyena vantāyē
toṭuvatanām anaivarukkum marupiravi tantuviṭṭāy
piravāta perunilaiyai tāyē nī aruḷvāyē

Show me the path of liberation, help me transcend the cycle of karma, You who have come to this earth embodying motherly love. Your touch has transformed so many, made so many feel reborn. Please bestow Your boon that I may go beyond birth and death

vallavēḷa palluyirum enatāka vēṇḍum ammā
nallatāka kāṇpatellom nalamāka vēṇḍum ammā

uḷḷoḷiyē pēroḷiyāy ulakenkum katiroḷiyāy
narpirappām ippirappil nān kāṇa vēṇḍum ammā

I should be able to see myself in others, I should be able to see the good in everything. Help me realize, in this life, that the light glowing within me permeates the whole universe.

ammā unakku palakōṭi vandanankaḷ

Mother, I prostrate at Your holy feet over and over again.

Nā hṛdi (Telugu)

nā hṛdi koluvanī nī padakamalam
darśiñcanī mātā nīdivyarūpam

Let my heart worship Your lotus feet. Mother, allow me to behold Your divine form.

nā kanureppalu kāru mabbulai
kurisē kannīru vāna jallulai
padunu tīranī eṭata bhūmini
molakettanī bhaktivittuni

When dark clouds form in my eyelids, tears flow down like rainwater. Let the ground of my heart become wet, so that the seeds of devotion can sprout!

viṣaya vāsanala kalupu mokkalanu
rāga dvēṣamula muḷḷa ḍonkalanu
dhruṭamagu nammika padunagu kattiga
perikivēyanī citta vṛttini

The weeds of materialistic vasanas, the thorny bushes of passion and hatred, the deep rooted likes and dislikes - let them all be eradicated by the sharp knife of unshakable faith in You!

bīṭṭalu vārina bamjaru bhūmula
avidya niṇḍina mānasa sīmala

sāgu cēyanī nī śaraṇāgati
virabūyanī ānanda vallari

The expanse of my ignorant mind is like a wasteland. Let it be ploughed by surrendering to You. Let eternal bliss bloom like a flower!

Naiyyā tērē (Hindi)

naiyyā tērē jīvankī
gumrāh kaisē hō gayi
sukhki or nikli thi
dukh sāgarmē khō gayi

How did the boat of your life lose its way? It started its course towards happiness, but got lost in the ocean of sorrow.

tan dhan par hī dhyān diyā
apnē sat kō bisrā diyā
parāyē kō tū apnā samjhā
apnē kō ṭukrā diyā

You paid attention to wealth and body alone, forgetting your true self. You thought a stranger to be yours, forsaking your own self.

ahankār kē jāl mētū
bandi bankar rah gayā
apnē andar kē hīrē kō
pahcānē binā tū rah gayā

In the trap of the ego, you became a prisoner, unable to recognize the jewel inside you.

na sōc din hē bahut
jānē kabh naiyyā dūb jāyē
kāl jō āyē dvār tērē
kal tak tū nahi ṭāl pāyē

Don't think there are endless days; who knows when the boat may sink? If tomorrow comes to your door, you will not be able to put it off to the next day.

Nāḷnallatākum (Tamil)

nāḷnallatākum kōḷ nallatākum
nātan tāḷ paṇintāl
nānenatennum māyai māyntē pōkum
nātan manam kanintāl

Auspicious will be the day, and all planets will become favorable when one prostrates before the Lord. The feelings of 'I' and 'mine' will disappear if the Lord showers grace.

siṭrinpattinil pattrinai nīkki
paraman pattrinai pattriṭuvōm
aritāyvāytta ummāniṭa piravi
payanuracceytē vāzhntiṭuvōm

Let us detach from fleeting pleasures and attach to the feet of the Lord. Let us live this rare human birth in a beneficial way.

tiruvaruḷālē manaviruḷnīnka
pōṭruvōm tillaināyakanai
tarumvarattālē kūttrinai māttri
kēṭaruppān nam kūttapirān

Let us praise the Lord of Chidambaram, that our ignorance be dispelled by his divine grace. With His boon, our Lord of dance can even change our destiny and remove our sorrows.

ellām vallavan ellām avanseyal
enṭruṇarntē sivan aṭipaṇivōm
innalkaḷ ellām maraintē pōkum
iruḷpōl katiravan oḷiyinilē

Let us understand that he is all powerful and everything is his will, and prostrate at Lord Shiva's feet. Like darkness disappearing in sunlight, our difficulties will also disappear.

ponnār mēniyanē puviyāḷum śankaranē
minnār saṭaiyōnē harahara mṛtyuñjaya śivanē

Shiva, Lord of golden effulgence, ruler of the world, Lord with matted hair, conqueror of death!

Nambinōr (Tamil)

nambinōr keṭuvatillai nānkumarai tīrppu
ambikaiyai tozhuvōrkku illaiyē irappu

The scriptures declare that those who believe in God will never come to any harm. Those who have faith in the Goddess will attain immortality.

ponkalvaittu vazhipaṭa aruḷ taruvāyē
māriyammanē uḷḷam amarntu oḷitaruvāyē
anputantu aruḷtantu aḷḷiyaṇaikkum māriyamma
amutamē arumaruntē śaraṇaṭaintōmē

Grant me the boon of worshipping You on Pongal (a festival dedicated to the Goddess). O Mariyamma, dwell in my heart and enlighten me. You shower love and grace on me, and embrace me. Goddess of immortality, sovereign remedy, we take refuge in You!

kuzhantaiyum taivamum ontrutānē
kuzhantayāy taivamāy guruvaṭivāṇavaḷē
aruḷkozhuntē mīnākṣiyē araśanin makaḷānāḷ
amutavaḷḷi nāvinālē piḷḷaitamizh tantāḷē

The innocent child is no different from God. For me, You are child, God and Guru. O benevolent One, Meenakshi, daughter of the king! Your innocent prattle in Tamil delighted everyone.

kōyilillā nagaramē narakamentru solvārkaḷ
kōyilāy manam māra sorkamākum enpārkaḷ
kōyilin karuvarai uraintiṭum māriyamma – mana
kōyilil vīttriruntu mangaḷam aruḷvāyē

It is said that a city without a temple is like hell, and a heart that enshrines God is heaven. O One who dwells in the inner sanctum of the temple, You reside in my heart and bestow auspiciousness on me!

maṭamayai nīkkiṭam magimaimiku māriyamma
mannāḷum māriyavaḷ tankiṭuvāḷ manatilē
anpenum malarkoṇḍu manatilpūja seyvōm
anpāna māriyavaḷ kaṣṭankaḷai kaḷaivāyē

O Mariyamma, capable of dispelling ignorance! O ruler of the earth, dwell in my heart! With the flowers of love, I shall worship You in my heart. O compassionate Mariyamma, please remove my troubles.

Nām japo (Hindi)

nām japo nit hari kā pyāre
nām se darśan milte nyāre

Dear one, chant the name of Hari. This name alone will reveal the form!

nām se hi cit kā ho śodhan
nām hi har sādhak kā sādhan
nām ki mahimā śiv hi jāne
nām ko rām se ūpar māne

The Lord's name is the only purifier for the mind and the means for every seeker. Shiva alone knows the glory of the Lord's name, as he gives greater importance to Rama's name than to Rama himself!

nām japat pāpom kā kṣay ho
nām raṭat man nāmī may ho
nām ki mahimā kahi na jāye
nām jape so hi gati pāye

By chanting the Lord's name, one's bad karma comes to an end and the mind merges in the divine. No one can express the glory of chanting that name. Whoever chants it reaches truth!

rām ne kuchko hi tārā thā
nām ne to lākhom tāre
sākṣi rahe he cānd sitāre
rām bhajo yā bhajo murare

Rama gave liberation only to a few in his lifetime, but his name has granted deliverance to millions. The moon and stars are witness to this - therefore, chant the name, be it Rama or Murari!

bolo rām rām rām sītā rām rām rām
bolo rām rām rām sītā rām rām rām

Hail Rama, Sita!

Namo namah (Telugu)

namo namah namo namah kāli caranālu
mā manasuna koluvaina kāli caranālu

Salutations to the holy feet of Mother Kali, which are enshrined in our hearts!

vairāgya sīmalo āḍu caranālu
kālidāsu pūjinche kāli caranālu
bangāru andela śyāma caranālu
mā manasuna koluvaina kāli caranālu

The feet that dance in the abode of dispassion, are worshipped by Kalidas (poet); those dark feet, that are enshrined in our hearts, are adorned by golden anklets.

yenalēni andāla jilugu caranālu
dharani dēvi cumbince kāli caranālu
manasune mōhinche madhura caranālu
mā manasuna koluvaina kāli caranālu

The holy feet, whose beauty is beyond measure, are kissed by Mother Earth; those sweet feet that capture the minds of devotees, are enshrined in our hearts.

bhaktiki muktiki gūdu caranālu
ārtula kalpa taruvu kāli caranālu
padilamuga koluvare talli caranālu
mā manasuna koluvaina kāli caranālu

The sacred feet are the nest for devotion and liberation, they are wish fulfilling tree to the destitute. With unwavering faith, let us worship this Mother's feet, that are enshrined in our hearts.

Namōstutē dēvī (Marathi)

namōstutē dēvī durgē mahēśvarī kāḷī

Devi, Durga, Maheshvari, Kali, our salutations to You!

ambā bhavānī bhagavatī mātā
mantra japunī tuja nāmācā
akhaṇḍa gāū tujhīca gāthā
karū tujhī prārthanā
dēvī karū tujhī prārthanā

Mother, Bhavani, Bhagavati, chanting the mantra of Your name and singing Your glories, we pray to You.

jaya jagadambē ambē mā !

Victory to Mother of the Universe !

lakṣmī sarasvatī jaya jagadambā
sarvasvarūpiṇī tujhēca cintan

mātē kadhī tū dēśīl darśan
karū tujhī archanā
dēvī karū tujhī archanā

Victory to the Mother of the Universe, Lakshmi, Sarasvati! All-pervading One, we meditate only on You. Mother, when will You give us Your darshan? We worship You, Devi!

Nānē ariyāta ennai (Tamil)

nānē ariyāta ennai
nanṭrāy arinta en tāyē
tānēyākiṭum uṇmai
dayaiyuṭan uṇara vaippāyē

O my divine Mother who knows me better than myself! Kindly bless me with the realization that the eternal truth is the Self.

vīṇē kiṭakkutu vīṇai – atai
virumbinī mīṭṭiṭuvāyē
tēnē tikazhātma dēvi
disaiyenkum inimai seyvāyē

O Mother, please lovingly play this veena (musical instrument) lying unused, spreading a sweet melody in all directions. O Goddess of honey, You are verily my inner self, the Atman.

mānē matiyīnattālē – maṇam
tēṭi alaivatupōlē
vīṇē vaiyam itil ōṭi
vizhalukku nīriraittēnē

Like a deluded deer in search of musk, due to my ignorance I am fruitlessly searching in this world, verily watering the weeds instead of the plants.

nīyē nizhalkoṇḍu neyta – nin
māya maraitannai māṭra
sēyāka untāḷ paṇintēn
śivaśaktī kāttaruḷvāyē

Shivashakti, this child of Yours falls at Your feet, seeking protection from this veil of illusion which You have woven by Your maya.

Nān enbatai (Tamil)

nān enbatai marandāl – tān
yārenbatai uṇarntāl
nanmaikaḷ pirakkum namvazhi sirakkum
vanmaikaḷ oḍunkum akavazhi tirakkum

When we forget the false 'I' and realize the true 'I,' good qualities will dawn, our destiny will become better, sorrows will end, and the inner eye of wisdom will open.

uḍal enḍrum idu nilaiyillai
āḍal atil muzhu niraivillai
āḍal muḍintu tanai venḍrāl ānandamayamākumē

The body is ephemeral. One cannot derive total satisfaction from pleasures. If we can curb the vacillating mind and control the ego, we will enjoy bliss.

tēḍal enbatu mana ēkkam
vāḍal enbatu guṇamayakkam
tēḍal muḍintu tanaiyarindāl tūya manam malarumē

It is the mind's nature to seek. Sorrows are illusory. If we attain God after seeking, the pure mind will blossom.

pāḍal enbatu akamakizhvu
nāḍal enbatu iraiyuṇarvu
pāḍalilmūzhka meyyidanuḷ paraviḍum amaidiyē

Devotional hymns are an expression of inner happiness. Seeking is a sign of awakening God-consciousness. If we can immerse ourselves in devotional singing, peace will pervade the body.

ānandam pērānandam ānandam paramānandam
ānandam nityānandam ānandam ātmānandam

Bliss, immense bliss, supreme bliss, eternal bliss, bliss of the Self!

Nānendu kāṇuve (Kannaḍa)

nānendu kāṇuve ninna divya rūpava kṛṣṇā
ninagāgi kādiruve bahaḷa dinagaḷinda
nānu gaidaparādhavēnu ninninda dūraviralu
ī agalike tāḷalāre bēga bā nannoḍeyā

When shall I see Your divine form, O Krishna? I have been waiting for so long! What did I do wrong to make You stay away from me? I cannot bear this estrangement. Please come quickly to me!

tōride ninna puṭṭa bāyoḷu viśvavanne yaśōdege
viśvarūpava tōride arjunage raṇarangadi
pāda sēvakanige nīḍu ninna bhavya darśana
karuṇe tōru kṛṣṇā ī caraṇa dāsana mēlē

You opened Your lovely mouth to reveal the whole universe to Mother Yashoda. You revealed Your universal form to Arjuna on the battlefield. Please grant Your servant Your darśan. I have been serving Your feet.

yādava nātha gōkula nāthā jagannāthā kṛṣṇā

O Krishna, You are chief of the Yadava clan, leader of the cowherd clan, and Lord of the universe.

dhruva prahlādage nīḍide nī divya jñānavā
paramamitra kucēlana dāridryava kaḷēdē
nanagāvudu bēḍa ninna darśana bhāgyava biṭṭu
taḍavinnēkē prabhuve kṛpeyā mādi uddharisu

You bestowed divine knowledge on Dhruva and Prahlada. You banished the poverty of Your dear friend Kuchela. I want nothing but Your darshan. Without further delay, please shower Your grace and liberate me.

Nanna hudōṭṭada (Kannada)

nanna hudōṭṭada mallige sampigē
ammani gāgiyē nagutālivē
nanna mane bīdiya podegaḷā hūgaḷu
ammanī gāgiyē araḷidāvē

The jasmines and champaks in my garden are smiling for Mother's sake. The flowers in bushes on my street have bloomed for Mother's sake.

nannayī ūrina maragiḍa baḷḷiyu
ammani gāgiyē kādidāvē
nannayī nāḍina hasirēle hūhaṇṇu
ammanī gāgiye biṛiyutīvē

The trees and vines and plants of my town are waiting for Mother's sake. The green leaves, fruits and flowers of my land have been borne for Mother's sake.

nannayī bhūmiya ondondu jīviyu
ammani gāgiye jīvisive
nannayī lōkada acarācara vella
ammani gāgiyē tapisutīvē

Each and every being of this Earth of mine are living on for Mother's sake. Every one of the moving and unmoving of this world of mine is longing for Mother.

sṛṣṭiya pūrṇṇate illide kēḷū
satyam śivam sundaram

Here lies the fulfillment of Nature. Listen - 'satyam shivam sundaram'.

Nannōḍeya (Kannada)

nannōḍeya tiruka nānavana sēvaka
bhaktigē oliyuva sumanōpama sumukha

My Lord is a vagabond , and I am His servant. The One who is delighted by devotion, the One with a charming face...

himada baṇḍe masaṇabhūmi ella avana nivāsa
rāgabhōgagaḷigē avanu sadā udāsa
nondu benda hṛdayakkella karuṇāmṛta varuṣa

He lives in the mountains and cremation grounds. He has no taste for the materialistic world and its luxuries. He comes as a shower of compassion for the hearts that are in pain.

śīva śiva śiva hara hara hara śambhō śankara
śīva śiva śiva hara hara hara śambhō śankara

Shiva, Hara, Shambhu, Shankara!

jñānaghananu prēmamayanu mugddha saraḷa mahimanu
maruḷanante tōrutiha pracaṇḍa taraḷanu
ātmaratiyu mahāyatiyu bhaktajanage gatiyu

He is the embodiment of knowledge. He is love incarnate. He is simple yet great. He pretends to be foolish, but He is all knowing, and has great depth. He always revels in His own consciousness. He is the greatest monk and is the only hope for His devotees.

oṁ namaḥ śivāya oṁ namaḥ śivāya
oṁ namaḥ śivāya oṁ namaḥ śivāya

Prostrations to Lord Shiva!

Nānu embudilla (Kannada)

nānu embudilla keḷu
nanna dembudilla
nannavarembuvarilla - satyadi
nā-nē embudē illā

Listen, there is no such thing as 'me' or 'mine'. Nothing is 'my own'. In fact there is no 'me' or 'You' at all.

tanuvu manavu nannadu endalli
tanuvu manavu daṇivudalla
tanuvige tāraṇa bāradalla
manasige mukti dorakadalla - endu

I may say the body and mind are mine, but then they are finite and get exhausted. The body cannot cross over (the sea of samsara) and the mind will never attain liberation.

tanuvu manavu ninnadu endalli
iha para dvandva innilla
ida nenedare dukhavilla - āga
nīnallade bērondilla ammā

On the other hand, if I make body and mind 'Yours,' then there will be no duality in life. Then I will have no more sorrow. At that stage, there will be none other than You, O Mother.

Narahari nārāyaṇa (Kannada)

narahari nārāyaṇa hari hari nārāyaṇa
narahari nārāyaṇa hari hari nārāyaṇa
yēnu heḷali ninna mahime yaṣtu hogaḷali
narasimha narasimha narahari narasimha

Narayana, what can I say about You? Your glories cannot be described enough. O Narasimha (man-lion form of Vishnu)!

rakkasanige brahmanitta varake jagavu añjuta
mundinagati tiḷiyade hedari hedari beccutā
vande tande nī nellara kṣēma samādhānake
varaprasāda niyama taradi konde avana bageyutā

When Brahma granted the boon of invincibility to the demon Hiranyakashipu, the world trembled, fearful of its fate. The demon sought immortality and asked that he be killed by neither man nor animal, neither inside nor outside, neither at daytime nor night-time, and by no weapon. Dear Father, for the good of everyone, You slew him at dusk with Your claws at the entrance of a building without violating the boon's conditions!

devā nārāyaṇa hari hari nārāyaṇa
devā nārāyaṇa hari hari nārāyaṇa

O Lord Narayana, Hari!

kanda prahḷādana śraddhe bhaktige nī maṇiyalu
nārāyaṇa nārāyaṇa nāma kūsu japisalu
kāde avana appanitta śikṣayinda hagaliraḷu
maguvina visvāśa kāgi prakaṭa vāde kamboduḷu

You were lovingly compelled by the darling Prahlada's faith and devotion. The little one's ardent calls of "Narayana, Narayana" were irresistible to You. You watched over Prahlada day and night, protecting him from his father, the demon Hiranyakashipu who plotted to kill him (enraged at his son's claim that the Lord resided everywhere). To disprove it, Hiranyakashipu struck at a stone pillar and lo! – the Lord appeared there in the fierce man-lion form of Narasimha. For that little child's innocent faith, You appeared in the pillar. O Lord Narayana!

mugdha muguva prēmabhakti varṇisalu asādhyavu
kūsu taḷeda hari nambike accari amōghavu
hē dēvā dayapālisu namagu ā bhaktiya
ninna nāma japisi bhajisi janma mukti rītiya

That innocent child's love and devotion are indescribable, the little one's trust in the Lord so fruitful! O Lord, if You grant us that devotion, we can chant Your name and thus attain liberation!

Narttana māṭō naṭarāja (Kannada)

narttana māṭō naṭarāja
kīrttana hāṭide bhutagaṇa

O Nataraja, dance! Your companions are singing for You.

takatayya-tayya śivāya namaḥ ōm
dhimi-dhimi kiṭatōm śivaśiva hara ōm
bam bam bōlā ō naṭarāja

I bow down to Lord Shiva, Lord of dance! O Lord of dance we adore You with the sounds of drums.

kālakāla kālabhairava
kaṭegāṇisō kāla
smaśānavāsi vyōmakēśi
samsāra dāṭisu bā
ō mahākāla ō bhavahara

O Lord who is death unto death itself, O Kalabhairava, do put an end to time. You dwell in the cremation ground, and the sky is Your hair! Help us cross over samsara.

dikkanne dharisida nīlalōhita
dāri tōrō dēvā
ruṇḍamāladhara ō rudrarūpa
rakṣisu śaraṇaranu
ō mṛtyuñjaya ō harōhara

O Lord with a blue throat, You wear the directions. Show us the way out! O Lord with a fierce form wearing a garland of skulls, protect us who have surrendered to You! Hail Lord Shiva! O conqueror of death!

sṛṣṭi sthiti marma bhēdisō
mahā. . . layakara
tāṇḍava kuṇiyo śiva śiva ō naṭarāja
mahālayakara śrī naṭarāja

O Lord, You cause the great dissolution. Please reveal the secrets of creation and preservation! O Nataraja, You perform the dance of ultimate dissolution.

ō naṭarāja tāṇḍava kuṇiyō śiva
ō naṭarāja tāṇḍava kuṇiyō śiva
ō jaṭadhāri tāṇḍava kuṇiyō śiva
triśūladhāri tāṇḍava kuṇiyō śiva

Please perform the tandava dance! O Shiva with matted hair, dance the tandava dance! Great dissolver bearing a trident, dance the tandava dance!

ō gangādhāri tāṇḍava kuṇiyō śiva
tripunṭradhāri tāṇḍava kuṇiyō śiva
ō sōmadhāri tāṇḍava kuṇiyō śiva
trinētradhāri tāṇḍava kuṇiyō śiva

One with matted hair, wearing the Ganga, dance the tandava dance! You wear sacred ash on Your forehead and the moon in Your hair, dance the tandava dance!

ō nāgadhāri tāṇḍava kuṇiyō śiva
ō tripurāri tāṇḍava kuṇiyō śiva
ō ḍamarudhārī tāṇḍava kuṇiyō śiva
trikāladhāri tāṇḍava kuṇiyō śiva

Lord with three eyes, wearing snakes as garland, dance the tandava dance! You destroyed the three cities, dance the tandava dance!

ō naṭarāja ō naṭarāja

O Lord of dance!

Navanitacorā (Hindi)

navanitacorā veṇugopālā jaya vṛndāvana bālā
mākhan de de nāc nacāve tujhko sab brajbālā

O butter thief of Vrindavan, everyone plies You with gifts of butter to keep You dancing.

pīt jhugaliyā tanpar sohe, mor mukuṭ māthe pe
kālī alke māthā cūme sab balihāri chab pe
tātā thaiyyā, tattata thaiyyā pag paṭte dharttī pe
pāv me kinkiṇi ruñjun bāje jūm uṭe braj sārā
jai vṛndāvana bālā jai vṛndāvana bālā
he citta corā gopa kumārā nand ke sundara lālā

All are bewitched by Your beautiful form - You wear yellow garments, a crown of peacock feathers and have long black hair. With anklets adorning Your feet, You dance and fill all of Vraj with divine joy. Victory to the child of Vrindavan, the beautiful son of Nanda!

śyām rādhe śyām rādhe śyām rādhe rādhe śyām

Victory to Krishna, victory to Radha!

naṭkhaṭ ki muskān manohar, jīt rahi man sabkā
māt yaśodā balaiyyā le par lālā pyārā braj kā
mākhan hi nahī cit bhī curāye mudit he man gopin kā
man hi nahi jo pighle nā sun aisi mohanī līlā
jai vṛndāvana bālā jai vṛndāvana bālā
he citta corā gopa kumārā nand ke sundara lālā

This naughty One's beautiful smile captures all hearts. Adored by his mother Yashoda, he is also the darling of all of Vraj. He steals not only butter, but also the mind; making the gopis enchanted by divine love. There is really no heart that does not melt before his bewitching divine play. Victory to the child of Vrindavan, the handsome son of Nanda!

Navavidha bhakti (Telugu)

navavidha bhakti mārgamulatō
jaganmātanu koluvavē manasā
bhaktivinā sanmārgamu ammanu
cēragaladē manasā. . .

O mind, worship the Mother of universe through the nine paths of devotion! O mind, is there a way better than devotion to reach the divine Mother?

amma bhāgavatamunu sadā śraddhatō
śravaṇamu ceyyavē manasā
ammā ammā anucu prēmatō
kīrttana ceyyavē manasā
ammā mantramu sadā smaraṇamu
cēsi tariñcu manasā. . .

Listen to the story of the divine Mother with all faith, O mind. Sing the glories of the divine Mother with love and ecstasy! Contemplate the mantra of the divine Mother and become sanctified, O mind!

amma pādamulanu yadalō nilupukoni
śaraṇu kōravē manasā
ammanu arciñci pujiñci pilaci
dhyānamu ceyyavē manasā
jagamunu ammagā cūsi vandanamu
cēsi sēvimpavē manasā. . .

Install the lotus feet of the divine Mother in your heart and seek refuge O mind! Perform archana to the divine Mother, invoke her through worship and meditate on her form, O mind! Perceive this world as the divine Mother by bowing down to it with reverence and service.

ambādāsuḍaina annī amma
kāryamu lagunu manasā
ammatō sakhyamu enni janmala
puṇyapalamō manasā
ammanu nīlō pratiṣṭhiñcukoni
amṛtapadam cēru manasā. . .

If you become Mother's servant, all your actions become the divine Mother's work, O mind! Intimacy with the divine Mother is the result of many meritorious deeds performed in previous births. By firmly establishing the divine Mother within, reach the abode of eternal bliss, O mind!

Navilu gariya (Kannada)

navilu gariya nayanada kṛṣṇa
nīlavarna navilina kṛṣṇa

Peacock feather eyed Krishna, blue colored peacock Krishna,

pancamadā kōgile kṛṣṇa ōdi bārō

Melodious nightingale Krishna, come running!

nagutaliruva navanīta kṛṣṇa
bāyoḷage brahmāṇḍa kṛṣṇa
beṭṭesāku beṭṭakke kṛṣṇa ōḍi bārō

Ever smiling butter Krishna, You show the entire universe in Your mouth. Come running Krishna, with Your finger that can lift the hill!

hare kṛṣṇa hare kṛṣṇa
hare kṛṣṇa hare kṛṣṇa

Chant the name of Krishna!

nātyavāḍe kāḷinganiruva
pavaḍisalu śeṣane baruva

haktikaḍale kṣīrasāgara ōḍi bārō

Kalinga is here for You to dance on, Sesha comes for You to lie on, come running from the milky ocean sea of devotion.

hokkaḷalli brahmane banda
brahmana amma nīnēnā
dēvakī yaṣodeyā muddu maga nīnā

Brahma himself came from Your belly, aren't You Brahma's mother? Aren't You the loving son of Devaki and Yashoda?

ādi antya ananta krṣna
āladeleya tēluva krṣna
ninna koḷalē satchidānanda viṭhala kṛṣṇa

You are the beginning, the end, and the eternal Krishna; You are the one floating on the banyan leaf, Your flute is truth, consciousness & bliss, O Vittala Krishna.

Neñcakaṁ ventiṭunnu (Malayalam)

neñcakaṁ ventiṭunnu - ammē
sañcitapāpa-tāpāl
vañcitanāyiṭunnu - innu
pañcēndriyaṅgaḷāl ñān

Mother, my heart is burning with the heat of accumulated sins. I am being betrayed by my five sense organs.

attal koṇḍende cittam - ēre
taptamāy nīriṭunnu
itramēl tāṅguvānāy - illa
kelppenikkantarangē

My heart is being seared with sorrow- I have no strength to withstand such pain.

en tāpaminnakattān – kṛpā-
sindhuvām nin hṛdantē
pontiṭēṇam-uṭanē – kṛpā-
vantiramālayonnu

To end my burning sorrow, a pure wave of kindness must arise from the ocean of compassion that You are.

Nēnu yavaranu (Telugu)

yā devī sarva bhuteśu
mātṛ rūpeṇa samsthita
namastasyai namastasyai
namastasyai namo namaḥ

Salutations to the supreme Goddess, who manifests Herself in all beings as the divine Mother.

nēnu yavaranu nēnu yavaranamma
nēnu nīvukākka inkevaranamma
inkevaranamma inke varanu amma

Who am I? Who am I, O Mother? "I am You!" "I am You!" Who else can I be other than You?

aham ityēva vibhāvayē mahēśīm

O supreme Empress, let me meditate on the thought, "I am nothing other than You."

nī caitanya kaṭalilōni
nīṭibuḍakanamma
nī divya tējasulōni cinnikiraṇam amma
nīvanē viśvavṛkṣapu cikuruṭākkunamma
nī sṛṣṭi hāramulōni maṇipūsanamma

O Mother, I am a tiny bubble in the infinite ocean of consciousness called 'You.' O Mother, I am a minute ray of light issuing from Your divine glow of brilliance. O Mother, I am a tender leaf on the all-pervading tree of the universe called 'You.' O Mother, I am a tiny pearl strung on the garland of creation called 'You.'

rāgadvēṣa mūlaku baddhuṭanaikinamma
śarīra sukha mūlaku vasuḍanaitinamma
māyaku lōpaḍi nīnu nivēnani
maracikinamma amṛtānandamē
na svarūpa mūkadamma

O Mother, I have become imprisoned by my likes and dislikes. Mother, I have succumbed to bodily comforts. Mother, captivated by illusion, I have forgotten that 'I am You.' O Mother, is not my real essence and form that of eternal bliss?

Nīla-kamala (Telugu)

nīla-kamala pādāla centana
oka tāmara mogganu nēnu
pūrtigā vikasiñci prēma
parimaḷamē prasarimpa
karuṇimpavē kṛpa varṣimpavē
ammā karuṇimpavē kṛpa varṣimpavē

I am a like a lotus bud at Your blue lotus feet. That I may fully blossom and spread the fragrance of love, shower Your grace, O Mother!

remma-remmalalō arpiñcetanu
janma-janmalā vāsanalu
okkō remmanē suguṇamugā mārci
śānti suvāsana vedajalla
karuṇimpavē kṛpa varṣimpavē
ammā karuṇimpavē kṛpa varṣimpavē

With every petal, I offer my negative tendencies accumulated through many births. To change each petal into a good quality and spread the fragrance of peace, shower Your grace, O Mother!

kṣaṇikamē ī jīvitam bhava
tāpamutō vaḍalenu vēvēgam
ī konta samayam nī pādāla nilici
nija ānandamē vyāpimpa
karuṇimpavē kṛpa varṣimpavē
ammā karuṇimpavē kṛpa varṣimpavē

The life is momentary, and may dry up soon due to the heat of samsara (world). That I may stay at Your feet for this short time and spread the joy of pure bliss, O Mother, shower Your grace!

Nīlakkadamba (Malayalam)

nīlakkadambamarachōṭṭil ninnu
koṇḍōṭakkuzhalu viḷichatārō?
kaṇṇā ennu viḷicha nēram – ponnin
kālchilambocha kēḷppichatārō?

Who is that standing below the blue kadamba tree and playing the flute? When I called out "Kanna!", who was it that made me hear the tinkling of golden anklets?

nīḷum niśatannariku patti kaṇṇa
nōṭi vanneṅgoṭṭu maṇḍi vīṇḍum?
ariyāmenikkende ponnukaṇṇā. . . ninne
uḷḷattil pēri naṭannīṭuvān

Night is progressing. Where did Krishna run off to yet again? O my darling Krishna, though You've run away, I know how to carry You in my heart!

rāvinu nīlimayērunnu vīṇḍumā
kilukilā ciriyum muzhaṅgiṭunnu

eviṭeyennōrāte ninnu rādha. . . mizhi
ttumbināl kāṭṭikkoṭuttambiḷi

The darkness of the night is deepening, but hark, the sounds of laughter ring out again. Radha stood, not knowing where the laughter was coming from. Ah, but the moonlight revealed where He was!

cārutta veṇmullavallitan pūvukaḷ
rāvin maṭiye alankarikkē
kaṇṇande tēnutta puñciri kaṇḍukaṇḍā-
nandamagnayāy ninnu rādha

The beautiful white jasmine flowers adorn the lap of the night. Gazing again and again at Krishna's nectarous smile, Radha became transfixed in rapturous bliss.

Nī tanda solleṭuttu (Tamil)

nī tanda solleṭuttu nān pāṭinēn
nilaiyaṭṭra vāzhvirkku poruḷ tēṭinēn
nān enṭrum nī enṭrum ēn pārppadō
nān unnil karaindiṭa nāḷ pārppadō

I sang with the words You gave me; I searched for the meaning of this illusory life. I think that You and I are separate; should I be thinking of the day when I will merge in You?

yandiramāy nānum iyankīṭinum
iyakkiṭum śaktiyinṭri iyakkamuṇḍō
seyalgaḷai nānum seydīṭinum
seyalpaṭum valimai unadanṭrō

Though I move around like a machine, I should know that even a machine needs power to operate. Though I perform many actions, I should realize that the power to act comes only from You.

viralkūṭa nīyinṭri asainditumō
vīṇāy ārpparittal maṭamaiyanṭrō
ulakattin asaivellām unadanṭrō
umaiyaval un pādam śaraṇamanṭrō

We criticize our karmas because of our foolishness. Even a finger will not move without You. All of the activity in this world is Yours alone. Mother Uma, I seek refuge at Your feet!

Okka maṇi (Telugu)

okka maṇi kānuka ivvālani
vedikiti aṇuvaṇuvuna dhariṇī
ammā ninu miñcina maṇi lēdani
telusukoṇṭini sarvēśvarī

I searched the whole world to find a suitable present for Mother only to realize that there was nothing worthy of Mother.

ō mutyam bahumati ivvālani
ammā sōdhinciti mottam kaḍalini
nī nētrālanu miñci mutyālu lēvani
grahiñciti satyam mātā bhavānī

I trawled the whole ocean to find a pearl for Mother. But the truth is that there is nothing more lustrous than Mother's eyes.

tallī tīyani tēnelu tēvālani
tirigiti palu kōnalu kānalani
ā vanālu telipē alasina nanu gani
amma palukula kannā lēvani

I looked here and there for honey that I could give Mother. When I became exhausted, the forest said, "There is nothing sweeter than Mother's words."

nī mungiṭa velugu nimpālani
ā candruni anduku tēvālani

śaśi telipē tanu pasi bāluḍani
amma mundu velavela bōyēdānani

I decided to bring down the moon to illuminate Mother's house. But the moon sighed that it was a mere child and that it would pale before Mother's luster.

Om mangalam (Sanskrit)

om mangalam
omkara mangalam
om namah śivaya
śri gurave mangalam

Om is auspicious, the syllable Om is auspicious. Salutations to Shiva. Sri Guru is auspicious.

na-mangalam
nakara mangalam
nada bindu kalātita
gurave mangalam

Na is auspicious, the syllable Na is auspicious. The Guru who is beyond sound and all form is auspicious.

ma mangalam
makara mangalam
maya moha bandha rahita
gurave mangalam

Ma is auspicious. The syllable Ma is auspicious. The Guru who is beyond maya and all attachment is auspicious.

śi mangalam
śikāra mangalam
śiva viṣṇu brahma rūpa
guravē mangalam

Shi is auspicious. The syllable Shi is auspicious. The Guru, who is in the form of the Trinity - Shiva, Vishnu, Brahma - is auspicious.

vā – mangalam
vakāra mangalam
vāda veda jñāna dīpa
gurave mangalam

Va is auspicious. The syllable Va is auspicious. The Guru who is the light of knowledge, of all debate and learning, is auspicious.

yā – mangalam
yakāra mangalam
yāga yoga sākṣibhāva
gurave mangalam

Ya is auspicious. The syllable Ya is auspicious. The Guru, who is witness to all action and sadhana is auspicious.

amba mangalam
jagadamba mangalam
annapurne śankarāngi
śakti mangalam

Mother is auspicious. The Mother of the world is auspicious. She is the granter of food, she is the better-half of Shiva, she is Shakti, and she is auspicious.

amba mangalam
jagadamba mangalam
mahalakshmi śaradambe
kali mangalam

Mother is auspicious. The Mother of the world is auspicious. She is Mahalakshmi, Goddess of Prosperity. She is Sharadamba, Goddess of Learning. She is Kali, Goddess of Dissolution.

amba mangalam

jagadamba mangalam
brahma rupe viśva rupe
devi mangalam

Mother is auspicious. The Mother of the world is auspicious. She is the form of ultimate Brahman, She is the form of the universe. She is Devi, she is auspicious.

Om śakti (Tamil)

om śakti om śakti om – parāśakti
om śakti om śakti om
om śakti om śakti om – parāśakti
ādi parāśakti om

Obeisance to the supreme power of the universe. Obeisance to the primordial energy of the universe.

ammā nān unnai marandālum, tāyē nī ennai marappāyō
kattrariyā uḷḷam tanai kaḷvanaippōl māttrinēn
pattrukaḷāl pāsamgaḷāl pāṭham kattruttērinēn
tīmaiyaitterindiuntum tīvinayāl keṭṭēn
nanmai ena arindum arukē pōnatillai

O Mother, even if we forget You, will You forget us? I've secretly tainted my pure and pristine heart. As a result of attachments and bonds, I have learned many lessons. Even though I knew it was bad, I did what was wrong. Even though I knew what was good, I did not act, and thus sullied my character.

nān ariyātennuḷḷē pukundu naṭattukirāy
nān arindēn ena ninaittāl pāṭāyppaṭuttukirāy
meypporuḷām dēvi unnai arivatu eḷitō
poyyulakam tannil ennai pōkaviṭātē

Without my knowing it, You steal into my heart and operate from within. If I think I know You, You crush my ego. Is it easy to fathom You, O Goddess, embodiment of truth? Please do not let me loose in the world of falsehood.

Ō naruḍā (Telugu)

ō naruḍā! ō naruḍā! nīvē śivuḍu rā
adi nīvē! adi nīvē! ani telusukō rā
sōham śivōham

O mortal being! You are Shiva! (eternal auspiciousness) Please know this truth - You are That! I am That, I am Shiva!

nīvu janiyiñcitivi śivuni nuṇḍi rā
nīvu layincedavu śivamu nandē rā
antā śivamaitē! nīvē śivu ḍaitē
nī rākapōkalu echaṭiki rā

Rise above the concepts of birth and death and know that You are Shiva - eternal consciousness and bliss.

jagamantayu śiva caitanya sāgaramē rā
nēḍu nīvokkacinna nīṭi buḍaga rā
rēpu nīvokkapedda alavuduvu rā
ī nāma rūpālu śiva kaṭalē rā

The whole universe is nothing but the ocean of the Shiva consciousness. Today You may be a little bubble on the ocean of consciousness. Tomorrow You may become a mighty wave in that ocean; rise above the concepts of name and form and know that You are Shiva.

nēnanu bhāvamutō sṛṣṭi nijamu nīku rā
ābhāvamē toligitē sṛṣṭi māyamagunu rā
jīvitacitrālu merisē venḍitera nīvu rā
nīvennaṭu mārppu candani śivānandamu rā

When the feeling of 'I' appears, this world seems real. It vanishes when the feeling of 'I' disappears. You are like a beautiful silver screen, where many life forms shine and disappear. Know that You are eternal, unchanging auspiciousness and bliss- Shiva.

sōham śivōham

I am That, I am Shiva!

Only love (English)

may the light of unity
dawn in our minds
every thought of understanding
opens our hearts

only love is our guiding light
only love can heal and unite
may the walls of separation
vanish in our love

every word of kindness
brightens up the dark
may forgiveness and compassion
grow in all we do
every deed of goodness
leads the way to peace

only love... is our light, only love... can unite
only love... shines so bright
only love can end this night

Ōrmmayil ninnurnnu (Malayalam)

ōrmmayil ninnurnnu vīṇoru kāvyaśīlil ñān ende
jīvitatte tōṇiyākki yātra-ceyyunnu!
kāttunilpillārum-ennuṭe yānapātratte ende
tōṇiyil ñān mātramāyi yātra-ceyyunnu!

I make my life a boat and journey along the flowing verse that seeps out of my memory. No one waits for me; I travel in my boat all alone.

ātma-nombaram āraarivū nīyorāḷenyē snēho-
dāraśīle! nīlavānam pōle-ninnuḷḷam
mānasappon tēril ñān-onnānayichōṭṭe ammē
nēraminnum ēreyāy nī āgamikkille?

O One who showers generous love! Who other than You knows the sorrows of my mind? Your heart is like the vast blue sky. Let me welcome You in the golden chariot of my mind. Mother, it is getting late. Will You not come?

uḷḷil ārdratayuḷḷa nīyennuḷḷu-kāṇille kaṇḍāl
uḷḷamīvidhamentin-ammē ventunīrunnu?
eḷḷileṇṇakaṇakku nīyennuḷḷiluṇḍelum uḷḷāl
kaṇḍariññallāte yeṇganeyuḷḷumārunnu?

Soft-hearted One, can't You see my heart? If You have seen it, why does my heart still burn? Though You reside in my heart like the oil in a sesame seed, without seeing You, how will my mind change?

cāriṭārillen-manassin jālakaṇgaḷ ñān premo
dāragānālāpamāy nī āgamikkille?
māntaḷirtottinde mārddavamuḷḷorennūḷḷam ninde
kālaṭippon tāmarattēn pūvū tēṭunnu!

I am not closing the windows of my mind. Will You arrive as a song of love? My mind, as soft as tender mango shoots, searches for the nectar of Your golden lotus feet.

Oru nāḷamma (Tamil)

orunāḷamma sēyākavaruvāy
sirupiḷḷai nānuntan tāyākavēṇḍum
aritāna muttinai varavēttru nānum
narumalar tūvi ānandam koḷvēn

O Mother, won't You come to me as a child one day? I want to be mother to that divine child. I shall welcome that precious child by blissfully showering flowers on Her.

sīraṭṭi pārāṭṭi muttamiṭuvēn
mañcaḷpūsi piñcumēni nīrāṭṭuvēn
piñcunakku paṭṭuṭutti talaivāri pūsūṭṭuvēn
kanakamaṇi kolusaṇintu kaivaḷaikaḷ pūṭṭuvēn

I shall hug, cuddle and kiss Her. I shall bathe Her cherubic body in turmeric powder. I shall clad the darling with silk clothes, comb Her hair and adorn it with flowers, and put on anklets and bangles.

kaṇmaṇikku maitīṭṭi sāntupoṭṭu vaittiṭuvēn
vairakkal mūkkutti nāsikayilē pūṭṭiṭuvēn
sinnañciru iṭayinilē oḍyāṇam aṇivippēn
minnum ponmakuṭam sirasinilē sūṭṭuvēn

I shall apply collyrium to Her eyes and sandal paste on Her forehead, and put on a diamond nose-ring on Her nose, a girdle around Her tiny waist, and a glittering crown on Her head.

puttanputu pūtoṭuttu maṇimārbil sūṭṭuvēn
muttazhaki sirippinilē ennai marappēn
nilavaikāṭṭi katai pēsi maṭiyamartti sōrūṭṭuvēn
toḷile tūnkavaittu tālāṭṭu pāṭiṭuvēn

I shall weave a fresh garland and place it around Her bejeweled neck. I shall forget myself in Her enchanting smile. I shall put Her in my lap and feed Her, while telling Her stories, pointing to the moon. Placing Her on my shoulder, I shall sing lullabies to Her.

anbē amutē ārārirārō, tāyē tankamē tālēlēlō . . .

Lullaby to You, O darling, embodiment of immortality! Lullaby to You, beloved Mother!

Orunāḷum piriyātta (Kannada version)

endendu ninagāgi hambalisi alede
huḍukāḍa deḍeyilla – amma
janmāntarakū jagadambe bēkentu
huḍukāḍa deḍeyilla – halajanma

gatigeṭṭa jīvitava nōḍu – enna
vijaya pratīkṣe baraḍāgide
taragele tharadali paravaśaḷāgi nā
dikkeṭṭu alediruvē – dāri
beḷakkāgi nī tōri bā

durmada ennali heḍe ettitō – ayyō
gati tappi naḍede durvidhiyindali
hagaliruḷēnnade hṛdayata ṭākadi
amṛtamaḷē surisū – amma
puḷaka rōmāncana tā

Oru piṭi cāramāy (Malayalam)

oru piṭi cāramāy maṇṇōṭu cērunna
manujā nī alayunnateviṭē ?
oru ceru nīrpōḷa pōle ī jīvitam
manujā nī ariyuvatentē ?
viruvilāy ozhiyunna ī lōka vēdiyil

vāzhvitu nāṭakamallē ?
verum śōkānta nāṭakamallē ?

O man, you will ultimately become a handful of ashes and merge with the soil. Where are you wandering? This life is like a tiny bubble. What do you really know? In this ever changing world, isn't our existence merely a drama? Doesn't this drama end in tragedy?

oru vākku connāl ozhiyēṇḍa gēham
oru nāḷil tannuṭētāmō ?
oru nōkkil onnō ariyunna lōkam
ozhiyunna kāzhchayatalle ?
nāḷeyennōtuvān oru pozhutuṇḍō ?
kaimutal innatu mātram -
ōrttāl pōyppōya kālam anantam

Will this body ever really be ours? We will have to relinquish it at a single word from the Lord of death. The world that we see in a single glance, isn't it just a fleeting image? Is there any value in saying 'tomorrow'? Only the present moment is in our hands. If we think about it, the time we have lost is infinite.

vasanaṅgaḷ pōle veṭiyunnu janmam
valayita mōhāndhakāram
pāritilennum pāloḷitūkum
paramātma tattvamē nityam
oru noṭi ozhiyāte ōraṇamuḷḷattil
ā mātṛ pādaṅgaḷ nityam
vāzhvin amṛtattvam ariyunna satyam

Just as we change clothes, we go through numerous births, caught up in the darkness of desires. All that is permanent is the Paramatman, the supreme self, that sheds light throughout creation. Without wasting a second, we should forever hold on tightly to the divine Mother's feet in our heart, for that is the eternal principle of life.

Oru soṭṭu kaṇṇīrāl (Tamil)

oru soṭṭu kaṇṇīrāl manakkovil abhishēkam
nibandhanaikaḷ illayē
noṭiyēnum dinamun manatil nān iruntāl
viṇveḷiyum toṭuvēn

With one drop of my tears, the ceremonial abhishekam is happening in the temple of my mind. There is no set rule there to do this kind of abhishekam. If You remember me even for just one second every day, from here I will reach and touch the sky!

marakkindra pōtunnai vāṭiya ilaipōl
kīzhē utirkindrēn
ninaikkindra pōtu azhutālum enkō
ārutal perukindrēn

Whenever I forget You I simply fall like a withering leaf. On the contrary whenever I remember You, though I cry at least in crying I find some consolation.

virikindra pūmukham ponnāna bhāṣaikaḷ
sintāmal nindriṭumō
ārātu neñcam ārātu anbē
tannuḷḷē tavikkindrēn

Here after will the blossoming flower-like face of Yours stop pouring forth golden words? I cannot bear it, my dear, I cannot bear it anymore. Restlessness is growing within.

Paccamalai pavaḷamalai (Tamil)

paccamalai pavaḷamalai paccamalai pavaḷamalai

O Murugan, who dwells in places such as the hills Pacca Malai and Pavala Malai.

paccamalai pavaḷamalai pazhaṇimalai marutamalai

tankamalai taṇikaimalai enkamalai svāmimalai
vāpatiyē bhupatiyē vandemmai kāpatiyē
mālmarugā vēl murugā bhaktarkurai tīr-murugā

O Murugan, who dwells in the hills Pazhani Malai and Maruta Malai. O Murugan, who abides in the hills Tanka Malai, Tanikai Malai, Enka Malai, and Swami Malai. Nephew of Lord Vishnu, bearer of the spear, deign to redeem us, Your devotees, of our shortcomings!

kumaranē guruparanē kuṭṭrankaḷai kaḷaipavanē
saravaṇanē ṣaṇmukhanē sankarī umaibālakanē
kandaiyyā suppaiyyā cinnaiyyā murugaiyyā
tāḷ pōṭri vēl pōṭri dēvēsēval pōṭri

O Kumara, the Guru, who forgives the mistakes of devotees, You are the son of Parvati. O Murugan, known also as Saravana, Sanmukha, Skanda, and Subramanya! Prostrations to Your holy feet, spear and emblem.

sandanam sandanam kandanukku vandanam
kāvaṭi kāvaṭi kandan tiruccevaṭi
āṭivā āṭivā anpōḍu āṭivā
tēṭivā ōṭivā muruganai ni naṭivā

Smeared with sandal-paste and carrying the kavati, (the ornamental arched pole) we prostrate at Your sacred feet. O Lord Muruga, come dancing lovingly before us. We seek refuge in You.

arōharā arōharā kandanukku arōharā
arōharā arōharā muruganukku arōharā
arōharā arōharā kumaranukku arōharā
arōharā arōharā bālanukku arōharā
arōharā arōharā kandanukku arōharā

Hail Skanda, Muruga, Kumara, Bala!

Pādāravindakē (Kannada)

pādāravindakē namipēśāradē mātē

I bow down to Your lotus feet O Mother Sharada (Goddess of knowledge).

saṅgītalōlini sakala vidyādātē
viṣṇusahōdari varadē vāgīśvari

Lover of music, bestower of all knowledge, sister of Vishnu, Goddess of speech!

śvētāmbaradharē śāśvatē śubhadē
caturvēda caturē vīṇāpāṇi
nārada janani nādabrahmāṇi
nāmapārāyaṇāmṛta karuṇisammā...
nāmapārāyaṇāmṛta karuṇisammā...

You are adorned in white, O eternal auspicious One. Wise one, You know of the four Vedas, and play the veena. Mother of Narada (ancient immortal sage), Goddess of sound, kindly grant us the grace to incessantly chant Your names.

kāruṇyasindhuvē paripūrṇṇa bandhuvē
śraddhēbhaktiya nīḍi paripālisammā
mamakāra naśisi vairāgya mūḍisi
pariśuddha jñānava nīḍu nī namagē
pariśuddha jñānava nīḍu nī namagē

Ocean of compassion, complete, eternal friend. Please destroy our attachments, let detachment and renunciation dawn in us. This way, bestow on us pure knowledge.

saṅgītalōlini sakala vidyādātē
viṣṇusahōdari varadē vāgīśvari

Lover of music, bestower of all knowledge, sister of Vishnu, Goddess of speech!

Pāṇḍuranga nām gyā (Marathi)

pāṇḍuranga nām gyā hoyī samādhān
dhyān je sundar dhyān manohar
pītāmbar śobhe pāṇī kaṭṭīvar
rang jo sāvḷā chāyā deyī
lekarās āss lāge jāvaḷ gheyī

Call out to Lord Panduranga from your heart and feel peace within. Panduranga, the object of my meditation, is indeed beautiful. Meditating on Him has helped me win over my mind. He wears a yellow robe around his waist, and has a complexion like that of dusk.

māi ji viṭṭāyī dūsarī rakhmāyī
paṇḍarapurā lābhlī atī puṇyāyi
galā ghāluni tuḷasī mālā
viṭṭāyī sād ghālī sakaḷā

Pandharapura is blessed with the presence of Lord Vittala and his consort Rukhmani. He wears a tulasi garland around His neck, indicating that he is detached towards the riches of royalty. He has become dear to everybody.

manī vase viṭṭāyī viṭṭāyī nī kṛṣṇāyī
dāṭṭale nām japu paṇḍurang nirantara
ek dhyān ek dhyās
pāṇḍurang pāṇḍurang pāṇḍurang

Vittala, who is Krishna, resides in our hearts; we chant the name of Panduranga constantly. One meditation, one thought: Panduranga.

pāṇḍurang pāṇḍurang pāṇḍurang pāṇḍurang
viṭṭala viṭṭala viṭṭala
viṭṭala viṭṭala viṭṭala

Panipaṭarnda malaiyin (Tamil)

panipaṭarnda malaiyin mīdu uruvamānavan
amaradīpamāy viḷankum amaranānavan
mēghankaḷ tālāṭṭum malaiyumānavan
dāhankaḷ taṇittiṭum gankaiyānavan

O Lord, You have taken the form of ice on the holy mountain Amarnath. You have taken the form of the ever-burning lamp of mount Amarnath. There, even the clouds are singing lullabies to You, You who embodies the form of the mountain. You quench the thirst of knowledge just as the Ganges quenches the thirst of people.

ēri varum makkaḷ tam kuraikaḷ tīrppavan
idayamozhikaḷ tannai kēṭṭu āśi tarubavan
uruvamāki aruvamāki tōttram tarubavan
paruvam tōrum kāṭci tantu bhakti tarubavan

You take care of the difficulties of devotees who come to You with intense faith. You hear their heartfelt prayers and bless them. O formless One, You appear to the devotees in form to enhance their devotion.

umaiyannai uḷḷam kavar kaḷvanānavan
sumaiyumāna vinaikaḷ nīkki mukti tarubavan
pāvam tannai pōkkiṭum punitavaṭivinan
tāpam tannai tīrttiṭum tāyumānavan

You're the One who has captured the mind of Goddess Uma, O Lord, You take care of those who unburden their heavy heart and take refuge in You. You rid them of their sins and difficulties, making them pure, just like a mother does for her child.

om namaḥ śivāya

Salutations to Lord Shiva!

Parayuvānāvatilla (Malayalam)

parayuvān āvatillammē neñcil
urayunna paritāpa pūram
nirayunna mizhikaḷil paṭarunna śōkam onnu
ariyuvān āvatillennō?

O Mother, I am unable to express the pain that has lodged itself in my heart. Can You not understand this from my wet eyes?

kanalinde tāpatte vellunnorīcuṭu
neṭuvīrppil eriyunnu janmam
karuṇatan kaṇamonnu karutiyīyaṭiyannu
coriyunna dinamennucērum?

The scorching heat of my sighs, hotter than embers, is burning my life. I am desperately waiting for the day when You will shower Your compassionate grace upon me.

iniyende manavīṇamīṭṭiṭuvān amma
tazhuki talōṭukilokkum
arutātta rāgaṅgaḷ ariyāte atilūrnnatu
aṭiyande pizhayonnu mātram

Only the caresses of Your touch can awaken music from the strings of my idle mind. It is my fault that, in the past, some dissonant notes issued from it.

taḷarukayilliniyonnukoṇḍum tava
karuṇāmśu avalambamennum
saphalamī yātrayum saphalamī janmavum
aviṭunnu arikattaṇaññāl

Having taken refuge in the light of Your compassion, I will not give up hope hereafter. The journey of my life will become fruitful when You remain with me evermore.

Parinamamamiyallatta (Kannada version)

pariṇāma villada paramēśvari - ena
paritāpa ninagē tiḷidillavē?
madanārī paramēśa patiyallave - ena
manadā iruḷannu kaḷeyamma nī

iruḷāgi kaḷēdu hagalallave - ena
iruḷantha hṛdayanina garivillave?
daḷavellā uduridā hūvādene?
daye tōralendu nī baralāreyā?

kirubaḷḷiga abhaya hem-maravallave? amma
kirumakkaḷ-abhilāṣe nīnallave?
nānēnu māḍali hēḷambikē
ninnalli ondāga bēkambikē

baraḍāda marubhuvil alediruvē nā - ammā
baralāradāgide nina sanihakke
nīḍamma enagendu dayadintali
nina pādadāśraya sarvveśvari

Pari pari (Telugu)

pari pari vidhamula tirigēṭi manasu
ūhala uyyālai ūgēṭi manasu

Many, many, are the ways for the wandering mind. A cradle of imaginative thoughts is this swinging mind.

oka pari bhakti tō cintiñcē manasu
maru pari rakti tō parigiḍē manasu
inkō paribhuktikai pākkulāḍē manasu
bahupari ceñcalamai urikēṭi manasu

One moment, it contemplates with the mood of devotion. Next moment, it runs in thirst for amusement. Another moment, it craves for sumptuous food. In many ways, it wavers, the ever oscillating mind!

oka pari gānamulō paravaśiñcē manasu
maru pari viṣayamulō vihariñcē manasu
inkō pari bandhamulō munugeṭṭi manasu
bahupari ahamulō ciketṭi manasu

One instance, it delights in the sweetness of melodious songs. Next instance, it detours into the worldliness. At another instance, it gets drowned in the bondage of relations. In many instances, it gets caught in the clutches of ego.

japa tapa dhyānamutō sthiramagu manasu
bahukāla sādhanatō nilicēṭṭi manasu
ammanu prēmiñci śuddhamayyē manasu
satguru śaraṇamutō tariñcē manasu

By repetition of holy names, austerity and meditation, the mind becomes calm; by making consistent effort for a long time, it becomes stable. By seeking Mother and loving Her, the mind becomes purified. By surrendering to the Guru, the mind becomes elevated and perfected.

Paṭṭave pādamu (Telugu)

paṭṭave pādamu gaṭṭigā manasā
paṭṭunu viḍuvaka niluvave manasā

O mind, hold onto Her feet with all your strength, stay there and don't let go.

penumāyala tera kamminagāni
palumārlu guri tappinagāni
suḍigālulu celarēgina gāni
bhavasāgaramuna munigina gāni

Although the dark heavy veils of maya surround you, although we may so often miss the goal, although tornadoes rage around you, even if you drown in the ocean of this world, hold on to Her feet.

śaraṇāgatulanu kāceḍi pādamu
bhaktajanulanu brēceṭi pādamu
nammina biḍḍala sākeḍi pādamu
viśva rūpamuna veligeḍi pādamu

Those feet protect whoever surrenders to You; they grace those who are devoted to You and nourish the children who believe in you. Those feet illumine the creation, showing it to be a manifestation of the cosmic form.

sṛṣṭiki mūlamu ā mṛdupādamu
hariharabrahmalu koliceṭi pādamu
muggurammalaku mūlapu pādamu
amṛtapadamu gamyamu pādamu

Those sweet feet are the primal cause of creation. They are worshipped by the trinity, and are the base of the three mothers. Those feet are the goal of the path to immortality.

Ponnammā en ammā (Tamil)

ammā undan tāy pāsam, dēsam ellām oḷi vīsum
rōjā malarin vāsam, undan varavai pēsum

Mother, the light of Your maternal affection is all-pervading. The fragrance of roses heralds Your arrival.

ponnammā en ammā sellammā nī ammā
pozhutellām unnōṭu nān irukkalāmā

O darling Mother, my Mother, may I spend my free time in Your presence?

kaivaḷaikaḷ kulunga kāl salangai siṇunga
suttri suttri azhakāy nī naṭanam āḍumpōdu

kaṇkuḷira un ezhilai nān rasikkalāmā?
mālaippozhutil marattadi nizhalil
manankavarum nal kataikaḷ nī uraikkum pōdu
kātinikka un mozhikaḷ nān kēṭkalāmā?

As Your bangles jangle and anklets clink while You dance enchantingly in circles, may I revel in Your refreshingly beautiful form? At night, in the shade of a tree, as You narrate captivating stories, may I listen to Your words, which are like music to the ear?

mazhalayai tūkki maḍiyinil amartti
makizhvuḍan un viralāl sōru ūṭṭumpōdu
nāvinikka un kaiyāl amudarundalāmā?
nakṣattira pandal kīzh nilavai nōkki nī
bhaktiyuḍan manamuruki pāṭal pāṭum pōdu
un bhakti mazhayil nān mey silirkkalāmā?

As You carry a child, place him in Your lap, and feed him, may I partake of the elixir from Your hand? Under the canopy of the starry sky, as You gaze at the moon and sing devotional songs that melt the heart, may I become ecstatically drenched in that rain of devotion?

Ponnūñcal āṭāyō (Tamil)

ponnūñcal āṭāyō ennammā
ponmēni siridē sāyndu koḷḷa

Mother, won't You come lean on the golden swing for awhile to play?

eṇṇattin ōṭṭamum aṭankiṭavē
untiru malaraṭi sērndiṭavē
eṇṇamatil nī enṭrum niraindiṭavē
unpāda sēvai nittam seytiṭavē

To calm my thoughts, to bless me, that I may merge in Your holy feet. To fill my mind forever with thoughts of You, to bless me to serve Your holy feet forever.

uḷḷattin kavalaikaḷ kaḷainditavē
uṇmaiyenum narpayir vidaittiṭavē
uḷḷamatum meypporuḷai uṇarndiṭavē
uṇmaiyāga vanda tāyum nīyallavō

To rid me of my mental agonies, to sow the seed of truth in my mind, to help my mind realize the Truth. Aren't You the real Mother who has come to us?

āṭāyō ennammā ponnūñcal āṭāyō

Will You not play, Mother? Will You not play on the golden swing?

Prabhū pyār kī (Hindi)

prabhū pyār kī jyot jalāvo
viṣayan kī citā sajāvo

Light the lamp of God's love, set the pyre of your desires.

mṛg tṛṣṇā mē jīvan khoyā
sach kā dhan barsāvo

You have lost your life in animal desires. Shower the riches of truth!

man sankalp vikalp mē uljhā
icchā prabal banāvo

The mind is confused between options and decisions. Make your will strong.

thak hārā me khel khilone
ab tum hiya bas jāvo

I'm tired and defeated, playing with these toys. At least now come and live in my heart.

mē nirbal nisāhay paḍā hum
bhuj mē āp uṭhāvo

I'm lying helpless and weak, take me in Your arms.

rūpo se tum man bharmātte
saty-rūp dikhalāvo

With Your different forms, You plunge my mind in illusion. Show me Your true form!

Prāṇeśvarī (Malayalam)

prāṇeśvarī prāṇatantriyil minnunnu
prēmāśrubindukkaḷ innanēkam
bhaktānuvarttinī! nityānuraktan
ninakkāy koruttiṭām tārahāram ninakkāy
koruttiṭām tārahāram

O Goddess who is my very life, the abundant teardrops of my love for You are flowing and sparkling from the rhythmic chords of life. Eternally in love with You, I shall weave You a garland of stars.

nirayunnu nayanam virakoḷvū kaṇṭham
ariyāte viṭarunnu hṛdayapatmam
vinayārdra cittam nukarum saharṣam
kanivārnnu nī tūkum amṛtavarṣam
kanivārnnu nī tūkum amṛtavarṣam

My eyes are brimming with tears, my voice is quavering, and the lotus of my heart is blossoming without my knowing. Melted by humility, my heart ecstatically sips the ambrosial nectar You shower compassionately.

uttunga saubhāgyajālaṅgaḷillātta
nissāra putranāṇennākilum
sundarī! nin divya lāvaṇyapūrattil
nirllīnamen hṛttil nityōtsavam
nirllīnamen hṛttil nityōtsavam

Though I am an insignificant son who is not graced by the noblest fortunes, I feel an eternal celebration in my heart. Beautiful one, my heart has merged in the fullness of Your beauty.

cintakkagamyayām cinmayarūpiṇī
citkalē saccidānandamūrttē
cintāmaṇisthitē nin sparśamēttorī
dhanyamām janmam ānandasāndram
dhanyamām janmam ānandasāndram

Embodiment of truth, knowledge and bliss, O Goddess of divine knowledge whom the intellect cannot apprehend, You reside in the chintamani (divine wish-fulfilling gem). Sanctified by Your touch, my life has become blessed and is steeped in bliss.

Prēma sāgara (Kannada)

prēma sāgara ninna mānasa sarōvarā
manassina cintēya nīgisuva sangītā
hṛdaya spandisuva mauna sandēśā
samarppisuvē nanna ī jīvitavu ninnalli

The lake of Your mind is like an ocean of love, like a gentle music soothing the turbulences of the mind. Your silent messages touch the heart; I offer my life to You.

ēkāntanāgi andhakāradalli cintisalu
ninna divya amṛtasāgara sēridē
amṛtatva sēvisalu hṛdaya spandisitu
ninna divya caraṇavē duḥkha nivāraṇavu

I was wandering lonely in deep ignorance- I came across Your divine, immortal ocean. My heart was touched, hearing Your immortal teachings. Your holy feet are the only cure for all misery.

ō ānanda sāgarā ninna svarūpā
dēhābimānā biḍisu dēvi mā
jñānajyōti beḷagu nanna cidrūpiṇī
mahāyōgini amṛtēśvarī ninna mahāsāgarā

Your real nature is divine bliss! Release me from the body-mind complex, O Goddess- light the lamp of knowledge, You whose form is consciousness absolute. You are the supreme yogini, eternal Goddess, in the ocean of love.

Puṭṭa kṛṣṇa (Kannada)

puṭṭa kṛṣṇa muddu kṛṣṇā
cikka kṛṣṇa celuva kṛṣṇā
puṭṭa kṛṣṇa muddu kṛṣṇā
cikka kṛṣṇa celuva kṛṣṇā

Baby Krishna, darling Krishna, little Krishna, handsome Krishna!

kṛṣṇa bandakṛṣṇa banda nōḍirō
bālakṛṣṇa bandā kaimugiyirō
ītanu sāmānyanalla teḷiyirō
ivana mahimē hāḍuvenu kēḷirō

Did you all see Krishna come? Young Krishna came with hands folded in prayer. Try to understand that he is not ordinary. I will sing his greatness. Please listen.

jananigē bāyalli jagavatōrisidā kṛṣṇā
śakaṭāsurapūtaniyara marddisidā kṛṣṇā
duṣṭa kāḷītuliyuta śikṣisidā kṛṣṇā
giriyetti gollara samrakṣisidā kṛṣṇā

Lord Krishna opened His mouth and showed His mother the entire Universe. He killed the demons Sakatasura and Putana. Krishna punished Kalinga, the poisonous snake, by dancing on its hood. Krishna lifted the Mount Govardhan and gave protection to all.

māva kamsa darppadhvamsa goḷisidanā kṛṣṇā
rāsalīlē gōpikaḷoṭan āṭinalita kṛṣṇā
mitrakucēlanigē accu meccāda kṛṣṇā
hogaḷalheccu padagaḷu siluganta kṛṣṇā

Krishna destroyed the ego of his evil uncle Kamsa. Krishna danced the 'rasa lila' along with the milk maidens. Lord Krishna, You are the favorite of Your friend Kuchela. We will glorify You until we reach Your lotus feet, O Krishna.

aguḷannadi yatigaḷudara tumbisidā kṛṣṇā
sabhayalidraupadi mānava kāppāṭida kṛṣṇā
gītōpadēśa nīḍi upakarisida kṛṣṇā
śaraṇara yōgakṣēma pālipa śrīkṛṣṇā

Lord Krishna uplifted the saints near the banks of the river Agula. Lord Krishna saved Draupadi from disgrace in front of the crowd. Lord Krishna gave us the Bhagavad Gita, the supreme treasure of knowledge. Lord Krishna takes care of the welfare of those who surrender to him wholeheartedly.

puṭṭa kṛṣṇa muddu kṛṣṇā cikka kṛṣṇa celuva kṛṣṇā
puṭṭa kṛṣṇa muddu kṛṣṇā cikka kṛṣṇa celuva kṛṣṇā

Baby Krishna, darling Krishna, little Krishna, handsome Krishna!

Queen of my heart (English)

queen of my heart, I have opened the door;
O when will you come to find me?

I await that day like the coming of the dawn,
when your eyes will meet mine finally.

though the night is drawing near,
your name is on my tongue
if it's my fate that we won't meet,
then in my heart I'll sing you this song.

light of the morning,
hope of the fallen,
goddess of all things,
please hear me calling.
durge mata, durge mata.

the night has come, still you're not here;
is there a hope for me?
of what worth is a life
that does not bring me to your feet?

Rādhā gōvinda (Telugu)

rādhā gōvinda kṛṣṇā kṛṣṇā
kēśava mādhava kṛṣṇā kṛṣṇā
kṛṣṇā kṛṣṇā kṛṣṇā kṛṣṇā

Victory to Radha, Govinda, Krishna!

vēdānta pāṭham mākēla kṛṣṇā
vēdāntam nīvaite kṛṣṇā kṛṣṇā
sṛṣṭi māyavādam mākēla kṛṣṇā
unnadi nīvē kādā kṛṣṇā kṛṣṇā

Krishna, in what way do Vedantic teachings help us? When You, the 'end of knowledge', are with us. Krishna, in what way do arguments about creation-illusion benefit us? When You, the all-pervading entity alone exist as creation.

mannu tinna nōru cūpu kṛṣṇā
viśvamē nīlō unnadi kṛṣṇā
jagamē nīlīlā svapnamu kṛṣṇā
brahmamu nīvē kādā kṛṣṇā kṛṣṇā

Please show us inside Your mouth with the mud You had eaten. What a wonder- the whole creation is within You Krishna! This ever changing world is Your cosmic play, a long dream. Krishna, You alone are the ultimate reality!

nī kathalē māku śravaṇamu kṛṣṇā
nī līlē mananamu kṛṣṇā kṛṣṇā
nī rūpamē māku dhyānamu kṛṣṇā
nī pai prēmanu ivvu kṛṣṇā kṛṣṇā

Listening to the telling of Your story *is* scripture. Krishna, Your playful acts are our scriptural contemplation. Krishna, Your wonderful form is our meditation. O Krishna! Please bless us with a mind that loves You forever.

Rādheśyām rādheśyām (Hindi)

rādheśyām rādheśyām
taṭpat hūn mem yād mem terī, nā jānū viśrām

Radheshyam, O Radheshyam. My mind is always pining for You, and it knows no rest!

bāvri kehke mīrā par sab haste hai
nirmohī ke jāl me phas gayī kahte hai
jānte hai vo phir bhī sab anjāne hai
rādheśyām rādheśyām

Everyone laughs at Mira and calls her a mad-woman. They tell her that she has fallen into a stone-hearted one's trap. They all know the truth, yet act as though they know nothing, O Radheshyam!

śyām binā man ekākī hai mele me
lāge nā man is duniyāke jamele me
kis se kahū me man kī vyathā koyi jāne nā
rādheśyām rādheśyām

Without Shyam, my mind feels lonely even in the crowd. Now I do not like the crowd of this world anymore. With whom can I share the pain of my heart? No one understands, O Radheshyam.

Rasikarāj (Hindi)

rasikarāj braja bhūmi bihārī
nanda dulāre natjanapāl
nīrajāvar nirmal nirupam
nityanirāmay bhajle
bhajle bhajle bhajle bhajle
bhaj bhaj bhajle bhajle bhajle

O Lord of all arts, wanderer of the land of Vrindavan, loving son of Nanda, friend of the gopas. Chant the name of the one with the lotus eyes, who is the pure self, beyond comparison, ever prevailing!

bhaj kṛṣṇa kṛṣṇa kṛṣṇa
bhaj bhakta citta cōrā
bhaj nityanṛtta lōlā
bhaj satya cit svarūpā
bhaj candana carchita
sundaradeha manōhara nandasuta

Chant the name of Krishna, the enchanting dancer who steals the hearts of the devotees! Chant the name of He who is the true self! Chant the name of He who is the talk-of-the-town, has a beautiful form, captivates the mind of all, and is the son of Nanda!

nīradsam śūbha angmanōhar
nirakh nirantar nainā
citt curāvan cārubilōcan
barasat karuṇā ham par

You are auspicious, attractive, and always look after the devotees. You steal the hearts of Your devotees with Your eyes that glance in all directions. Please shower Your grace and compassion!

śūka nārada sanakādi munīśvar
śūbha mangal nit gāve
bansumbhūṣit madana gopāl jō
manmē nitya birāje

All great saints such as Suka, Narada and Sanak always sing Your glory. You are adorned with wild flowers, O cowherd, and always reside in the heart of Your devotees.

brajbanitāṣat nāce gāve
murali bajāvē kānhā
kōṭikōṭi kandarp lajāve
rūp nihāri nihāri

All the people of Vrindavan are singing and dancing, as Krishna is playing the flute. Thousands and thousands of gopis are blushing, constantly gazing at the beauty of Krishna!

Rāt din ḍalatī jāy (Hindi)

rāt din ḍalatī jāy
na kōyi khabariyā śyām kī āyē

rāt din ḍalatī jāy. . .

The days and nights go by. There is no news of Shyam. Yet the days and nights go by.

nīr bahē naynōm se jaise
vraj me dūsarī jamunā
pūchū me har jīv jāl sē
kab āyēnge kānhā

My tears flow like another Yamuna (name of a river) in Vraj. I ask every creature when my Kanha will come.

haste he sab kahke mujhkō
pagalī śyām divāni
hāl mērā yē dēkh kānhā
kaisī tērī mamāni

Everyone laughs at me calling me mad, the lover of Shyam. Look at my state O Kanha, see what You have brought upon me.

Sāgara cēpaku (Telugu)

sāgara cēpaku teliyadu dāhamu
jijñāsa lēni nī centa un
nī biḍḍanamma! nī biḍḍanamma!

The fish swimming in the ocean does not know thirst. Although living in Your divine presence, this child of Yours lacks spiritual enthusiasm.

vajrapu viluva bāluḍiki teliyadu
candanapu vāsana varāhamerugadu
dīpapu kānti tana nīḍana sōkadu
māyalōni nāku nī mahima kānadu

A baby does not know the value of a diamond. A pig cannot appreciate the fragrance of sandalwood. The light from a lamp does not illumine its own shadow. Blinded by maya (cosmic delusion), I cannot perceive Your divinity.

pāhi parātparē jagadambā
śaraṇam śankari jagadambā

Mother of the universe, protect us; grant us refuge.

voḍḍuna paḍi vilavilalāḍē
cēpaku telusu nīṭina sukhamu
sādhana cēsi manassunu gelavani
jijñāsiki telusu sadguru mahima

Only a fish out of water gasping for breath appreciates the happiness of living in water. A seeker who has failed to control the mind even after vigorous sadhana (spiritual practice) alone appreciates the greatness of a Satguru.

samsāra kolanulo īdeṭi nannu
amṛtasāgaramulo paḍavēsi nāvu
arhatalēni ahambhāvinaina
dayacūpinannu kāpāḍavamma

I was swimming in the pond of worldliness. Now, You have put me in the ocean of immortality. Egoist that I am, I do not deserve to be here. O Mother, be compassionate to me and protect me.

Śakti tā jagadambā (Tamil)

śakti tā jagadambā
bhakti tā jagadambā
anbai tā jagadambā
nambikkai tantennai kāttiṭuvāy

O Mother of the universe! Give me strength, give me devotion. O Mother of the Universe! Give me love. Give me faith, and protect me!

anaittuyirum nīyena nān
anmbuṭan paṇi puriya
aṇuvēnum nīyinṭri
asaiyātena uṇarum
bhakti tā jagadambā

O Mother of the universe! Grant me devotion that will enable me to serve all living beings with love, and see them as Your form. Nothing, even an atom can move without You.

nikazhvatellām nin seyalāy
nittam ninaindurugum
anbai tā jagadambā

O Mother of the universe! Give me supreme love, that my mind may melt every moment with the knowledge that everything in this world is Your lila (divine play).

tāy karattil piḷḷaiyena
dayavuṭan kāppāy ennum
nambikkai tantennai kāttiṭuvāy

O Mother! Give me the faith that You will protect me with compassion, just as a mother cradles her baby in her arms.

Sāmbasadāśiva (Tamil)

sāmbasadāśiva sāmbasadāśiva
saccidānandanē sāmbaśivā

O ever auspicious Lord accompanied by Mother Shakti! You are the embodiment of existence-knowledge-bliss.

poyyāṁ ulakaṁ purindiṭavē
meyyāy unpadaṁ puṇarndiṭavē
nādan un mahimai pāṭukirēn
namaḥ śivāya ena kūrukirēn

To know the illusory nature of the world and to attain Your feet which itself is truth, I sing Your praises and chant 'Namah Shivaya.'

vēdattin nāyakanē dēvā
mādorubhāgan ānavanē
māl ayan kāṇā pēroḷiyē
ālayamāguṁ ānandamē
sāmba sadāśiva... sāmba sadāśiva...
sāmba sadāśiva... sāmba sadāśiva...

O God, You are the Leader of the Vedas, and you are half of Shakti. Your effulgent form was not seen even by Lord Vishnu and Lord Brahma. You are the bliss in which all beings merge.

Samsāramanu (Telugu)

samsāramanu kānalō cikkina
pasidānni kāvaga rāvammā
moravini brōvaga rāvammā
karuṇatō kāpāḍa rāvammā

O Mother, listen to the prayers of this little one who got caught in the forest of samsara. Come to protect her with Your compassion.

pāpapuṇyamulu taskarulu
satyasampattunu dōcēnu
nā nijasaudhamuku dūramujēsi
dēhāraṇyamuna vidhicēnu – ammā
kāvagarāvammā

The thieves called merits and demerits have stolen the real wealth. They took me away from the true home and left me in the forest called this body. O Mother, come to protect this little one!

rāgamōhamulu kannulu kappenu
cittabhramalu cētulu kaṭṭenu
ciṭṭaḍavilō cikkina prāṇi
dikku tōcaka ākrōśincenu - ammā
kāvagarāvammā

Blind-folded by desires, bound by wrong understanding of the Truth, caught in this thick forest, not knowing the directions, this being is grieving. O Mother, come to protect this little one!

ēdi gati nāku evaru rakṣa nāku
trāṇamucēyuna devaru evaru
dikkū telipi dāri cūpēdevaru
vilapincē jīviki sāntvanamevaru - ammā
kāvagarāvammā

Who is my refuge? Who will look after me? Who will protect me? Who will show me the directions and the way? Who will console this grieving soul? O Mother, come to protect this little one!

Sānnu pīkh (Punjabi)

sānnu pīkh pāde māyiye sānnu pīkh pāde mā
terī pagtī dī ō mayyā sānnu pīkh pāde mā
de dātī de dātī terī pagtī sānnu de dātī

O Mother, we are hungry for Your devotion. Please grant us devotion to You.

o sānnu hiknāl lāle māyiye
dukh dard miṭāḍe māyiye
sāḍhi ghālī cōḷi par de - sānnu pīkh pāde mā
de dātī de dātī terī pagtī sānnu de dātī

Mother, please always keep us close to You. Please remove our sorrows and sufferings. Fill our hearts with devotion for You. O Mother, please grant us this devotion!

ō azi maneyā azi pāpī
sānnu bakṣi ō dātī
mā bacheyām tōnni rusdī
bacheyānnu lā chāti
de dātī de dātī terī pagtī sānnu de dātī

We know we are sinners. O Mother, please forgive us. Please do not be upset with our faults. Keep us close to Your heart, Mother, please grant us devotion.

pesā ṣoratnayi mangde
saccepagtā de kis kam de
caraṇā vicc lele māyiye
sānnu pīkh pāde mā
de dātī de dātī terī pagtī sānnu de dātī

O Mother, we do not seek money or fame. We only want to be truly devoted to You. Grant us Your refuge. Mother, please grants us devotion to You!

o din rātī... tere dātī...
tere pairī... karāmātī...
harṣetom... tere nā di...
khaṣbo he... mā āmdī...
de dātī de dātī terī pagtī sānnu de dātī

O Mother, day and night we want to be Yours only. Every moment, whether in happiness or sorrow, we want to remember You alone. Mother, grant us devotion to You!

Santāpa hṛttinnu (Malayalam)

santāpa hṛttinnu śānti-mantram
sandēha hṛttinnu jñāna-mantram
samphulla hṛttinnu prēma-mantram
anpārn-norammatan nāma-mantram

For a grieving heart, You are the mantra of peace. For an inquisitive mind, You are the mantra of knowledge. For the blossoming heart, You are the mantra of love.

centāraṭikaḷil ñān namippū
cintāmalaratil nī vasikkū
sandēhamillātta jñānamennum
samphulla hṛttil teḷiññiṭaṭṭe

I prostrate at Your lotus feet. You reside in the flower of my thought. Let that absolute knowledge reflect in my heart in full bloom.

ennōṭenikkuḷḷa snēhamalla
ninnōṭenikkuḷḷa prēmammē!
amma-hātṛkkazhal tārillello
manmanaḥ ṣaḍpadam-āramippū

The love that I have for You is greater than the love I have for myself. O Mother, the bee of my heart rejoices at Your divine lotus feet.

vārmazha-villaṅgu māññupōkum
vār tinkaḷ śōbhayaliññutīrum
māyukayill-ātmāvil ennum-amma
ānanda saundarya-dhāmamallo

Rainbows will wane away, splender of delighting moons will melt away. But You who are the very abode of enchanting beauty and bliss of the soul will never fade away from my heart.

Satyam jñānam (Tamil)

satyam jñānam anantam brahmaḥ

Brahman (the supreme) is truth, wisdom and infinitude.

kāṇum yāvaiyum māruvatuṇḍu
māttrattin pinnē mārātatonḍru
mārum poruḷin tēṭalai viṭṭu
mārā onṭril manadai niruttu

All that we see is subject to change. Behind all change lies the changeless. Forsaking the pursuit of the changing, fix the mind in the changeless.

arivenḍrarivatu pulanarivākum
aribavan tānē arivin svarūpam
uṇḍāna arivellām edanoḷiyil oḷirum
uṇarndadai arindiṭu un manadatil patittiṭu

All that we perceive is only knowledge from sense organs. Real knowledge is none other than the knower. Realize that by which all knowledge is illumined, and fix Your mind on it.

tōnḍrā onḍru maraiyādirukkum
tōttrattirkkappāl nilaiyāyirukkum
tōnḍruvatellām atilē tōnḍrum
tōttram viṭṭu atilē oṭunkum

The Self can never cease to be. It remains eternal, beyond all manifestations. All that manifests emerges from it, and dissolves again into the unmanifest.

arivin vaṭivadu amṛta vaṭivē
ānanda vaṭivadu ananta vaṭivē
unnaiviṭṭillaiyadu ulakil uḷadeduvum
unadu mey vaṭivadu un manadatil patittiṭu

True knowledge is immortality, bliss and eternity. All that exists in the world is not separate from You. That is Your eternal nature. Fix Your mind on this truth.

Satyattin sāram (Tamil)

satyattin sāram
vāzhvirkkādhāram
nimmati tarum nādam
śivāyam śivāyam

Shiva's name is the essence of truth and the substratum of life. The sound of His name gives peace of mind.

aṭiyārkaḷ pāṭum, iṭaiviṭātinnādam
kalankum manatirkku upāyam
śivāyam śivāyam śivāyam

Shiva's name is sung by devotees constantly. This name is the sole refuge for the restless mind.

vēṇḍuvōrkkatu rūpam, nāṭuvōrkkatu tañcam
vīṭupettrai vazhankum śivāyam
śivāyam śivāyam śivāyam

For those who worship, the name is form. For those who seek, the name is refuge. Shiva's name is the one that gives Self-realization.

śivamentra akṣaram, śivanirukkum akṣaram
uṇmaiyāna akṣaram śivāyam
śivāyam śivāyam śivāyam

Lord Shiva lives in the word Shivayam. The real word is Shivayam and it is imperishable.

Seḷeyadirali ninna (Kannada)

seḷeyadirali ninna kaṇṇōṭṭa mōhakate
bedarisadirali ninna bhīkarate
pādāravinda makaranda dāhi maridumbi nānamma
maridumbi nānu
maridumbi nānamma
maridumbi nānu

O Mother, may I be neither drawn by the attraction of Your eyes, nor be terrified by Your fierceness. I am a mere honey bee, thirsting for the nectar of Your lotus feet.

jayakāra jayakāra mahākāḷi
jayakāra jayakāra bhadrakāḷi
hrīmkāḷi mahākāḷi bhadrakāḷi

Hail to You, O Mahakali, Bhadrakali! Hail to You, Hrimkali, Mahakali, O Bhadrakali!

puṭṭa kāḷi beṭṭa dantha śivana meṭṭi nintaḷu
rakkasara bechisalu katti śūla hiḍidaḷu

Little Kali stands on Shiva who is like a mountain. For the sake of terrifying demons She holds sword and spear.

kattaleya nungi kāḷi seṭedu koṇḍu nintaḷu
raktajinugo jihveya cācci tōrutiruvaḷu

Swallowing the darkness, Kali stands stiff, stretching and showing off her blood-dripping tongue.

caṇḍa muṇḍa nāśini muṇḍa māla dhāriṇi
śumbhādi daityara madavimarda nartini

Slayer of demons such as Chanda and Munda, slayer of demons such as Shumba, O Kali who dances in mirth!

bīja asura dhvamsini mahiṣa asura mardini
ahanmkāra dvēṣini saddharma vardhini

Slayer of demons such as Bijasura and Mahishasura, She hates the ego. She is the upholder of virtues and dharma.

Śēr pe savār (Punjabi)

śēr pe savār hōnevālī
pyār se sabko nihārnevāli
madhukaiṭabh vadh karanevāli
tū hī hai natjanpālini maiyyā
ō. . . ō. . . ō. . . ō. . .
ō maiyyā. . . ō maiyyā. . .
ō. . . ō. . . maiyyā

O Mother who rides a tiger, You gaze upon everyone with love, You destroyed the demons Madhu and Kaitabha (signifying the destruction of the ego); You are indeed the one who takes care of all, O Mother!

śūmbhaniśumbhaki bairini yōgini
bhīkararūpiṇi tum ho sanātani
śailanivāsini śūlini mālini
tū hi kapālini kāli ḍarāvani

You destroyed the demons Shumbha and Nishumbha! You are in eternal meditation, have a fierce form, and are eternal. You dwell in the mountains, wield the trident, and wear a garland of skulls, O Kali, whose fierce form instills fear.

pralay kī agan mē nāc kē tū nav
srajan kī bāriś ban ke barasati
bhuvan ko siraj ke mōhit karti
māyājāl me sabko phasāti

You whirl in the dance of the destruction and then create new universes, You ensnare everyone with the power of Maya (illusion).

janam maraṇ bhava bandhan mōcan
sab he mā tērī mōhan līlā
mahiś ke māthē pē nācnevālī
mē ab tēri śaraṇ hu maiyā

Life, death, the bonds of the world, all these are Your play. You danced on the head of the demon Mahisha, I am now in Your refuge, O Mother!

Sēvaiyenum (Tamil)

anbōṭu anaittuyirkkum nām seyyum sēvai
atutānē ammāvin tiruppāda pūjai

Loving service performed for all beings is worship of Mother's holy feet.

sēvaiyenum arumarundu
pāvamadai migaviraindu
tīrttiṭumē idaiyarindu
dinantōrum nī arundu

The rare remedy of service immediately rids one of sin. Know this and consume it daily.

āsaiyilē arivizhandu
kōpattilē guṇamizhandu
tān seyda tavaruṇarndu
tayankāmal nī tirundu

Having lost your discrimination because of desire, and virtues because of anger, realize your folly and change over a new leaf without any hesitation.

arivennum agal uṇḍu
anbennum ney koṇḍu
atan tiriyāy nīnindru

aṇaiyāda oḷisindu

There is a clay lamp of knowledge, with love as its ghee. Become its wick and radiate an inextinguishable light.

tannalamillā sēvai seyyum manamē
tandaruḷvāyē tāyē enḍrum nīyē

O Mother, bless us forever with a mind for selfless service.

Silukisadiru nī (Kannada)

silukisadiru nī ī lōkadi - enna
silukisadiru nī ī lōkadi

Do not let me be caught in this world.

bandhana bēḍige bedari nā baḷalide
bhaktiya muktiya nīḍenage

I am frightened of the handcuffs of attachment. Hence grant me devotion and liberation.

sūryanu beḷakina maneyante - nīnu
arivina beḷakina gurumāte
manadali manemāḍi marevege dūḍi
nagutide nōḍamma māyāndhakāra
nagutide nōḍamma māyājālā

Just as the sun is home to all light, You are to the light of knowledge, O Mother Guru. The darkness of maya, this net of maya, has secretly made my mind its home, caught me up in forgetfulness, and laughs at me, teases me. See, Mother!

rāgadi biḍisu vairāgyadi nilisu
mōhadi biḍisu premadi nilisu
kāmane biḍisu karuṇāmṛta harisu
śōkadi biḍisu śaraṇāgati nīḍu

Release me from attachment. May I be established in detachment. Release me from attachment. May I be established in love. Release me from desire. Let the nectar of immortal bliss flow from You. Release me from sorrow and grant me surrender.

Sinnañciru kuzhandai (Tamil)

sinnañciru kuzhandai ammā tuṇayārumillai ammā
undan maṭi tañcamena viḷaiyāṭi makizha ēnkudammā

Mother, I am Your infant. I have no support other than You. I yearn to play in Your lap.

undan tiruccēvaṭikaḷ nān paṇiya vēṇḍumammā
undan tirumandirattai nāvuraikka vēṇḍumammā
un punita sindanaiyil manamuruka vēṇḍumammā
unnai maravāmal piriyāmal vāzha vēṇḍumammā

Mother, may I worship Your feet. May I chant Your sacred names. May I always remain immersed in thoughts of You. May I never forget You or live apart from You.

kālam seyda kōlam enne alaipāya vaikkudammā
māyai ennai tākkudammā taṭumāra vaikkudammā
kālam ennai nāṭi varum kālamum nerunkudamma
kāpāṭṭra tāyē nī karuṇai koṇḍu viraivāyē

The changes that time wreaks have disturbed me. Maya, the power of cosmic illusion, has created obstacles in my path. The time of my death is drawing near. Mother, please come quickly and save me with Your compassion.

kaṇkuḷira unnai kaṇḍappin kaṇ mūṭa vēṇḍumammā
en uyir un sēvaṭiyil sērndamara vēṇḍumammā
pirappirappillā appērinba nilaiyaṭaiya
tāyē gati nīyē mahāmāyē hṛdayēśvariyē amṛtēśvariyē

May I die only after gazing at You to my heart's content. May my life become one with Your feet. Mother, great illusion, Goddess of my heart, only You can help me attain the blissful abode beyond life and death.

Siṭrinbam nāṭum (Tamil)

siṭrinbam nāṭum sirumatiyinai
sīrākki sīrārum pērinba amutinai
aḷḷittarum annaiyē arputamē - un
porpadamē em narpadamē

O Mother, You are a great wonder! You mend our little minds that seek petty pleasures and provide immortal bliss in plenty. Your golden feet are our ultimate refuge!

azhiyāta ānandam taruvāḷ
annayiṭam aṭaikkalam aṭaintiṭuvōm
nilayillā ulakil irundālum
nilayāna tuṇayāy irundiṭuvāḷ

Let us seek refuge in our Mother who gives eternal bliss. She remains as our permanent support in this ever-changing world.

vazhikāṭṭa nīyum maruttuviṭṭāl
vazhimāri pōyviṭuvōm tāyē
takuti illāmal irundālum
untāḷkaḷ nāṭiyē vandōmē

O Mother! Should You ever refuse to guide us, we would go astray. Though we know we are utterly unqualified, we have come seeking protection at Your holy feet.

gativēṇḍi ēngiṭum unsēygaḷ
vidhitūṇḍum vazhiyil sellāmal
matimayakkam tannai teḷivākki
ativēgam untan tāḷsērppāy

O Mother! Your children are yearning to reach the supreme state. Protect us from falling into evil paths driven by fate. Please provide clarity to our confused minds, and gather us at Your holy feet without delay.

Śivanē śankaranē (Kannada)

śivanē śankaranē jayasāmbasadā śivanē
harahara mahādēva śiva śiva mahādēva

Hail to the great Lord! Victory to Lord Shiva!

praṇavasvarūpanē praḷayāntakanē
karuṇāmayanē paripālisu dēvanē

O Lord, You are of the nature of the pranava mantra and Lord of cosmic dissolution. Filled with compassion, You protect us all.

smaśānavāsiyē kailāsavāsiyē
hṛdayanivāsiyē sarvantaryāmiyē

You dwell in the cremation ground. Your abode is also Mount Kailash. You dwell in the heart, and You pervade the whole universe.

jai namaḥ pārvati patayē harahara mahādēva

Salutations to the consort of Goddess Parvati. Hail to the great Lord!

Śivaśakti aikyave (Kannada)

ōm namaḥ śivāya śivāyyai namaḥ ōm

Prostrations to Shiva and Shakti.

śivaśakti aikyave sṛṣṭi sthiti rahasya
samacitta bhāvave ātmika rahasya
ihapara eraṭilla iruvundodātma

yātake ahamkāra mereve jīvātma ?

The union of Shiva and Shakti is the secret of creation and its maintenance. Equanimity of mind is the secret of spirituality. There are no two as 'this world' and 'that world'. There is just one Atma. Why do you show off your ego, O individual soul?

hindina sukṛtava induṭṭuṇa bēkātma
indina karmava munduṇa bēkātma
phaladāse toredalli migilāda phalavunṭu
sankalpa śakti ninadāgali ō ātma

The fruits of the past shall be enjoyed in the present, just as the fruits of the present shall be enjoyed in future. If You give up the desire for fruits, then, there is a greater fruit. May you have a strong will, O individual soul!

apajaya jayagaḷu nāṇyada mukhagaḷu
priyavu apriyagaḷu eṭabala kaigaḷu
paravaśavāgi nī ēkāgra manadi
paramārtha paratatva nene sadā ō ātma

Success and failures are two sides of the same coin. Likes and dislikes are like both hands. Transcendent them, and with a one-pointed mind, meditate on the Supreme, O individual soul.

manuja, ni alpanu lakṣyahīnanu saha
mānava janmavu amūlyavu kēḷu
māṭuvu dellavu yōgavē āgali
mahātmage śaraṇāgi kai mugi jīvātma

O Man, you are a mere one with no sense of direction. Listen, this human birth is very precious. May everything you do relate you to the Supreme. Surrender to the Mahatma, and offer Him prostrations, O jivatma!

Śivke (Hindi)

śivke bāyē śōbhit śakti
tum deti hō bandan mukti
har jīvōm ke antaryāmi
tumre āgē mastak ṭekkum

Adorning Shiva on his left, You free us from bondage. O indweller of all beings, I bow down to You.

śivaśakti svarupiṇī, ānandarupiṇi, prēmasvarupiṇī māte

Mother, You are of the embodiment of Shiva-Shakti, of ananda (bliss) and of love.

nabh hai terā śīrsh bhavāni
dhartti pe tu per rakhī hai
sab jīvōm me cetan tuhi
bhavbādhā kō dur kare mā

With the sky as Your head, You keep Your feet on the earth. You are life in all beings. You remove of worldly sufferings.

jai māte, jai devi, jag māte, jagadambe...

Hail Mother, hail Goddess, hail Mother, O Mother of universe!

jananī terī sarjan kelī
bujhtti nā ye sṛṣṭi pahelī
tumhī jāne tatva anōkhā
nit nīrāgētup nirālā

O Mother, it is impossible to solve the riddle of Your creation. You alone know the wondrous essence of this ever changing creation.

bagtōm kō tu premamayī hai
dukhiyōm pe kāruṇya dikhātti
muniyōm mē tu gyān jagātti
danujōm kō niśśeṣ harātti

You are full of love towards Your devotees, and You shower Your compassion on the afflicted. You are the source of knowledge in the sages. You are the destroyer of evil.

Śri dēvi laḷitā (Tamil)

śri dēvi laḷitā paramēśvari
śricakraṁ vīttiṭum laḷitēśvari
ulakin annaiyē anpunāyaki
umai ambikē dēvi kanyākumari

You are Lalita Paramesvari who is Goddess of wealth and Supreme Goddess. You are Goddess Laliteshvari who resides in Sri Chakra. You are the Mother of Universe and the Queen of compassion. You are Goddess Uma Parasakti in the form a maiden.

kayalvizhi karuṇaimiku mīnākṣiyē
kāśipuraṁ jñānamaruḷ viśālākṣiyē
karimbuvillēntum kāmākṣiyē
arumbu malaraṭi śaraṇam tāyē

You are compassionate Goddess Meenakshi with fish shaped eyes. You are Goddess Visalakshi from the city of Kashi, bestowing knowledge. You are Goddess Kamakshi holding the sugarcane bow. O Mother! We take refuge at Your feet which are as soft as flower buds.

āyiram itazhmītē kamalāmbikē
ātmavidyaiyaruḷuṁ vimalāmbikē
anaittuyirai anpāl piṇaittavaḷē
anbu malaraṭi śaraṇam tāyē

You are the Goddess sitting on thousand petaled lotus. You are the Goddess giving the knowledge of Atman. You have connected all souls with love. We take refuge at Your feet that are like flowers of compassion

ūnamatai akattum umāśankariyē
vīṇai nādaṁ mīṭṭiṭuṁ maṇgaḷāmbikē
prāṇa śaktiyākum karppakāmbikē
praṇava rūpiṇi śaraṇaṁ tāyē

You are Goddess Uma Sankari who saves us from the cycle of birth and death. You are Goddess Mangalambika who plays the veena. You are Goddess Karpakambika who has become pranic energy. You are in the form of pranava - we take refuge in You.

śaraṇaṁ śaraṇam śaraṇam laḷitā paramēśvari
śaraṇaṁ śaraṇam śaraṇam gaurikṛpākari
śaraṇaṁ śaraṇam śaraṇam śrībhuvanēśvari
śaraṇaṁ śaraṇam śaraṇam rājarājēśvari

Mother Lalita, supreme Goddess, fair one, gracious one, supreme Empress of the universe, we take refuge in You!

Śrī kṛṣṇā deva (Malayalam)

śrī kṛṣṇā deva caitanya vihāra
prēma varṣadayālō prēma varṣadayālō
māyā bandha vimōcananē hari
rādhakṛṣṇā sukumārā, rādhakṛṣṇā sukumārā

O Lord Krishna, refuge of Chaitanya. Kind-hearted One, You shower divine love. O Hari, who releases us from the bondage of illusion, ever youthful Radha Krishna!

kāliṇakūppum mānava hṛttil
ānandatte uṇarttum
dīna dayāmayā kāraṇapūruṣa
māmaka mānasa lōla

You awaken bliss in the hearts of those human beings who stand before Your feet with folded hands. You are kind towards the helpless, You are the primordial cause. You entertain my mind.

trētā yuga śrīrāma-raghūttama
dvāpara yādava kṛṣṇā
kātaramām kali kāla matilvann-
ādhiyakattuka dēva

In the Treta Yuga You came as Rama. In Dwapara Yuga You came as Krishna. In this fierce Kali Yuga You come and remove all worries.

jñānālaya śrī sādhuśarīrā
gānālaya mama dēvā
kātaranāmen mānasa vāṭiyil
vāzhū nī dayaśīla

You are the abode of knowledge, the embodiment of truth. You are the abode of music, my Lord. I am weak. O merciful One, please reside in the garden of my mind!

Śrī rāma nāmamē (Tamil)

śrī rāma nāmamē sonnāl
ankē varuvān hanumān
kṣēmaṅgaḷ yāvum taruvān
śrī rāma bhakta hanumān

Whenever we chant Lord Rama's name, Hanuman manifests himself. Hanuman, who is Lord Rama's devotee, bestows auspiciousness on all.

śrī rāma rāma jaya rāma rāma
śrī rāma rāma jaya rāmā

Hail Lord Rama!

ilankayai vālāl erittavan – anta
lankāpatiyai etirttavan
añjana makanavanām
śrī rāma bhakta hanumān

He razed Lanka with his tail. He defied the Lord of Lanka (Ravana). Hanuman, son of Anjana, is Lord Rama's devotee.

sañjīvani malayai koṇḍu vandavan
sirañjīvi ennum peyar pettravan
añjana makanavanām
śrī rāma bhakta hanumān

He brought back the Sanjivani mountain. He earned the name of Ciranjivi (immortal). Hanuman, son of Anjana, is Lord Rama's devotee.

Sṛṣṭi vēru (Telugu)

sṛṣṭi vēru sṛṣṭi karta
vēru kādura
dēvuḍu jivuḍu
vēru vēru kādura
mahāvākyālu cebuttunna-didērā

Creator and creation are not separate from each other. God and the self are not separate from each other. All the mahavakyas (words from the Vedas) speak the same eternal truth.

prajnānam brahma
ayamātmā brahma
tatvamasi aham brahmāsmi

Knowledge of the Self is Brahman. The individual self is Brahman. Thou art that. I am Brahman.

maṇṇu vēru kuṇda vēru
vēru kādura
nāṭyamu nartaki
vēru vēru kādura

The clay and the clay pot are not separate from each other. Dancer and dance are not different from each other.

kāntini sūryuni vēru ceyyalēmura
mādhavuḍu mānavuḍu
vēru kānē kādura

Sun and sunlight can never be separate. God and humankind can never exist as separate entities.

parikaramul-ennunna vidyut okaṭerā
vigrahamul-ennunna daivamokaṭerā
ī bhinnatvamu-lonē ēkatvam-undira
ēkam nundi anēkamē sṛṣṭi tirurā

So many instruments yet only one electric current. So many deities yet only one God. There is unity in this apparent diversity. One becomes many – this is how creation unfolds itself.

Sukh kartā (Hindi)

sukh kartā tum ho
duḥkh hartā tum ho
he bhāgyavidhātā
gaṇanāthā tum ho

O Lord of the ganas, giver of happiness, vanquisher of sorrows, Lord of my fate...

gaṇapati bāppā moryā
mangaḷa mūrtti moryā

Hail to our Father Ganesha, hail to the auspicious One!

manmohak hai rūp terā
omkārasvarūp terā
hai bhakton pe dhyān terā
karuṇādr hṛday terā

Your form is that of the sacred syllable Om, Your form is enchanting. Your compassionate heart is always dwelling on Your devotees.

man jo hai bada cancal
tere smaran se ho niścal
bhakti bhav karde prabal
janam merā ho safal

The temperamental mind becomes calm and stable with Your remembrance. O Lord, please strengthen my devotion to You, that this life of mine become worthy and fruitful.

mūṣak par ho savar
tum ho jag ke ādhar
kṛpa kar hai pālanhār
darśan iccha ho sakār

Your vehicle is the mouse. You cut the bonds of ignorance, taking us to supreme freedom. You are the support of the world. Bless us, O Lord, that our desire to behold You is fulfilled.

Sundara vadanā (Hindi)

sundara vadanā kanhā – man
mandir me tū ānā
cañcal citvan se tu – merā
sankaṭ sab har lenā

O Kanha with the beautiful face, please come to the temple of my mind. With Your mishchievious gaiety, please destroy all my woes.

śyām śyām śyām jai jai
śyām śyām śyām
śyām śyām śyām jai jai
śyām śyām śyām

Victory to Shyam!

nandakumāra devā – terī

bāsuri me tu bajānā
mōhan rāg surīlā - sunke
mōhe man - vṛndāvan

O son of Nanda, please play sweet notes on Your flute, that I might be enchanted and feel Vrindavan in my heart.

dil ke kuṇjan me āke - tū
rās racāvegā tō
prem ki jamunā laharāyegi
nāc uṭhegī jaldī

If You would only come to my heart and play the Ras (Krishna's famous dance of eternal love), a Yamuna (name of a river) of love would awaken and dance in my heart.

terā dars dikhāne me ab
derī kuch bhi na hōgī
merā man kehtā hai - tū
apanā ban jāyegā

Now I know that there will be no delay in Your darshan (vision). My heart says that You will be mine.

Sundari jaganmōhini (Kannada)

sundari jaganmōhini kuḍi nōṭava bīrutali bā
ātma samsātake bā bāreyā karuṇāmayi

O beautiful One, enchantress of the world! Do come, throwing love-glances. Give companionship to my soul. Won't You come, O Mother of compassion?

mangaḷē sukhakāriṇi janma pāpavināśini
enna mārgadarśini bhavāniye mṛdubhāṣiṇi
ambike jagadambike janma pāvani dēviyu ni
ninna maḍilali malagisiko kōmalē vimalāmbikē

O auspicious One who comforts, You destroy the sins of this lifetime. You show me my path, O Bhavani, soft spoken One! Mother, Mother of the world, You are the Goddess who makes our lives blessed. Take me in Your lap, O sweet One, pure Mother.

candrikē bhavatāriṇi bhava bandhana biḍisutali
nava santasa nīḍuta bā bāreyā jaganmāteye
śāradē vidyādēviye jñāna dēviye vandisuvē
nīḍu bhaktiya varavēnagē dēviyē paramjyōtiyē

O Mother, cool like moonlight, O Mother who takes devotees across the world of transmigration, release me from all worldly ties. Give me new joys, come. Won't You come, Mother of the world? O Sharada You are the Goddess of learning. You are the Devi of knowledge. My prostrations to You. Grant me the gift of devotion, O Devi, highest, resplendent One.

lakṣmiyē kamalāmbikē ellā sṛṣṭiya oḍatiyu ni
kaiyya mugiyuta vandisuvē māteye mamatāmayi
durgiyē lalitāmbikē nitya prēma kaṭākṣavē bā
satya jyōti prakāśavē bā kāḷiyē amṛtēśvari

O Lakshmi, the Goddess bearing the lotus, You lord over all of creation. I join my hands and bow to You. O Mother who is full of love for Your children! O Durga, O Lalitambika. O one who throws love-glances all the time, do come. O light of truth, come.

Sūryanobbane (Kannada)

sūryanobbane upameyamma
sūryanobbane upameyamma
sadā jagavabeḷaguva
sūryanobbane upameyamma

Mother, only the sun can be compared to You, the sun which forever brightens the world with its radiance.

hagalilla iruḷilla dinakara yogige
hagaliruḷilla śubha karininage
avanalle nintu līlegaiyyuvanalla
avani geragi nī sevisalande
ammā nī nallave pratyakṣa daiva

There is no day or night for the sun who is the best karma yogi, the cause of day. O Mother, cause of auspiciousness, there is also no day or night for You. He enacts His play from where He stands- but You have descended in order to serve. O Mother, are You not the Goddess present before our very eyes?

tānalli beḷagi bānallī beḷagi
kōṭi kōṭi jīva poreva o ravi
anantakōṭi hṛdayava beḷagi
sajjanikē cirabhuviyali harasuva
ninage sūrya candraresākṣi

He shines from up there. He illumines the sky and nurtures innumerable lives. But You brighten innumerable hearts and make the river of goodness flow on Earth. O Mother, only the sun and moon are witness to all this play!

Śvāsamellām un peyarē (Tamil)

śvāsamellām un peyarē
nēsamellām un uruvē
pāsamellām unniṭamē – ennammā
pūjaiyellām un aṭikkē – ponnammā

Your name is within every breath of mine. All my affection flows towards Your form. All my attachment is only for You, my Mother. Darling Mother, all my worship is only to Your feet.

ānālum en akattil
azhukkellām maraiyavillai
vīṇāga kazhikiradē – ennammā
vidhiyinai māttriṭuvāy
vinaikaḷai pōkkiṭuvāy
tuṇaiyena vandiṭuvāy – ponnammā

Still, the impurities in my mind have not disappeared. Days are wasted, Mother, please change my destiny. Darling Mother, please help me by removing the results of my bad actions.

koṇḍu vandatonṭrumillai
koṇḍu pōvatonṭrumillai
iṭaippaṭṭa vāzhvinilē – ennammā
iṭipaṭṭu nondu viṭṭēn
innum nī kāṇalaiyō?
unnanbē kāvalammā – ponnammā

I brought nothing with me, I will not take anything away with me. Nothing have I brought, and nothing I will take. I'm stuck in this life, suffering in agony. Do You not see me? Darling Mother, Your love is my protection.

cindaiyellām cellammā un ninaivē
pūjaiyellām ponnammā tiruvaṭikkē

Darling Mother, only thoughts of You are in my mind. Beloved Mother, all my worship is only towards Your holy feet.

Taḷarnnuraṅgukayō (Malayalam)

taḷarnnuraṅgukayō? iniyum
viṣādamūkatayō?
manujakōṭikaḷ viṣayagaraḷam
nukarnnuraṅgukayō! tammil

marannuraṅgukayō?

Why are you sleeping in exhaustion? Why are you so sad and depressed? Why are the millions of human beings imbibing the poison of materialism and sleeping? Why have they forgotten each other?

kālattin kaiviraltṭumbāl viracicca
chāyā citraṅgaḷō... manuṣyan
uyarttiyatalakaḷ! tāzhttiya talakaḷ
viraḷunna – viḷarunna mukhaṅgaḷ! eviṭeyum
maraviccu-maruvunna manuṣyan?

Are we just pictures drawn by the finger tips of time? Men with upright heads, men with downcast faces, pale and scared faces - everywhere men are living frigid lives.

niṅgalkku kaṇikāṇān niṅgaḷe kaṇikāṇān
innī jagattil manuṣyaruṇḍō?
uṇḍenkiloru tāmara-malarmoṭṭupōle
mizhiyaṭaccuraṅgunnatentē... hṛdayam
itaḷ-viṭarttīṭāttatentē?

Are there human beings in this world for you to see when you wake up? Are you there for them to see when they open their eyes? If so, why are you closing your eyes and sleeping like a lotus bud? Why does your heart not open up its petals and bloom?

Tañcamena vantōm (Tamil)

tañcamena vantōm dayaipuri vēlā
vañcamilā neñcamatil
mañcamkoḷḷa vārāy - murukā

O Muruga! We have come seeking refuge, please be compassionate, holder of the spear. O Lord, come and stay in our innocent hearts.

arivirkkaṇiśēr aranār makanē
piravippiṇitīr piraiyōn makanē
turavikaḷ paṇiyum maraiyin poruḷē
iruvinai nīkkum saravaṇabhavanē

You are the son of he who adorns a snake around his neck, You are the supreme truth that adds beauty to all knowledge. Cure us of the disease of birth and death, O Son of Lord of Shiva, who wears the crescent moon. The sages bow down to You, You are the essence of the Vedas. O Saravana Bhava, You free us from the effect of our actions.

anpin vaṭivē arivin suṭarē
iruḷai akaṭri oḷiyai perukkiṭu

Embodiment of love, flame of knowledge. Please remove this darkness by shedding light upon us!

aṭiyārkkaruḷ sēr jñānakkumarā
eḷiyār maruḷtīr śaktikkumarā
oruvāy mozhiyilai unpēr anṭri
varuvāy vēṇḍiṭa manatil onṭri

Embodiment of wisdom, please shower Your grace on Your devotees and remove the fear of this less fortunate son of Shakti. I am unable to utter anything but Your holy name. O Lord, You come to us whenever we pray whole-heartedly.

inpam tunpam imai marumai
irumai akaṭri orumai uṇarttiṭu

Please remove the dualities of sorrow and joy, of this birth and of the next one, and make us realize Your glory!

vēlvēl murukā veṭrivēl murukā
vaṭivēl azhakā śakti umai bālā

Glory to You, O Muruga, holder of the spear, beautiful One, son of Uma!

Tañcam undan (Tamil)

tañcam undan pādamenṭru
śaraṇaṭaindēn dēviyē... nān śaraṇaṭaindēn dēviyē
neñcam undan kōyilenṭru
nī amarvāy dēviyē... adil nī amarvāy dēviyē

O Goddess, Your holy feet are my only refuge. I surrender to You. Make my heart Your temple. Please reside within my heart.

munnam seyda vinaikaḷ ellām
muṭṭimōdippārkkutē... enai muṭṭimōdippārkkutē
enna solvēn undan seviyil
ēzhaiyin kural kēṭkutā – inda ēzhaiyin kural kēṭkutā

The fruits of past actions are trying to torment me. What shall I tell You, O Mother? Please listen to the helpless musings of this poor one.

enda niramtān undan niramō
enakku colvāy dēviyē... nī enakku colvāy dēviyē
enda vaṭivam undan vaṭivō
eṭuttu colvāy dēviyē... nī eṭuttu colvāy dēviyē

O Goddess tell me which color is Your true color? O Devi, please show me which form Your true form is.

kaṇkaḷ ceyta payan anṭrō
kāḷi unnai kāṇpadu – annai kāḷi unnai kāṇpadu
paṇ amaittu pāṭum inda
bālanai nī kāttiṭu... inda bālanai nī kāttiṭu

Beholding Your form would be the true merit of having eyes. Please protect this child of Yours who is singing Your glories!

Tandam tānannai (Malayalam)

tandam tānannai tānai tandanai
tānai tandanai tānannā
tandam tānannai tānai tandanai
tānai tandanai tānannā
veḷḷi malamēlē vāṇaruḷunnoru
indu kalādharā kaitozhunnēn
bhūtiyaṇiññuḷḷa bhūtavidhāyaka
bhūvitinennum abhayamēkū

Salutations to the One who resides on top of the silver mountain, wearing the crescent moon on his head. To He who is smeared with vibhuti all over His body, who commands the ghosts and spirits, we pray to give refuge to the whole earth.

mūnnu purangaḷerichuḷḷa mukkaṇṇan
mōdamāy ceyyunna narttanavum
viśvatteyākeyaṭakkum svarūpavum
viśvanātha prabhū kumbiṭunnēn

The three-eyed one, who reduced the three cities of Tripura to ashes, is dancing enchantingly. Salutations to the One who controls the entire universe.

tandanittannāna tānai tānai tandam tānittannāna
tandam tānittāna tānai tandam tānittānnānā – teyyattām
pīlittirumuṭiyum māril tūvanamālikayum
ōṭakkuzhalumēnti kaṇṇan uḷḷam kāvarnnu nilkkum

Peacock feather in his hair, a beautiful garland on his chest, with flute in his hand, stands Lord Krishna, who has stolen our hearts.

gōpījanapriyanē giridhara gokula pālakanē
rādhikā vallabhane murārē nityam namichiṭunnēn

Beloved of the gopis, the one who raised Govardhana mountain, protector of the gopis, Radha's Lord, slayer of the asura Mura, we pray to You.

tannēnāne nanē nānē tannannānā tāne
tānānai tānakatittai tannannānā - takitai
rāma nāmam japichīṭu kōṭi puṇyam - janmam
ennumennum ariyunna kāruṇyapūram - tai tai

Chant the name of Lord Rama to acquire punya (merit) which will bestow a shower of compassion all through your life.

janmamākum alayāzhi taraṇamceyyān - bhakta
hanumānde pādamennum abhayamākum tai tai

In order to cross over the ocean of life, the holy feet of the great devotee Lord Hanuman are the only refuge.

vāṇiṭunna vāṇīdēvi uḷttaṭāttil - ennāl
vāṇaruḷum arivallō abhayamākum - tai tai

When Goddess of Wisdom, Saraswati, resides in your ardent heart, then discriminative knowledge will be bestowed.

mangaḷangaḷ bhavichīṭān tozhutīṭuka - lōka
mangaḷattināy nityam namichīṭuka - tai tai

Bow down for blessings and auspiciousness in one's life and also for the whole world.

Tāṇḍavamāṭi (Tamil)

tāṇḍavamāṭi dayāpari varuvāy
dharaṇiyil piravippiṇi tīrkka
tāmarai malarmītē vīttiṭum mā dēvi
tāmarai idayattil naṭamāṭi vā kāḷi

Compassionate One, come dancing, to remove the cycle of birth and death! Mother Devi, sitting on lotus flower, Mother Kali! Come dancing to my lotus heart

vañcanaiyāl enkum adharmam perukutē
nañcāka koṭuñceyalē enkum vaḷarutē
kāḷiyāy vantu nī dharmam uṇarttavē
adharmmattai ozhittiṭa tāṇḍavamāṭi vā

Unrighteousness spreads everywhere due to deception. Cruelty grows everywhere like a poison. Come as Mother Kali to make us realize righteousness. Come dancing to remove unrighteousness!

jadi colli kavipāṭa kaḷiyāṭa manamāṭa
dēvi nīyō naṭanamāṭa
salankai kiṇukiṇunka virikūntalāka
kaṇṇāyirattāl āṭum tiruttāṇḍavam
dēviyāṭu... ādiparāśaktiyāṭu

My mind is in joy with rhythmically composed poems. O Mother Devi – You are dancing, with anklets tinkling and Your hair flowing freely. O thousand-eyed Goddess who dances so divinely! It is Mother Devi, primordial energy!

māyā svarūpiṇi māyaiyil vaśappeṭṭē
māyayai āṭṭivaikkum ādiparāśakti
manattirai vilakkiyē māyai kaṭattiṭavē
maṇṇulakil dharmam tazhaikka vanta tāy nī

You are the form of maya (illusion) and You at the same time You are under maya. You govern maya – O primordial One, You have come to Earth to unveil the mind and remove maya! In this way righteousness will flourish.

maṇṇāti uyirkaḷum makizhntē āṭiṭa
maṇṇilum viṇṇilum mankaḷam niraintiṭa
dēvādi dēvarum iśaimīṭṭi malar tūva
tiruḷḷattōṭu nī āṭum pukazhttāṇḍavam

For earthly beings to dance happily, for auspiciousness to fill the earth and heaven, for the showering of flowers to the sound of divine music by the gods- the dance You are dancing is a much-praised one!

Tapamanu (Telugu)

tapamanu dhanuvanu cēpaṭṭu
manasanu śaramunu sandhiñcu
brahmamanu lakṣyamu bhēdincu
ēkatvamune sādhincu

Take up the bow of austerities, fix the arrow of mind, shoot the goal of Brahman, and gain oneness with Brahman.

bhavabandhamulu māyākaṭṭlut
gaṭṭivi vāṭini temputṭaku
puṭṭuṭṭa giṭṭuṭṭa kāraṇamaina
pāpapuṇyamula tolagiñcu

Worldly bonds are illusory bondages, but very strong to cut free. Rid yourself of both merit and sin; they are responsible for the cycle of birth and death.

manasulō cintalu malinamulu
madilō dēvuni marapiñce
maruguna paṭina mādhavu neruga
avidya teranu tolagiñcu

Thoughts in the mind are like dirt covering up the Lord inside the heart. Remove the curtain of ignorance, to find the veiled Lord.

Tāraka nāma (Kannada)

tāraka nāma mahā mahimā śrī rāma
jaya-rāma raghu-rāma sītā-rāma

The glorious name of Rama enables one to transcend samsara, the cycle of birth and death. Victory to Rama of the Raghu dynasty, consort of Sita!

manavemba markaṭa – ō rāma
nina nāma dinda nina prēmadinda
nina dhyāna dinda nina sēveyinda
manavemba markaṭa āyitalla hanuma

O Rama, the mind is like a monkey. O Rama, by chanting Your name, loving You, meditating on You and performing selfless service, the monkey mind attained the state of Hanuman!

jaya-rāma raghu-rāma sītā-rāma

Victory to Rama of the Raghu dynasty! Victory to Rama, consort of Sita!

kānana kusuma – ō rāma
nina nāma dinda nina prēmadinda
nina dhyāna dinda nina pūjeyinda
kānana kusuma āyitalla śabari

O Rama, by chanting Your name, loving You, meditating on You and worshipping You, Shabari who was like a wild flower, became a renowned devotee.

jagadagala carisi carācarava porede
jaṭāyu sampāti jāmbavara porede
manujara porede amānuṣara porede
nammante nakke nammante atte
nammante silukade viśva-vibhu-vāde

You traversed the entire world. You nourished all beings, moving and unmoving. You nurtured Jatayu, Sampati, and Jambavan. You looked after the welfare of both human and non-human beings. You laughed and cried just like us, but You did not get caught in the world. You became Emperor of the universe!

Tāraka nāmamu (Telugu)

śrī rāma rāma rāmēti
ramē rāmē manōramē
sahasranāma tattulyam
rāma nāma varānanē

Meditate upon Sri Ram as Sri Rama Rama Rama. The thrice recital of Rama's name is equal to the recitation of the thousand names of Lord Vishnu (Vishnu Sahasranama).

tāraka nāmamu taluvara manujā
bhava-nāśaka mantramu maruvakurā

O Man, without forgetting, chant the name of Rama, which is capable of taking one across this ocean of samsara.

kancarla gōpuni kācina mantram
rāmadāsugā mārcina mantram
annamācāryulu nutincinadi
śabarī-mātaku varamaina mantram

This mantra protected Kancharlagoppanna and changed him to Ramdas. This mantra was praised by the great poet Annamacharya. This mantra was Shabari's boon.

bhōgā-saktuni tulasīdāsuni
yōga-yuktuni cēsina mantram
pōtanā-mātulya brōcina mantram
tyāgarājula madi koluvuṇḍinadi

This mantra turned worldly-minded Tulasidas into a great devotee. This mantra protected the poet-devotee Potana and also was established in the heart of Tyagaraja.

duḥkhālalō dānini viḍuvakurā
sukhālalō asalu maruvakurā
anni vēḷalā taluvara manujā
adiyē manaku ēkarakṣrā

O Man, don't leave it during your difficult times, don't ever forget it during your good times, chant it at all times, that alone will rescue us.

rāmā rāmā jaya jaya rāmā
rāmā rāmā jaya śrī rāmā
gaṭṭiga piluvara rāmā rāmā
prēmatō palukara rāmā rāmā
bhaktitō piluvara rāmā rāmā
śraddhatō taluvara rāmā rāmā

Chant loudly, Rama Rama! Chant with love, Rama Rama! Chant with devotion, Rama Rama! Chant with faith, Rama Rama!

Taṭaikaḷai nīkkiṭum (Tamil)

taṭaikaḷai nīkkiṭum dēva dēvā
taḷarum manankaḷai kākkum dēvā

O Lord who removes all obstacles in life, the One who protects an exhausted mind!

varam onṭru kēṭṭēn vallabhanē
varadā undan ninaivuṭan vāzhndiṭa
vallamai pettriṭa vaiyyagam pōttriṭa
vaḷankaḷ yāvaiyum vāri nī tandiṭa

O Lord, I asked for only one boon from You, to always live in Your remembrance, thus making my life meaningful. Without that boon, which is the real wealth, I will not be able to lead a prosperous life.

piravi mēl piravi eṭuttu calittēn
piravā varam vēṇḍum enṭrunnai tudittēn
nallavai nāṭiṭa tīyavai tēyndiṭa
nanneri nāṭiyē nānilam uyndiṭa

I am tired of taking endless births. I pray to You to liberate me from this cycle of birth and death. O Lord, let my mind always see only good in everything and let the negative tendencies wither away from me, thus making me a worthy recipient for Your grace.

gajamukha vadanā gajānanā
garvita madahara śubhānanā
pārvati nandana parātparā
paripālayamām pāpaharā

O Elephant-faced One, destroyer of ego, auspicious-faced One, O son of Goddess Parvati, supreme One, protector, You are the destroyer of all sins.

Tāyenḍru azhaikkavā (Tamil)

tāyenḍru azhaikkavā tandaiyenḍru azhaikkavā
guru enḍru azhaikkavā daivamenḍru azhaikkavā

How should I address You – as mother, father, guru or god?

aravanaittu anbai tandāi
azhumpōtu ārutal tandāi
atanāle nī endan tāyallavā
artavaru seytāl kaṇḍittāyē dayavuṭan mannittāyē
atanālē nī endan tandaiyallavā
enakku ellāmē nītān ammā

You love me through embraces, and console me when I cry. Therefore, aren't You my Mother? You chastise me when I err, and forgive me compassionately. So, aren't You my Father? O Mother, You are everything to me!

manam teḷiya mandiram tandāi
makkaḷkkutava sēvaikaḷ tandāi
atanālē nī endan guru allavā
eḷiyavarin tuyaram tīrttāi
ellōreyum sēyāi nēsittāi
atanālē nī endan daivam allavā
enakku ellāmē nītān ammā

To purify the mind, You gave me a mantra. For the welfare of humanity, You offered selfless service. Therefore, aren't You my guru? You assuage the sorrows of the suffering, and love everyone as Your child. So, aren't You my God? O Mother, You are everything to me!

tāyum tandayum nītān ammā
guruvum daivamum nītān ammā

Mother, Father, Guru, God– my Mother, You are everything to me!

Taye tava (Kannada version)

tāye ninna makkaḷali
kāruṇya tōrammā
tāpadi hṛdaya tapisutide
kāruṇya rūpāngane

mōda bandu divākara prabheyu
mareyāguvantē
mōhakkai siluki nāsōlladirali
kāruṇya rūpāngane

taruvu lateyū jalavu akhila
jīva jālagaḷū
nina sṛṣṭi entu nānintu arite
kāruṇya rūpāngane

Teyyōm taka (Malayalam)

teyyōm taka tārōm tittōm ttaka
teytaka tārōm tittōm
rārikkam rārō rērikkam rērō
rārikkam rārō rērikkam rērō
nalluma maintanallē murukā valli maṇāḷanallē
māmala mōḷilāyi vāzhunnoru māmayil vāhakanē
murukā ninpadam kumbiṭunnēn

O Muruga who rides on the great peacock, we worship Your feet. Son of Parvati, O Lord Muruga, groom of Goddess Valli. You reside on top of great mountains.

nal paḷanimalayil murukā vāzhunnadēvatamē
māmarutāmalayil amarum dēvasēnāpatiyē
murukā ninpadam kumbiṭunnēn

You reside in the Palani temple and live in Marutha malai as the commander in chief of the gods. Muruga, we worship Your divine feet!

kāvaṭicintupāṭām murukā āṭiyulaññiṭāmē
pālkkuṭakāvaṭiyāy kumārā kōvilaṇaññiṭunnē
murukā ninpadam kumbiṭunnēn

We sing the Kavadi Sindhu (a devotional folk song) for You, and dance with milk kavadi (a devotional apparatus), and we are reaching Your temple, Muruga. We worship Your feet!

āraṇa rūpanallē murukā nīraṇa āryanallē
vēlēnti villēntiyum murukā ērivarikayillē
vēlā ninpadam kumbiṭunnēn

O Muruga, You have six heads and are a great warrior. You hold a bow, arrow and spear- are You not coming? We worship Your divine feet.

tārakabhañjakanē mānasa tārilamaraṇamē
pāritaruḷuvōnē murukā jñānamaruḷiṭaṇē
vēlā ninpadam kumbiṭunnēn

O You who killed the asura Tharaka, please reside in our hearts. You bestow grace to the world, please give us wisdom. We worship Your divine feet.

Tintaka tintaka (Malayalam)

tintaka tintaka teyyam tārō taka
tintaka tintaka teyyam tārā
kaṇṇottu nōkkuvān pattunnatallende
kaṇṇende ceytikaḷattaramē
kuṭṭittaraṅgaḷāṇenkilumammaykku
tiṭṭattil vīṭṭilirunniṭāmō

In order to see Krishna, two eyes are not enough. His lilas are like that. Even if those plays are like a child's play, is it possible for His mother to stay inside the house?

muttattu ninnonnu cuttikkaḷicciṭum
tettannu kāṇilla pinnavane
veṭṭattil ninnonnu māriyālāyavan
cettennu kāṭakamēriṭumē

The baby Krishna plays all around the courtyard, and the next moment he disappears. If He disappears from the open space, in another moment He is climbing in the forest.

kalluṇḍu muḷḷuṇḍu kuññinde kālaṭi
ennuḷḷa cintayavaykkuṇḍāmō
kuṇḍukaḷ pārakaḷuṇḍava kāṭṭilāy
kuññavanennavayorttīṭumō

There are thorns and sharp edged stones there. Do they know that it is a child's tender foot that is stepping on them? There are pits and rocks in the forest. Do they remember that He is a kid?

paikkaḷōṭottavanōṭi kaḷikkumbōḷ
payyeyirunnatu nōkkiṭāmō
payyummarannavanōṭi kaḷikkumbōḷ
vayyennu connaṅgirinniṭāmō

Can You see Him from afar when He plays with the cows? The cows too are playing with Him, forgetting everything.

veṇṇa kavarnnavanuṇṇum parātikaḷ
peṇṇuṅgaḷeppōzhum conniṭunnu
kaṇṇanennallavar collunnatippōzhāy
kaḷḷanennākiliṅgentu ceyyum

The ladies from Vrindavan always come complaining that He is stealing their butter. Instead of calling him Krishna, they are now calling Him a thief.

taṇḍupiṇaccuḷḷa pīliyumāycennu
talluvānonnu tuṭaṅgiyālō
taṇḍukaḷ kāṭṭi kaṭannu pōminnavan
paṇḍillātuḷḷoru bhāvamāṇē

When He starts with a fighting stance with a peacock feather twisted on the end of it, He now moves on with a show of pride never before seen in Him.

cellakkārkoṇḍatil pīlitirukumbōḷ
cinnicciriccavan vanniṭumbōḷ

onnu koṭuttiṭumōṭattaṇḍonnināy
allāte colliyāl ettiṭilla

While inserting the peacock feather in His crown, when He comes close with an innocent smile, then I give Him one with His flute (hollow stick), otherwise He'll never listen to me.

maññayuṭuttavan celammē ciriccukoṇḍ-
ammēyennōtiyaṭuttiṭumbōḷ
ellām marannaṅgu ninnupōmuḷḷilāy
ammayennuḷḷoru puṇyamallē

Wearing a yellow cloth, when He comes near calling 'mother'. All His mischief will be forgotten inside, that is the merit of being His mother.

ambāṭi paitalām nīlakkārvarṇṇanum
ammayumārnnuḷḷa līlakaḷe
ambōṭeyōrkkunnu mānasameppazhum
ambāṭiyāyi vilasiṭunnu

The child of Ambadi, the blue cloud-colored one's lilas with his mother. By lovingly remembering little Krishna's lilas, the mind becomes Ambadi itself!

Tori koler chele āmi (Bengali)

tori koler chele āmi
ori doyay khāi-pori
shongshar mājhe karmo kore
dekhish tore bhule na jāi

I'm a baby in Your lap. I get my food and clothing by Your grace. Please ensure that I don't forget You and become immersed in worldly tasks.

ekti shukno patar mato
hava dilei jhore jaai

mātir shonge jabo mishe
bidāy na chai tore bhule

With a slight breeze I fall off like a dry leaf and get absorbed in the soil but I don't want an end like that - forgetting You completely.

ekla pother pothik āmi
mayar shuray neche jāi
hāriye moner pralobhane
poth hāriye chede na jāi

I am a lonely wayfarer on a lonely path. I keep dancing to the tune of maya. I should not get distracted and lose the way, tempted by the mind.

ghare eka bandho kopāt
kāndbo tore mone kore
ghadir kanta thamlo bole
āy ma chole amāy nite

Remembering You I'll shed tears in a room alone with the door shut. The clock is about to stop (death is about to come), please come to take me away with You.

Ulagankaḷ yāvum (Tamil)

ulagankaḷ yāvum nalamāga irukkaṭṭum
uyirinam yāvum vaḷamāga vāzhaṭṭum
kalahankaḷ nīnkiyē ottrumai ōnkaṭṭum
kaliyugam sattiya yugamāga māraṭṭum

May all the worlds be happy. May all beings be contented. May strife disappear and harmony take its place. May this Kali Yuga (age of unrighteousness) thus become transformed into Satya Yuga (age of righteousness).

lokah samasta sukhino bhavantu

May all beings in all the worlds be happy.

vānam mum māriyē mazhaiyinai peyyaṭṭum
vaiyyagam āṭaiyāy pasumaiyai aṇiyaṭṭum
kanivōṭu tiraikaṭal nanmaiyē puriyaṭṭum
kaliyugam sattiya yugamāga māraṭṭum

May the skies shower rain at the right times. May flora proliferate on Earth. May the oceans protect us compassionately. May this Kali Yuga thus become transformed into Satya Yuga.

māndarum aravazhi kaṭamaikaḷ puriyaṭṭum
matiyoṭu idayamum kaikōrttu naṭakkaṭṭum
kāvalāy annaiyām kāḷiyē nirkkaṭṭum
kaliyugam sattiya yugamāga māraṭṭum

May humanity follow dharma. May our hearts and intellects move hand-in-hand. May Mother Kali watch over everything as our guardian. May this Kali Yuga thus become transformed into Satya Yuga.

lokah samasta sukhino bhavantu

May all beings in all the worlds be happy.

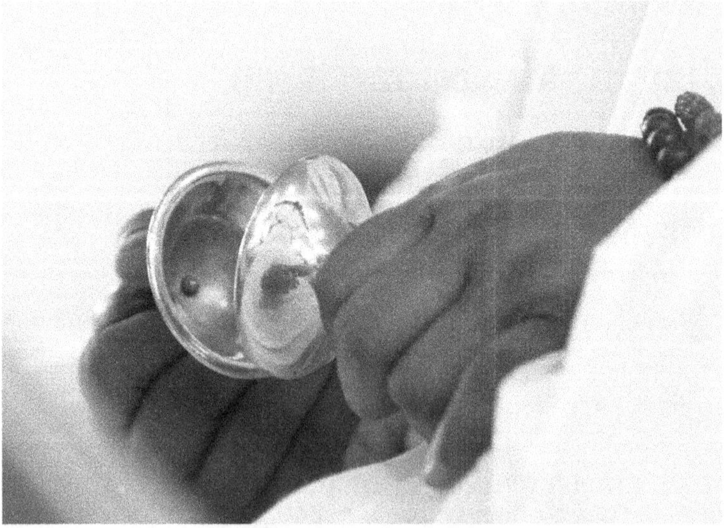

Ulagamāga māri nirkkum (Tamil)

cētanā adhiṣṭhitam jagat sarvam
inda pārellām paramporuḷin palarūpangaḷ

The whole universe is supreme consciousness. All that we see in this universe are manifestations of this supreme.

ulagamāga māri nirkkum ulaga annaiyē
inda ulagam vēr nī vēr embatillaiyē
idanai ariyum nāḷvarayil amaidiyillaiyē
idai arinda pinnar ariṇḍiṭavē onṭrum illaiyē

O Mother who is both the universe and the universal Mother, You are not separate from this universe, You are the universe itself. There is no peace till one realizes this truth. Once one realizes this truth, there is nothing more to achieve in this world.

arindu seyyum pizhaikaḷum agalavē illaiyē
ariyāda pizhaikaḷum vilagavē illaiyē
unnai nānum arindiṭa vāyppum illaiyō
vidhiyai māttrum unnaruḷ enakkillaiyō

I have not been able to get rid of the errors committed knowingly, nor have the unknowingly committed errors ended. Is there no way I can realize You? Am I not worthy of Your grace to change my fate?

aṭankāda manadil nī oḷirvadē illaiyē
manadai aṭakkum vazhiyum teriyavē illaiyē
vāzhum nāṭkaḷ ovvonṭrum undan maṭiyilē
un dayavanṭri vērēdum vazhiyum illaiyē

You don't shine forth in an uncontrolled mind- nor do I know how to control my mind. Every day of my life is on Your lap. There is no other way to obtain Your grace.

Ulakāḷum nāyakiyē (Tamil)

ulakāḷum nāyakiyē ōmkāra rūpiṇiyē
uḷḷanpāl manamkuḷirum navagraha nāyakiyē
umayavaḷē karpagamē paruvattu māriyē
uṇarvinil kalaintiṭum karuṇaimiku māriyammā

Goddess who rules the world, Your form is that of the Omkara. You rule over the nine planets and delight in our love. Uma (Shiva's consort), Goddess of richness, Goddess of seasons. You are Mariyamma who is woven into my life and experience!

māriyammā muttumāriyammā
vārivazhankum aruḷ māriyammā
varuvāy malarvāy anpu malarē
paramē tiruvē kanivuttāyē

O Mariyamma, bestower of grace! Please come and make the flower of my love blossom. You are the compassionate Mother, the eternal One.

jñāna oḷi cintiṭum ulakin ponnoḷiyē
pannezhuta tunnaipuriya tī pantam ēntiyē
kaviyin karam turitamāy kannattil iśayavē
kavitayinai azhakura inmukhamāy mozhintāy

You are the golden effulgence of this universe, spreading the light of knowledge. You are holding a lamp to help me write poetry. As I write the poems, You immediately sing them. You sing the poems beautifully with love.

ūśikkuttum iṭamillātē niraivāyē muttāka
iśaikēṭkka mēniyilē āṇmīka vittāka
āśaiyuṭan vantiṭuvāḷ anpāna viruntuṇṇa
diśayeṭṭum niraipavaḷē kāvalākum māriyammā

Mariyamma, You completely permeate me with pearls of spiritual wisdom. Please come lovingly to feast on my devotion. You stand in the eight directions and become my protector!

āyiramkaṇ pānayilē māviḷakku arppaṇam
āyimakamāyikku tamaraiyāl arccanam
agnikalaśam tānkiṭavē agni rūpamākavē
muktinalam cērttiṭavē jñānavaṭivākavē

I offer lamps made of flour (traditional prasad) in thousand-eyed pots. I perform archana to Mariyamma with lotus flowers to hold the fire of knowledge and to attain liberation, becoming knowledge itself.

māriyammā muttumāriyammā
māriyammā enkaḷ kāḷiyammā

Goddess Mariyamma, our Mother Kali!

Ulakattin tāyenṭru (Tamil)

ulakattin tāyenṭru unaipōttriccolvārē
uttamarellōrum tāyē - atan
uṭkaruttariyēn un sēyē
uṭalukku tāyāka ulakattil palaruṇḍu
uyirukku tāyānatālē - enkaḷ
ulakattāy ānāyō nīyē

The great ones praise You as the universal Mother. The significance of this is not clear to this child. There are many biological mothers. Are You the universal Mother because You are the mother of life itself?

pullirkkum pūvirkkum bhuvitannil yāvirkkum
purikinḍra mozhiyonḍru tāyē - adai
purindanbai pozhipavaḷ nīyē
kallirkkum uḷḷēyum īrattai kaṇḍinku
kanivōṭu anaittiṭum tāyē - emmai
karaisērkkum tōṇiyum nīyē

There is one language understood by all beings in creation (love); knowing this, You shower love on all beings. O Mother, You lovingly embrace even the stone-hearted.You are the boat which takes us ashore from this ocean of samsara.

nimmatiyai tēṭi nirkkāmalē ōṭi
niraivinḍri māniṭam taḷarum - tan
ninaivizhandiravil kaṇ āyarum
tammirkkuḷ tāmākum tanitta annilaiyilē
tavarāmal nī vandaṇaippāy - amaidi
tarukinṭra muttam padippāy

Humanity is relentlessly running in a fruitless search for peace. Exhausted from this search, man enters the state of deep sleep. In this state, where there is no duality, You unfailingly come and kiss us, bestowing peace upon us.

Unai maravā varamonḍru (Tamil)

unai maravā varamonḍru unniṭam kēṭṭēn - unai
enḍrum vaṇankiṭum nal manamonḍru kēṭṭēn

Please grant me a boon that I may never forget You. Grant me a heart that ever bows down to You.

sollonnā tūyarattil tūvaṇḍiṭum pōtum
cañcalankaḷ en manadai sūzhndiṭumbōtum
piravāda nilai kāṇa vazhiyinai kāṭṭi
piraviyadu kaṭaittēra padamalar taruvāy...

When my mind is tormented by endless sorrows, when desires engulf my mind, show me the way out of the cycle of birth and death by granting me refuge at Your lotus feet.

ulakirkku unaiyanṭri uyvadu uṇḍō
uyirukku unaiyanṭri uravadu uṇḍō
sērāda iṭam sērndu uzhanṭriṭum ennai

sērttiṭuvāy un pādakamalattil inḍru...
sērttiṭuvāy un pādakamalattil inḍru

Is there any refuge for the world other than You? Is there any near and dear one for this soul other than You? Even as I languish in the midst of unsuitable company, may You merge me unto Your divine feet.

manamōhana madhusūdhana rādhā ramaṇā
kaṇṇā kaṇṇā...

O Krishna of enchanting beauty, slayer of demon Madhu, beloved of Radha.

Underneath a kalpataru (English)

underneath a kalpataru
wish granting banyan
I pray for it to listen to me
pray for it to see
deep into my heart and hear it
sing a distant melody
take me in your arms devi,
take me back to thee

I wish there would be harmony
and within it a place for me
I wish I had the eyes to see
the oneness around me

aranyani aranyani
goddess of this banyan tree
take me in your heart devi
take me back to thee

I wish the world would pray with me
and think about our destiny
I wish we could be like this tree
giving shade impartially

Unmatta pañcakam (Tamil)

unmatta pañcakam pāṭiṭuvēnō
janmattin payan tanai tēṭiṭuvēnō
eṇpattum oru viradam irundiṭuvēnō
kaṇpotti kaḷikkum kaṇṇā nī solvāy

Will I sing five hymns that were written in divine intoxication? Will I attain the purpose of human birth? O You who play hide and seek, tell me.

solvatellām seyvatuṇḍō
seyvatellām solvatuṇḍō
uyyum vazhi ētum uṇḍō
un pādam tozhuvatanṭrō
tozhuvatonṭrē vazhiyākum
azhuvatu tān abhiṣēkam – atu
kazhuvum pāvamellām – atil
karayum vinaikal ellām

Do we do whatever we say? Do we say whatever we do? Is there any way to transform myself? Your lotus feet are the only way for transformation; the only way is to worship You. My tears, a ceremonial worship to You, will remove all my sins. My karma will melt away in that worship.

vinai tīrndāl ānandam
sollāmal akattil varum
akattil uḷḷa ānandam – enṭrum
azhiyā pēttrai tarum

pēratanai nān peravē
perumai migum padam paṇindēn
pērinbam nilai peravē
piḷḷai unai caraṇ pukundēn

When all my sins are absolved, inner peace will come to me of its own accord. That bliss alone will give immortality. To attain immortality, I worship Your honored lotus feet and take refuge in You.

Unnarumai (Tamil)

unnarumai mukham kāṇa kaṇṇā nān tavamirundēn
untanatu varavālē en piravippayanaṭaindēn
kaṇkaḷum kāṇāmal gangayāy ponkiyatē
kaṇḍapinnum mārāmal ennilaiyai solliṭutē

O Krishna, I have been doing penance in order to behold Your divine face. When You finally came, I felt my life had been fulfilled. My eyes filled with tears like the ever-flowing Ganges. But because of this I could not see You, thus demonstrating my pathetic state.

un madhura nāmamatai uṇavāga uṇḍirundēn
uḷḷam kavar un ninaivai uyirāga koṇḍirundēn
kanavilum kaṇḍatellām un mukham adanālē
kanavilum kaṇḍatellām un mukhamē adanālē
kanavō itu nanavō enṭru nānum mayankukinṭrēn

Your sweet names were like food to me. I survived only because of the enchanting thoughts I had of You. Even in my dreams I could only see Your divine face. I became confused as to whether I was dreaming or awake, as in both states I could only perceive Your holy face.

mālaiyēndi unakkāka nāninku kāttirundēn
mālaitōrum mālaivāṭa nānuminku vāṭi ninṭren
pūmālai kōrkkavillai unaikkāṇum innēram
pūmalai kōrkkavillai unnaikkāṇum innēram
pāmālai ennuyiril kōrtteṭuttu cūṭṭukinṭrēn

Everyday I waited for You with a garland, but by evening when You had not come, the flowers had drooped along with my face. When You came today, I had not made a garland, so I am garlanding You with heart-felt songs of Your praises.

Uṇṇi gaṇapatiye (Malayalam)

uṇṇi gaṇapatiye uḷḷam vaṇaṅgānāy
entaṭā kuññāṇē nammaḷum pōvēṇḍē

O little brother, shouldn't we also go to worship baby Ganesh with all our heart?

uḷḷamazhiññu tozhām meyyitulaññu tozhām
uḷḷilezhunniṭaṇē uṇṇi gaṇapatiyē

We pray with fervor, we pray as we sway. O baby Ganapati, please be present within us.

mālarum mauli tozhān mānattil nōkkiṭunnē
pārāte pādam tozhān pāritil vīṇiṭunnē

To bow down to His purifying crown, we look up to the sky. To bow down at His feet, we look down to the earth.

ambiḷikkīraṇiyum vambezhum kēśabhāram
tumbōṭu kaṇṇariññē mumbāyikkaitozhunnē

We bow down, beholding his thick hair adorned with a crescent moon.

embāṭu mumbartozhum mānpezhum nalpadaṅgaḷ
vembalakattiṭānāy nambivaṇaṅgiṭunnē

To remove grief, we bow down with faith to His feet which are worshipped by the gods.

tumbamakanniṭānāy tumbikku kumbiṭunnē
imbamiyanniṭānāy kumbayum kaitozhunnēn

To remove sorrows we bow down to His trunk. To acquire joy, we bow down to His belly.

vambezhum kombatinē anpināy kaitozhunnēn
lambōdharanivane ambōṭu kumbiṭunnēn

For grace we bow down to his tusk; we bow down with love to this large-bellied Ganapati.

nallavil śarkkarayum veṇmalar kēramatum
nanpezhum nalpazhavum mātaḷam nīḷkarimbum

We offer You beaten rice, jaggery, puffed rice, coconut, excellent plantain bananas, pomegranates, and sugarcane.

nallaṭa mōdakavum kalkkaṇḍa muntiriyum
añcāte nēdichiṭām ayyanē kāttiṭanē

We offer You rice pancakes, modaka, rock candy and grapes. Please protect us!

nalluma yankamatil ārnnirunnennumennum
nanmayaruḷiṭaṇē uṇṇivināyakanē

O little Ganapati, seated on the lap of Goddess Parvati, bestow goodness on us always.

ādi vaṇaṅgiṭuṇē ādhikaḷattiṭaṇē
śankara nandananē śakti nīyēkiṭaṇē

We bow down at the very beginning to remove all our anxieties. O son of Lord Shiva, give us strength!

Ūraṭankum (Tamil)

anpu kuzhantai urankiṭa tālāṭṭum annai
āruyirai tālāṭṭi uḷḷam teḷivākkum kāḷī
imaippozhutum kāppāḷ enum nambikkaiyilē
īndra makkaḷ urankiṭukaiyil ulāvarudam makākāḷī

Mother sings a lullaby for the dear child to sleep. Mother Kali sings a lullaby for the soul, to make the mind clear. When Her children are sleeping with the faith that She will always protect them, Mahakali goes on a promenade.

ūraṭankum vēḷayilē ūrvalamāy vārāḷē
uttamiyām bhattirakāḷi namme kākka vārāḷē
urakkamatu vizhitazhuva akamuṇara umāśankarī
urankātu nammiṭaiyē ānandamāy vārāḷē
ammā om kāḷī makākāḷī
ammā om śaktī parāśaktī

When it is dusk and the city retires, She comes in a procession. Bhadra Kali, an embodiment of purity, is coming to protect us. For sleep to embrace our eyes and make us realize - the consort of Lord Shiva comes to us happily, without sleeping Herself. O Mother, Kali, primordial energy!

pañcam paśi tīravē gaṇapati tāy vārāḷe
mañcamākum manatinilē paḷḷikoḷḷa vārāḷē
añcum manatai amaidiyākka vārāḷē
pañcabhūtam āḷpavaḷāy vārāḷē

The Mother of Lord Ganesha is coming to remove poverty and hunger. She is coming to sit in the seat of the mind. She is coming to put the fearful mind at peace. She is coming to rule the five elements of nature.

kanimālai tānkiyē kanivuṭanē vārāḷē
piṇitīra vēppilai vīśi vēlavan tāy vārāḷē

paccaipayar śezhittiṭavē vārāḷē
icchayellām kaḷaintiṭavē vārāḷē

She is coming with compassion and bearing garland of fruits. The Mother of Lord Muruga is coming and waving neem leaves to remove disease. She is coming to grant a good harvest of crops. She is coming to rid us of desires.

muḷaippāri śiram tānka bhaktiyāka vārāḷē
viḷainilattai ponnilamāy māttriṭavē vārāḷē
bhānakāram paṭayalērka vārāḷē
manataiyāḷa makēsvarī vārāḷē

She is coming with devotion to bear the mulaipari (traditional earthen pot filled with sprouts of nine different grains) on Her head. She is coming to change the farmland into a golden land. She is coming to accept offerings of spicy beverages (traditional). Goddess Durga is coming to rule our mind.

Uṭayavaḷ (Malayalam)

uṭayavaḷ umayennu ninaykkum uḷḷam
upakariccīṭum-ārkkum- onnupōle
orikkalum-uzharilla bhaya kōpādikaḷilla
sukha duḥkha bhāva bhēdam onnumilla

The mind that considers Uma as the most intimate will be beneficial equally to everyone. It will not go astray, nor will it succumb to fear and anger. The mind will be free of the differences arising from opposites such as happiness and sorrow.

uṇarvvinnāyuttu nōkkum
unmatta bhaktarkkellām
unnati nalkum nīyammā parāśakti
unnati nalkum nīyammā

For the ecstatic devotees who look up to You for enlightenment, Mother Parashakti, You grant exaltation.

uṭalenna bōdham viṭṭu uttavaḷ nīyennōrttāl
uṭanōṭi ettunnavaḷ nī parāśakti
uṭanōṭi ettunnavaḷ nī

O Parashakti, You immediately come running to those who no longer identify with the body and consider You as the most intimate.

ulakellām-udippiccu ūnamattu kaḷiyāy kāttu
uḷḷilotukkunnavaḷ nī parāśakti
uḷḷilotukkunnavaḷ nī

Creating the whole universe as a play, O Parashakti, You protect it and then dissolve it into Yourself.

uḷḷatonnāyuṇḍatu uḷḷiluṇḍennu kaṇḍāl
uttungaparam-ānandam parāśakti
uttunga param-ānandam

There is one reality that exists. If we see that it is within, O Parashakti, we get supreme bliss!

Uyara uyara (Tamil)

uyara uyara pōkum manam āzhntu pōkavē
sōrntu pōyviṭāmal atai nī kākkavē
vāzhkayil uttama tattuvam nī
makattuvam nirainta māmaṇi nī

The mind that is soaring upwards must also dive into the depths. While doing that, please protect me so that it will not lose vigor and become listless. O Master, You are the supreme truth in one's life. In You lies the pearl of excellence.

ganamāna ninaivukaḷ varumbōtellām
guruvē un vārttaikaḷ itamānatē
mārā vicāraṇai seytīṭavē
vairāgyaṁ nī tūṇḍa nalamākutē

Whenever I am in the throes of my own spiritual seeking, O Guru, Your words of comfort alone give me strength. You are instigating the determination in me so that the ceaseless enquiry will go on within.

anubhavamām peru vīthiyil naṭattum guruvē
pūvō vazhi mūḷḷō viral piṭi pōtumē
ituvē nān nitaṁ seyyuṁ or prārtthanai
guruvē un aruḷ vākku balamānavai

In this expanded world of experiences, You are leading me on the path where there may be thorns and there may be flowers. No matter how the journey is, as long as You are holding onto at least one finger of mine, that is enough for me. This is my everlasting prayer to You. Please always give me strength with Your grace-filled words.

Uyirōṭuyirāy (Tamil)

uyirōṭuyirāy uṇarvōṭuṇarvāy
uravāṭiṭa vā kaṇṇā
siraiyil piranda maraiyin poruḷē
piravippayanē kaṇṇā

O Krishna! Come and be one with my being and consciousness. You, who were born in a prison, are the essence of the Vedas and the fulfillment of life.

pettravar anbum suttravar tuṇaiyum
uttravanum nī kaṇṇā
kattratu koṇḍu pattradu viṭṭu
pettradum unaiyē kaṇṇā...
pettradum unaiyē kaṇṇā

You are the embodiment of parental affection, of help from kith and kin. You are the intimate One. You are attained by dispassion that is obtained through knowledge.

akalāden manam tudittiṭum un padam
ānirai mēykkum kaṇṇā
ayarādoru kaṇam ninaittiṭum un mukham
ālilai tuyilum kaṇṇā...
ālilai tuyilum kaṇṇā

O Krishna, cowherd boy! My mind steadfastly worships Your feet. O Krishna who sleeps on the banyan leave! My mind tirelessly remembers Your face.

kaṇṇā... kaṇṇā... kaṇṇā... kaṇṇā...

Vandan gaurī (Hindi)

vandan gaurīnandanā –
tujhe vandan sukhamandira
sankaṭ sab harttā terā cintan gaṇanāyaka

My salutations to You, O son of Gauri. Salutations to the giver of happiness, You who destroys all woes for those who meditate on You.

jai manōjñavigrahā jai trilōkapālakā
jai munīndravanditā jai maheśanandana

Victory to the one with the beautiful form, victory to the Lord of the three worlds. Victory to the one worshipped by the sages, victory to the son of Mahesha!

mangal sab detā hai tū sang tere ham cale
ānand hai rūp terā andar ā base... tū ā base

O One who showers prosperity, we walk along with You. May Your form of bliss be enshrined in my heart.

bālak ham tere pās āye hai karanā kṛpā
saṇcit santāp sabhī āj dūr kare... tū dūr kare

We are Your little children who have come to You. Protect us! Please take away all our worries and sorrows.

Vandavar ettanai (Tamil)

vandavar ettanai cenṭravar ettanai
janmankaḷ ettaneyō?
vāzhndavar ettanai? vīzhndavar ettanai
māyndavar ettaneyō?

How many people have come, how many have gone, and how many lifetimes have passed! How many people have prospered, how many have fallen into bad times, and how many have died!

ettanai svantankaḷ ēdēdō bandankaḷ
ettanai sōdanaigaḷ ēdēdō vēdanaigaḷ
mīṇḍum mīṇḍum tāybandam
viṇḍu pōgum sēybandam
koṇḍu pōgum nōynoṭigaḷ
namakku inkē yār sondam

How many relations, how much bondage, how many tests and how much pain there is! Time and again, the mother-child relation has been forged, only for this bond to dissolve. Given that disease will eventually take us all away, who do we have to call our own?

vāzhum murai turanduviṭṭu
kurai śollal murai tānō
vāzhum pōdu pala uravu iranda pinnē yār uravu
manamadu kōyilām uḷ uraivadu kāḷiyām
dinamadai nām uṇarndu vaḷarachaiyvōm irai uṇarvu

Is it right to abandon one's dharma and then blame God for the consequences? While living, we have many relatives. After death, who is there to call our own? The mind is a temple. Kali is enshrined therein. Remembering this always, let us awaken God-consciousness.

Var de (Hindi)

mānav janm diyā hai tu ne
terī carano ki chāv bhī
bas var ye tu de de maiyā
saphal ho jīvan merā bhī
ek prārthanā sun le merī
nisvārth bhāvanā bhar de
aisā mujh ko var de mā
aisā mujhkō var de

You have given me a human birth; and also a shelter at Your feet. Please listen to my prayers, O Mother, and fill me with the attitude of selflessness, making my life successful. I seek such a boon, O Mother.

var de var de - maiyyā
var de var de - aisā
var de var de, vardān tū de

Grant me a boon Mother!

var de mā
man aisā de
duḥkh duḥkhiyōn kā
jān sakū

Grant me a boon, O Mother, that I may have a mind that can recognize the problems of the distressed;

var de mā
samajh aisā de
duḥkh aurō kā
samajh sakū

Mother, grant me a boon that I may understand others' sorrow.

aisā var de aise vichār de
aurō kā bhalā soch sakū
nisvārth cintan jagā sakū

Grant me a boon, grant me thoughts that I may invoke selfless thoughts.

var de mā nain aise de
duḥkh aurō ka dekh sakū

Grant me a boon, O Mother, that I may have eyes that can see others sufferings.

var de mā kar aisa de
dukhiyon ko sehlā sakū

Grant me a boon that I may have arms that can caress and console the distressed.

aisā var de dil aisā de
dūsron ko apnā sakū
nisvārth karam nibhā saku

Grant me a boon, grant me a heart that can accept others as my own and that I can carry out selfless actions.

Vaṭavṛkṣmām (Malayalam)

vaṭavṛkṣmām ninnil paṭarān kotikkunna
oru ceruvalli ñān ammē...
onnu taḷiriṭṭu pūviṭum munpe nī
vēraruttīṭarutē... enne
vērōḍe nīkkarutē

I am a tiny creeper that yearns to climb the banyan tree that You are. Please do not uproot or tear me away before I sprout and flower.

etrayō nāḷayi ñān pūjiccu nin pādam
bhakti ennil ankuriccū...
taḷiriṭṭu pūviṭṭu kaniyāy nin padatāril
patiyānāy ennē anugrahikkū... ammē
patiyānāy ennē anugrahikkū

After worshipping You for so long, the bud of devotion has sprouted in my heart. O Mother, bless me so that I may sprout, flower and bear fruit, which can be offered at Your feet.

azhalinte veyilēttu vāṭumen taṇḍum
taḷirum nīyillāte pōyāl
viṭarātaṭarumen moṭṭukaḷ vyathayōḍe
kēzhum nīyillāte pōyāl... vāḍi
vīzhum nīyillāte pōyāl

If You don't come to me, my stem and leaves will wilt under the scorching heat of sorrow. My buds will wither away and fall even before blossoming.

picca naṭakkuvānāvātta kuññine
mātāvu kaiviṭṭu pōyāl...
oru tuḷḷi pālināy kēzhumā kuññinte
vazhiyentu? pizhayentendammē... piñju
kuññinte gatiyentendammē

O Mother, if You leave this toddling child, who is crying for a drop of milk, what will it do? What wrong did I do? What will the lot of this tiny babe?

Vazhimēl vizhi (Tamil)

vazhimēl vizhi vaittu pārttirundēn
varuvān kaṇṇan ena kāttirundēn
manadil avan amara puttirundēn

malaraṭi en neñcil sērttirundēn

With my gaze fixed on the path, I waited in anticipation for Krishna. The flower of my heart blossomed to enshrine the lotus feet of the Lord.

karunīla niramellām avan terindān
kaḷḷamillāchirippil enai kavarndān
manatinil avan maṭṭum niraindirundān
matiyinil ninaivukaḷāy uraindirundān

I beheld Him in all that was cloud-blue. He captivated me through every innocent smile. He alone filled my heart, rooted as memories in my mind.

rādhayāy nāninku ēnki ninṭrēn
nandanai emmanatil tānki ninṭrēn
kaṇṇanin kuzhal kēṭṭu enai marandēn
karutiyen arukil vara ninaivizhandēn

I stood longing like Radha, my mind engrossed fully in thoughts of Him. I forgot myself in the melody of His flute. When He came near unexpectedly, I became transfixed.

Vettrivēl (Tamil)

vettrivēl! vīravēl! śaktivēl! jñānavēl!

Victory to Lord Muruga, the valorous, omnipotent and omniscient One!

aṭipaṇiyum aṭiyavarkku vettritarum vettrivēl
aṭuttuvarum tuyarkaḷaiya vīram tarum vīravēl
akhilattkkē sēvai seyya śaktitarum śaktitarum
anaittuyirum tannuyirāy kāṇavaikkum jñānavēl

You grant victory to those who seek refuge in You. You impart courage to face trials and tribulations in life. You impart strength to serve the world. You teach us how to see the One in all.

veḷḷivēl! tankavēl! muttuvēl! vairavēl!

O bearer of the silver, golden, pearl and diamond spear, victory to You!

veḷḷaiyuḷḷam koṇḍavarkku nallatuṇai veḷḷivēl
vēdanaikaḷ varumbozhutu tānkinirkkum tankavēl
munvinaiyai muzhuvadumāy azhittiṭumē muttuvēl
varuvinaiyai pōkki nalla vazhi seyyumē vairavēl

You are the eternal refuge of pure hearts. When in pain, You are the support. You negate the karmic consequences incurred in the past. You also avert the suffering one is destined to experience, and lead us along the right path.

kandavēl! kumaravēl! azhagvēl! murugavēl!

O Skanda (another name for Lord Muruga), Kumara (young one), Azhaga (beautiful one), Muruga, victory to You!

kaṇkaḷtannai kalvi tandu tirandvaikkum kandavēl
karpagampōl selvam tandu kāttu nirkkum kumaravēl
muyarchiyonṭrē azhagu enṭru uṇarttiṭumē azhagu vēl
muyarchiyellām tiruvinaiyāy ākkiṭumē murugavēl

You bestow wisdom on us, thereby openning our third eye of knowledge. You bestow all auspiciousness, and protect us like the Kalpaka Tree (wish-fulfilling tree). You help us appreciate the value of self-effort. You fulfill our efforts with divine grace.

vettrivēl - vēl vēl
vīravēl - vēl vēl
śaktivēl - vēl vēl
jñānavēl - vēl vēl
vettrivēl! vīravēl! śaktivēl! jñānavēl!
vettrivēl! vīravēl! śaktivēl! jñānavēl!

Vighnanāśaka śrīvināyaka (Kannada)

vāgīśādyāḥ sumanasaḥ
sarvārtthānām upakrame
yam natvā kṛtakṛtyāḥ syuḥ
tam namāmi gajānanam

You are worshipped by all the gods before any undertaking. Blessed by You, they gratefully pay obeisance to You, O Gajanana (elephant-headed god).

vighnanāśaka śrīvināyaka
mudati pālisunammanu
ninnabēḍuta stutiyagaivevu
sumukhane surapramukhane

O Ganesh, destroyer of obstacles, take care of us with love. We ask this of You as we sing Your praises. You have a beautiful form and are the leader of the Ganas (celestial followers).

pārvatisuta pāpa nāśaka
pāśānkuśadhara pādasevita
pāhi pāhi lambodara
sumukhane surapramukhane

Son of Parvati, destroyer of sins, You bear the noose (symbolizing the power of divine love) and goad (which restrains the forces of evil), we worship You. Protect us, Lambodara (large-bellied one – represents the acceptance of all things with awareness). Your form is beautiful and You are the leader of the Ganas.

kleśagaḷaniśśeṣa harane
śaraṇu śaraṇusarvātmane
caraṇakeraguve śūrppakarṇṇane
sumukhane surapramukhane

You are the destroyer of all conflict, we take refuge in You, all-pervading one. We worship Your holy feet. You have large ears, Your form is beautiful and You are the leader of the Ganas.

vignanāśaka jai jai jai śrī vināyakā jai jai jai
pāvanacaritā jai jai jai mokṣadāyakā jai jai jai

Victory to the destroyer of obstacles, victory to the pure One, the giver of liberation!

Vimmum kural (Tamil)

vimmum kural kēṭṭilayō?
vizhinīrai pārttillayō?
vimbum neñjai arindillayō?
vēdanai tān purintillayō?

Did You not listen to my cries? Did You not see my tearful eyes? Did You not understand my longing heart? Can You not understand my pain?

kanḍrin kural kēṭṭa pinpum
kanintiranga pasuvum uṇḍō?
onḍrivida tuṭikkum ennai
odukki vaittāl muraitānō
varuvāy varuvāy ena eṇṇi nān
engi nirkka kaṇḍa pōdum
pāramukham enammā?

Is there any cow whose heart will not melt when her calf cries? When I want to merge in You, is it appropriate for You to keep me away? Having seen that I am waiting for Your arrival with longing, still, O Mother, You have not looked at me.

viḷayāḍa poruḷ tanḍāy
viḷayāṭṭil mūzhkiviṭṭēṇ
arul pasiyai alittiduvāy

arul amudai parikiduvēn
kuraivellām nirayum
kuyilotta un vākkāl
varuvatellām nalamākum
vañji untan kaṇ nōkkāl

You gave me the toys to play with, so I became immersed in that game. Give me that hunger for Your grace. I will drink the nectar of Your grace. All my shortcomings will be removed with Your sweet, melodious words. When You gaze at me, whatever will come will be for my good.

Vināyakane vinay tīrtarulvāy (Tamil)

vināyakane vinay tīrtarulvāy
vaḷangal peruka vāzhkai shezhikka

Please remove the obstacles so that my life may blossom and good fortune may come to me.

om enum mandira
vaḍivam tāngi vandāy
odum maraikalil
uṭporulāki ninḍrai

Your form itself carries the message of the mantra 'Om'. You are the essence of the four Vedas.

malaimakal maindane malaraḍi nāḍukirōm
aḍiyavar manadinil nimmadi nilaittiḍa

O son of Parashakti, I come to Your lotus feet. Give this slave of Yours peace of mind.

vēzha mukham kanḍāl vēdanai tīrndiḍumē
vēnḍum varangalum vēnḍāmal kiḍaitiḍume

When we look at Your elephant-like form all our sorrows vanish. Even without our asking, You will give all that we need.

ulakattin nāyakane uvappuḍan pōṭrukirom
punnakai mukhattoḍu puvitannai kāttḍa

O King of the world, we praise You. With Your smiling face You will save the universe!

Vināyaka enkaḷ (Tamil)

karuvizhi umaiyāḷ tirumaganē
virisaḍai śivanārkkiniyavanē
karimukha kaṭavuḷ gaṇapatiyē – un
tiruvaṭi vaṇanki paṇindōmē

Son of Uma who has beautiful black eyes, darling of Shiva who has matted locks; O Ganapati, elephant-faced Lord, we prostrate at Your holy feet.

vināyaka enkaḷ vināyakā
vinaikaḷai tīrppāy vināyakā
vināyakā enkaḷ vināyakā
vettriyai taruvāy vināyakā

O Vinayaka, remove the effects of all our bad deeds, make us victorious!

alayum manadai aṭakkenḍrē
eli vāhanattāl uṇarttukirāy
adhikam kēḷ nal vākkenḍrē
ānaiceviyāl uṇarttukirāy

Through Your vehicle, the mouse, You indicate to us to control the wavering mind. You awaken the awareness of listening to wise words through Your elephant ears.

siruvāhanamum peruntalayum
sīrāy ceppumun tattuvamē
nuṇṇiyatil nī nuṇṇiyanē

periyatil ellām periyōnē

Your tiny vehicle and huge head symbolically represent this principle: that You are the subtlest of the subtle and mightiest among the mighty.

tōrkkum karaṇam māyaiyadan
īrkkum piṭiyil enḍruṇarndē
tōppukkaraṇam pōṭṭiṭavē
kākkum daivam gaṇapatiyē

We realize that our sense organs are blinded by the bewitching spell of maya (delusion). O Ganapati, we bow down to You. You are our savior.

Viśvam nīlō (Telugu)

viśvam nīlō unnadā?
viśvamulō nīvunnāvā?
nijamēdō telusukō dhīrā dhīrā

O hero of subtle intellect, know which is true: is the world within you, or are you in the world?

nīvanē caitanya kaṭalilō
īdēṭī dēhālanē cēpalennō
nīvanē cidākāśame
dēhamanē kuṇḍalōni ākāśamu
kāyamanēkuṇḍa pagilitē
migilēdi nīvanē cidākāśamē

You are the ocean of consciousness in which many fish called bodies are swimming. The all-pervasive space of consciousness which is You is the same space contained within the pot called the body. When this pot-like body breaks, what remains is nothing other than 'You' – the all-pervasive space of consciousness.

jāgṛtilō ī dṛśyajagamu
manō indriya nimittamē kādā
svapnamulō ī viśvamu
nīlōnē gōcariñcu cunnadi kadā
suṣuptilō prapañcamu
nīku māyamu aynadi kadā

In the waking state, isn't the perceived world caused and limited by the mind and five senses? In the dream state, doesn't the whole universe appear within you? In deep sleep doesn't the whole creation disappear to you?

nīvu dēhamanē bhrāntitō
viśvamulō bratikē ō jīvirā
nīvu sarvātmavaina
nīlōni sṛṣṭiki sākṣirā
turīyam idērā dhīrā
nijamidē telusukō ō muktuḍā

You are living as a creature in this world, deluding Yourself as the body. Realize your nature as the all-pervading atman, and you will witness the entire creation within yourself. O hero! This state of awareness is called turiya. This is the ultimate truth, O eternally liberated one!

Viṭhal smaraṇ karā (Marathi)

om śrī aho! ṣaḍguṇ aiśvaryai sampann
bhāgyavantā ahō! ramākāntā śrī viṭhalā

Om Sri! You are full of the six divine qualities, consort of Lakshmi, O Sri Vitthala!

viṭhal smaraṇ karā, viṭhal bhajan karā
pāvan nām śrī harī smaraṇ karā

Remember Vithala, sing the glory of Vithala! Remember and chant the pious name of Sri Hari!

yuga yugānantar narjanm miḷālā
niścit nāhi hā yōg parat hōyīl
lābhlēlā janm viṭhal caraṇī lāvā
nāmsmaraṇ karuṇ sārtaki lāvā

After many thousands of years, you got this human birth. But it's not certain that this good fortune will come to you again; therefore, always seek the lotus feet of Vithala. Accomplish the very purpose of life by chanting His name.

viṭhal viṭhal pāṇḍurangā
jaya hari viṭhal pāṇḍurangā
viṭhal viṭhal viṭhal viṭhal viṭhal viṭhal pāṇḍurangā

Victory to Vithala! Chant the name of Panduranga! O Vithala, Panduranga!

uṭhā uṭhā jan ho calā bhakti mārggāvar
sādhan sajjan sakhya kāhi prāpt hōyīl
paṇḍarīnāthācā nām sankīrttan svar
sōbat nija sadgurucī kṛpā lābhē

Wake up, wake up, O Man! Proceed on the path of bhakti yoga. If you are lucky you could get the company of virtuous men, take this opportunity to sing the glory of Pandharinatha. Get the benefit of grace from the real Sadguru!

mānav janmācā param uddēś kēvaḷ
muktī nirvāṇ sādhaṇē, dusarē nāhī
sōḍu avidyā bhrānti viṣaya sukh
samaj re manuja tu harinām sarv kāhī

Know that the true purpose of human birth is freedom from the cycle of birth and death. Therefore, give up ignorance, illusion, passion. Realize, O Man! Hari's name is everything in life.

Vizhi kiṭaikkumā (Tamil)

alaimōdum kaṭalinilē turumbāy nān tavikkayilē
nilaiyāna padam sēra nīyē en tuṇaiyammā

Like an insignificant particle tossed uncontrollably by the waves of the ocean, the endless ocean of transmigration is tossing me about. O Mother, take me and give me refuge at Your divine feet.

vizhi kiṭaikkumā kaṭaikkaṇ vizhi kiṭaikkumā
vāzhkaiyyil munnera vazhi pirakkumā
tāyē vazhi pirakkumā

Will I get Your divine glance that will allow me to progress in this life?

iṭam kiṭaikkumā, enakkōr iṭam kiṭaikkumā
unmanam tanilentrum iṭam kiṭaikkumā
enakkōr iṭam kiṭaikkumā

Will I get a place in Your heart?

karam kiṭaikkumā abhaya karam kiṭaikkumā
tuyarattil tuṇaiyāga karam kiṭaikkumā
undan karam kiṭaikkumā

Will You give me Your supporting hand, my sole refuge?

padam kiṭaikkumā malarppadam kiṭaikkumā
vāzhvinil karaisēra padam kiṭaikkumā
undan padam kiṭaikkumā

Will I get refuge at Your lotus feet to help me come out of this ocean of transmigration?

ōm śakti ōm śakti ōm śakti ōm
ādiparāśakti śivaśakti ōm
ōm śakti ōm parāśakti ōm
śiva śakti aikya svarūpiṇi ōm

O primordial power, eternally supreme power, You are the union of Shiva and Shakti in a single form.

Vṛndāvana kuñjavihāri (Hindi)

vṛndāvana kuñjavihāri
gopī jan sang milā hai
bansī dhun cheḍ rahā hai
brajme madhu baras rahā hai

The Lord of Vrindavan is with the gopis (the cowherd women of Vrindavan). He is playing a melodious tune on his flute, showering sweet nectar on the holy land of Braj. (The flute - the eternal call of the supreme to all.)

jai rādhika pyāre gopabāla nanda nandanā
śyāma sundarā bansi gāyakā
hare kṛṣṇā hare śyāma muraḷi mohanā

Victory to the beloved of Radha, cowherd boy, son of Nanda! Beautiful and dusky like the evening twilight sky, flute-player. Hail to Krishna who is dark in complexion and plays the enchanting flute.

kālindi thirak uṭhī hai
malayānil mand bahā hai
rettīle jamunā taṭpar
bāsantī rang jamā hai

The river Kalindi has risen joyfully in dance. There is a gentle soothing breeze from the mountains. On the sandy shores of river Yamuna, the lovely colors of spring rejoice.

rāsotsav maṇḍal sohe
gopījan nāc rahī hai
muraḷīdhar maddhya khaḍā hai
rādhājī sāth juḍī hai

All the gopis are dancing, gathered in rasa lila celebration. Holding the flute, He stands in the center along with Radha.

madhuban kā nāc sabhī ke
nainon ko soh rahā hai
devon ko jogījan ko
bhagaton ko moh rahā hai

This divine dance is so pleasing and mesmerizing to all – devas (demi-gods), yogis, renunciates and devotees are all enchanted by it.

kalpon se calttā āttā
rāsotsav manko bhāttā
merī yeh cāh kanayyā
nācūm sang tere mein bhī

The divine dance of love has been happening for ages, enchanting all. It is my desire O Krishna, that I too may dance this divine dance with You.

Table of Contents

Abhivandanam (Telugu) 4
Ādidaivamā (Telugu) 4
Adi sṛṣṭi lōpamā (Telugu) 6
Aintezhuttu (Tamil) 7
Akamanatin kāriruḷai (Tamil) 8
Akatārilennennum (Malayalam) 9
Akatāril oru nēram (Malayalam) 10
Ālā bhāgyāca kṣaṇ (Marathi) 11
Amala bharatam (English) 12
Ambapaluku (Telugu) 12
Ambā śāmbhavī (Sanskrit) 13
Ammā ammā enum (Tamil) 15
Ammā dēvī (Kannada version) 16
Ammā dēvi (Tulu version) 16
Ammā hāsattu (Konkani) 17
Ammā nāpai (Telugu) 17
Ammā ninna prēmakāgi (Kannada) 19
Amma nīvē sākṣi (Telugu) 19
Ammē enuḷḷu (Malayalam) 20
Amṛtalayam ānandalayam (Malayalam) 21
Ānandamē ānandam (Tamil) 22
Annaiyē unnaiyē (Tamil) 23
Antardarśanattinuḷḷa (Malayalam) 24
Anudinamum (Tamil) 25
Aparādham-endētu (Malayalam) 26
Āreyāṇāreyaṇiṣṭam (Malayalam) 28
Aridu aridu (Tamil) 29
Arikiluṇḍenkilum (Tamil version) 30
Arivenum akakkaṇ (Tamil) 31
Ariyāte ceytoraparādham (Malayalam) 32
Aśrutīrtthattāl (Malayalam) 33

Āṭalarasē (Tamil) 34
Āṭi bā ō ranga (Kannada) 35
Āvo mā ammā (Gujarati) 36
Āyā he sārā (Hindi) 37
Āye hān tvadde (Punjabi) 38
Āyī bhavāni tū (Marathi) 39
Azhagukku azhagu (Tamil) 40
Azhaku azhaku (Tamil) 41
Azhalingu puzhayāy (Malayalam) 43
Azhutāl unnaiperalāmē (Tamil) 44
Bā bhṛngavē bā (Kannada) 45
Balē ambikē (Tulu) 46
Bandaḷō bandāḷō (Kannada) 47
Bandaḷō bandāḷō (Gujarati version) 48
Bandhamu nīttō (Telugu) 49
Bandu biḍabāradē (Kannada) 50
Bārayya śiva (Kannada) 50
Barutihaḷu (Kannada) 51
Beḷḷi beṭṭadoḍeya (Kannada) 52
Beyond the most beautiful words 53
Bhaktigē sōpāna (Kannada) 54
Bhuvanasundarī (Tamil) 55
Birhā ki in (Hindi) 56
Callaga cūḍu (Telugu) 57
Candracūḍa (Telugu) 58
Cēnmilē (Hindi) 59
Cinna cinna kaṇṇā (Tamil) 60
Cuṭṭri cuṭṭri (Tamil) 61
Ḍam ḍam ḍum ḍum ḍamarū bōle (Gujarati) 62
Dānavāntakā rāmā (Kannada) 64
Dayānidhiyē (Kannada) 65
Dayatoru hē kāḷikē (Kannada) 66

Dayayālē urukoṇḍu (Tamil) 67
Dēvādidēvā (Telugu) 68
Dēvi dayākari (Kannada) 69
Devī mahādevī (Hindi) 70
Devī triloki (Hindi) 71
Dil me terī (Hindi) 73
Durge durgati (Hindi) 74
Ēkantatayuṭe āzham (Malayalam) 75
Ēlappulayēlō (Malayalam) 76
Ēlō ēlō (Malayalam) 77
Enakkuḷḷē nīyum (Tamil) 78
Enkirundu vandōm (Tamil) 79
Engum annaiyun (Tamil) 80
En mannassiloru maunam (Tamil) 80
Ennadu yāvudammā (Kannada) 81
Ennai nān maranda (Tamil) 82
Ennō ennō (Telugu) 82
En piravi muṭindiṭumō (Tamil) 84
Etayō tēṭi (Tamil) 85
Ettanai vēdanai (Tamil) 85
Gajānanā he gajānanā (Tamil) 86
Gaṇanāthā he gaṇanāthā (Tamil) 87
Gaṇaṅgaḷin nāthā (Tamil) 87
Gaṇapati guṇanidhi (Hindi) 88
Gōkula bālā gōvindā (Malayalam) 90
Gopiyara usirē (Kannada) 91
Gōpiyarkaḷ (Tamil) 91
Gōpiyarkaḷ uḷḷankaḷai (Tamil) 92
Gopiyarkoñcum (Tamil) 93
Hanumat bal do (Hindi) 94
Harē śankha cakra dhāri (Kannada) 96
Harē tū hamārē (Hindi) 97

Harim śyāmavarṇam (Sanskrit) 98
Harsut akhila (Hindi) 99
Hē mañjunāthā (Konkani) 101
He śrīnivāsa (Kannada) 102
Holi hai āyī (Hindi) 103
Hṛdoye ācho mā tumi (Bengali) 104
Illāmai enbatilum (Tamil) 105
Indu nammamma (Kannada) 106
Iniyoru janmam (Kannada version) 108
Inkē irukkum (Tamil) 108
Īrattē tūpanāru (Tulu) 109
Iyarkaiyammā (Tamil) 110
Jagajjananī (Marathi) 111
Jai jai rāma (Kannada) 112
Jamuna kināre (Hindi) 113
Janmāntarapathikan (Malayalam) 114
Japo re (Hindi) 116
Jaya jaya hō! (Telugu) 116
Jaya jaya rāma jānaki rāma (Kannada) 118
Jaya māt bhavāni (Sanskrit) 119
Jhala jhalavena (Tamil) 120
Jñānakkaṭaltannai (Tamil) 122
Kab āye gā (Hindi) 122
Kadiranu enagende (Kannada) 123
Kalamurali (Tamil version) 124
Kāḷī kāḷī kāḷī (Gujarati) 125
Kāḷi māteyē (Kannada) 126
Kallum avanē (Tamil) 127
Kanasu maṇigaḷa (Kannada) 128
Kaṇḍariyātana (Tamil) 129
Kandarppakōṭi sundarā (Telugu) 130
Kaṇṇan kaḷḷa kaṇṇan (Tamil) 131

Kaṇṇeḍuttu pārammā (Tamil) 132
Kaṇṇē kalankātē (Tamil) 134
Kaṇṇinakattoru (Malayalam) 135
Kaṇṇirāl kaṇṇā (Malayalam) 136
Kaṇṇīruṇangātta (Malayalam) 137
Karayallē paitalē (Malayalam) 138
Karumaiyilē (Tamil) 139
Karuṇaiyil pirandu (Tamil) 140
Kāruṇya murtte (Kannada version) 141
Kārunya rupiṇi (Malayalam) 141
Kaṭaikkaṇ pārvai (Tamil) 142
Kāttrāka nān (Tamil) 143
Kāvaṭiyām kāvaṭi (Tamil) 144
Kayilaiyilē śivaperumān (Tamil) 145
Kazhaliṇayil (Malayalam) 146
Kēḷiraṇṇā (Kannada) 148
Kēśava nāmamu (Telugu) 149
Kōṭṭaiyenṭrē (Tamil) 150
Kṛṣṇa kanaiyyā (Malayalam) 151
Kṛṣṇā ninnā bāla līle (Kannada) 152
Kṣaṇakṣaṇavu (Kannada) 153
Kuraiyellām nīkki namma (Tamil) 154
Kurumbukkāra (Tamil) 155
Kuzhandaiyena (Tamil) 156
Lālāli lālalē (Malayalam) 157
Lallē lallē (Malayalam) 160
Lemmu nara kiṣōramā (Telugu) 163
Madhura mohanam (Sanskrit) 164
Mādhuri (Gujarati) 165
Māhā nāṭakam (Telugu) 167
Māi bhavānī (Marathi) 167
Mā jai jai mā (Hindi) 168

Manakkōyil (Tamil) 169
Manamenḍrum undan vīdu (Tamil) 171
Manamirukka ahankāram (Tamil) 172
Manan karo man (Hindi) 173
Manasavāca karmaṇā (Kannada) 174
Mānasavīṇiya (Telugu) 175
Manasē kēḷū (Kannada) 176
Manassil nīla sarasil (Malayalam) 176
Mangaḷa nāyaki (Tamil) 177
Mangal vadana (Hindi) 178
Manitā iraivan (Tamil) 179
Mano nā visāri (Punjabi) 180
Manujkāy hāthī (Hindi) 181
Mā o mā (Gujarati) 182
Māriyamma māriyamma (Tamil) 183
Māya lōniki neṭṭak-amma (Telugu) 185
Māyā ulagam (Tamil) 187
Mayilirakaṇi mādhavanē (Tamil) 188
Merā mujh main (Punjabi) 188
Mere guruvāṅ di vāṇi (Punjabi) 190
Mizhinīrilāzhnna (Malayalam) 190
Mōkēda ammanu (Tulu) 192
Mother nature (English) 193
Muraḷīgānamutirkkunnu (Malayalam) 194
Muraḷī manohar (Hindi) 195
Murugā vēlmurugā (Tamil) 195
Muttu mūkkutti (Tamil) 197
Nā hṛdi (Telugu) 198
Naiyyā tērē (Hindi) 199
Nāḷnallatākum (Tamil) 200
Nambinōr (Tamil) 201
Nām japo (Hindi) 202

Namo namah (Telugu) 203
Namōstutē dēvī (Marathi) 204
Nānē ariyāta ennai (Tamil) 205
Nān enbatai (Tamil) 206
Nānendu kāṇuve (Kannaḍa) 207
Nanna hudōṭṭada (Kannada) 208
Nannōḍeya (Kannada) 209
Nānu embudilla (Kannada) 210
Narahari nārāyaṇa (Kannada) 210
Narttana māṭō naṭarāja (Kannada) 212
Navanitacorā (Hindi) 214
Navavidha bhakti (Telugu) 215
Navilu gariya (Kannada) 216
Neñcakaṁ ventiṭunnu (Malayalam) 217
Nēnu yavaranu (Telugu) 218
Nīla-kamala (Telugu) 219
Nīlakkadamba (Malayalam) 220
Nī tanda solleṭuttu (Tamil) 221
Okka maṇi (Telugu) 222
Om mangalam (Sanskrit) 223
Om śakti (Tamil) 225
Ō naruḍā (Telugu) 226
Only love (English) 227
Ōrmmayil ninnurnnu (Malayalam) 228
Oru nāḷamma (Tamil) 229
Orunāḷum piriyātta (Kannada version) 230
Oru piṭi cāramāy (Malayalam) 230
Oru soṭṭu kaṇṇīrāl (Tamil) 232
Paccamalai pavaḷamalai (Tamil) 232
Pādāravindakē (Kannada) 234
Pāṇḍuranga nām gyā (Marathi) 235
Panipaṭarnda malaiyin (Tamil) 236

Parayuvānāvatilla (Malayalam) 237
Parinamamiyallatta (Kannada version) 238
Pari pari (Telugu) 238
Paṭṭave pādamu (Telugu) 239
Ponnammā en ammā (Tamil) 240
Ponnūñcal āṭāyō (Tamil) 241
Prabhū pyār kī (Hindi) 242
Prāṇeśvarī (Malayalam) 243
Prēma sāgara (Kannada) 244
Puṭṭa kṛṣṇa (Kannada) 245
Queen of my heart (English) 246
Rādhā gōvinda (Telugu) 247
Rādheśyām rādheśyām (Hindi) 248
Rasikarāj (Hindi) 249
Rāt din ḍalatī jāy (Hindi) 250
Sāgara cēpaku (Telugu) 251
Śakti tā jagadambā (Tamil) 252
Sāmbasadāśiva (Tamil) 253
Samsāramanu (Telugu) 254
Sānnu pīkh (Punjabi) 255
Santāpa hṛttinnu (Malayalam) 257
Satyam jñānam (Tamil) 258
Satyattin sāram (Tamil) 259
Seḷeyadirali ninna (Kannada) 260
Śēr pe savār (Punjabi) 261
Sēvaiyenum (Tamil) 262
Silukisadiru nī (Kannada) 263
Sinnañciru kuzhandai (Tamil) 264
Siṭrinbam nāṭum (Tamil) 265
Śivanē śankaranē (Kannada) 266
Śivaśakti aikyave (Kannada) 266
Śivke (Hindi) 268

Śri dēvi laḷitā (Tamil) 269
Śrī kṛṣṇā deva (Malayalam) 270
Śrī rāma nāmamē (Tamil) 271
Sṛṣṭi vēru (Telugu) 272
Sukh kartā (Hindi) 273
Sundara vadanā (Hindi) 274
Sundari jaganmōhini (Kannada) 275
Sūryanobbane (Kannada) 276
Śvāsamellām un peyarē (Tamil) 277
Taḷarnnuraṅgukayō (Malayalam) 278
Tañcamena vantōm (Tamil) 279
Tañcam undan (Tamil) 281
Tandam tānannai (Malayalam) 282
Tāṇḍavamāṭi (Tamil) 283
Tapamanu (Telugu) 285
Tāraka nāma (Kannada) 286
Tāraka nāmamu (Telugu) 287
Taṭaikaḷai nīkkiṭum (Tamil) 288
Tāyenḍru azhaikkavā (Tamil) 289
Taye tava (Kannada version) 290
Teyyōm taka (Malayalam) 291
Tintaka tintaka (Malayalam) 292
Tori koler chele āmi (Bengali) 294
Ulagankaḷ yāvum (Tamil) 295
Ulagamāga māri nirkkum (Tamil) 297
Ulakāḷum nāyakiyē (Tamil) 298
Ulakattin tāyenṭru (Tamil) 299
Unai maravā varamonḍru (Tamil) 300
Underneath a kalpataru (English) 301
Unmatta pañcakam (Tamil) 302
Unnarumai (Tamil) 303
Uṇṇi gaṇapatiye (Malayalam) 304

Ūraṭankum (Tamil) 306
Uṭayavaḷ (Malayalam) 307
Uyara uyara (Tamil) 308
Uyirōṭuyirāy (Tamil) 309
Vandan gaurī (Hindi) 310
Vandavar ettanai (Tamil) 311
Var de (Hindi) 312
Vaṭavṛkṣmām (Malayalam) 313
Vazhimēl vizhi (Tamil) 314
Vettrivēl (Tamil) 315
Vighnanāśaka śrīvināyaka (Kannada) 317
Vimmum kural (Tamil) 318
Vināyakane vinay tīrtarulvāy (Tamil) 319
Vināyaka enkaḷ (Tamil) 320
Viśvam nīlō (Telugu) 321
Viṭhal smaraṇ karā (Marathi) 322
Vizhi kiṭaikkumā (Tamil) 324
Vṛndāvana kuñjavihāri (Hindi) 325

www.ingramcontent.com/pod-product-compliance
Lightning Source LLC
Chambersburg PA
CBHW070136100426
42743CB00013B/2727
* 9 7 8 1 6 8 0 3 7 7 1 2 5 *